YOU'LL NEVER WALK ALONE

LIVERPOOL
FOOTBALL CLUB

EST·1892 ®

MR LIVERPOOL
RONNIE MORAN
THE OFFICIAL LIFE STORY

MR LIVERPOOL
RONNIE MORAN

THE OFFICIAL LIFE STORY

with Paul Moran

By Arnie Baldursson
and Carl Clemente

Sport Media

To my children Elena, Leon and Nói.
They are all Reds through and through,
which means they were raised properly.
Everything would be impossible without
having my lovely wife, Ásta Sól, beside me.
Love you all to bits!

— Arnie Baldursson

Dedicated to my beautiful children Carlos
and Natividad and my loving wife Nati. I'm
so grateful for your eternal support and love.

— Carl Clemente

Written with Carl Clemente and Arnie Baldursson.

First published in Great Britain and Ireland in 2017 by
Trinity Mirror Sport Media, PO Box 48, Old Hall Street, Liverpool, L69 3EB.

www.tmsportmedia.com
@SportMediaTM

Trinity Mirror Sport Media is a part of Trinity Mirror plc.
One Canada Square, Canary Wharf, London, E15 5AP.

1

Hardback ISBN: 978-1-910335-69-7
Trade paperback ISBN 978-1-910335-70-3
eBook ISBN 978-1-908319-73-9

Photographic acknowledgements:
Ronnie Moran personal collection, Mirrorpix, PA.

Book editing: Roy Gilfoyle
Text proofing: Chris Brereton
Jacket design: Rick Cooke & Colin Sumpter

Printed and bound by CPI Group (UK) Ltd, Croydon, CR0 4YY.

CONTENTS

Foreword

Roy Evans

IT has often been stated by former players that during our time on the Liverpool coaching staff, I was known as good cop and Ronnie Moran was the bad cop. However, Ronnie's stern approach on and off the training field was more than needed at a football club where trophies were won on a yearly basis.

During my 35 years at Liverpool Football Club, Ronnie was always around. Even before I joined Liverpool in 1963 as an apprentice, I would watch Ronnie play left-back for the first-team from the Boys' Pen next to the Kop. We then went on to play in Joe Fagan's reserve team together and in 1974, when I joined the coaching staff, myself and Ronnie would go on to work hand in hand for the following 24 years.

Ronnie used to refer to the first-teamers as the Bigheads and would coach them well in order for them never to get carried away with their success. I remember when Ronnie used to hand out medals to the players on the first day back at pre-season. There were never any presentations or anything. He just made them think it was their job to be doing this and nothing special was ever made of it. Ronnie would just say something along the lines of: 'These don't mean anything now, same again this season, lads.'

Ronnie was very level-headed and had the right balance to be a successful coach. He was straightforward and treated everyone the same. He gave all the players an equal chance, whether it was a young apprentice starting out or one of the Bigheads.

Ronnie's coaching methods were a continuation from Bill Shankly's way of playing the game, keeping things simple. In them days it was all about Liverpool, what we did on the pitch and it was never about the opposition. Ronnie made the players become fearless; the Liverpool Way was the only way! The players would always conduct themselves as professionals on and off the pitch and Ronnie would always let them know that they were not just representing Liverpool Football Club, but the people of Liverpool too, just as Bill Shankly would have preached to Ronnie on many occasions.

Much of Liverpool's success throughout the seventies and eighties was down to Ronnie; not only as an excellent coach but also the discipline he instilled around the place. Yes, there were times he needed to give players a telling off, but it was always deserved. Without this discipline, the players wouldn't have been able to keep their feet on the ground and ultimately wouldn't have achieved as much as they did.

Every game was a big game for Ronnie and he prepared the players to go about their business in exactly the same way, whether we were playing a second round League Cup tie or a European Cup final. He gave so much to the club that means so much to him and rightly deserves the title 'Mr Liverpool'.

Foreword

Phil Thompson

I REMEMBER when I was a kid; I used to write all the names of the Liverpool players in coal on the walls of the coal shed at my mum's house in Kirkby. As players moved on from the club I would rub their names out and add new ones when players came in. I never rubbed out 'Moran'.

When I first joined Liverpool in 1969 as a 15-year-old, I would go on Tuesday and Thursday evenings to Melwood to train and Ronnie Moran was one of our coaches. I soon realised how super fit he was as he always participated in the practice games. He had a great footballing mind and knew the game inside out. Ronnie never missed a trick; he was all eyes and ears. He was very straight up, honest and genuine, as well as demanding and extremely vocal.

I started to get to know Ronnie better when he would take me from Melwood after training and drop me off at The Crown pub on East Lancs Road. I could then get the bus back to Kirkby and he would go back home to Crosby. We would always talk about football, but never about my progress as I didn't want to get too personal.

Liverpool Football Club was the best club side in the world; we had a lot of big characters and we needed someone with a certain fear factor to keep us in line. Ronnie Moran was everything and everywhere, the voice, the whistle. Ronnie was the constant, going back to when Bill Shankly was in charge.

Ronnie Moran is probably one of the most important people Liverpool Football Club has ever had. He played a major part in everything we achieved during my time there. In my eyes he is right up there with Shanks, Joe, Bob and Kenny. For all they achieved at the club as managers, you needed someone in behind, keeping that clock ticking, day in day out, making it special and Ronnie was that man. Without Ronnie we wouldn't have enjoyed the success we had and Liverpool probably wouldn't be the club it is today.

Ronnie was extremely demanding and always wanted the best from people. He was always there for me, just like Bill, Bob and Joe were. Ronnie was fantastic and helped me immensely. When I was on the coaching staff myself, later on, I would implement his tactics into my own training. Even when I was the assistant manager and manager in the absence of Gérard Houllier, he would come and chat to me about what had happened. Still, to this day when I do speeches at the academy, I always tell the kids what Ronnie told me when I was starting out.

On a personal level, I owe everything to Ronnie Moran, the way he guided me and brought me through the youth ranks, into his reserve team and then finally into the first-team. I've always said that Bill Shankly is my hero but Ronnie Moran was certainly my mentor.

'Even though my dad's memories are fading, I'm proud to be able to carry them on.'

Introduction

by Paul Moran

I HAD always planned on producing a book about my dad's 49-year career at Liverpool Football Club, but until now I had never got round to it. A call from my friend Carl Clemente got the project going and him and Arnie Baldursson did all the hard work in making this book possible.

There's no doubt my dad's career in football was a unique one. Few have served one of world football's greatest clubs for so long in so many different roles, and it's likely no-one will ever do so again.

From 1949-1998 he saw so many big changes at the club and in the wider world of football, and worked with so many top-class managers and players, his career is one to admire and envy.

He had a reputation as the bad cop of the dressing room, taking no prisoners and being as tough on the most famous players as he was with the apprentices.

However he did it, he was part of a Bootroom team that produced a trophy-winning machine. And his methods were ultimately appreciated by the Anfield staff and players who queued up to pay tribute to him on the pages of this book.

If my dad's life was unique, then I also appreciate how being his son meant I got to see and experience things that most of my peers couldn't.

From getting behind the scenes at Anfield and Melwood, to meeting the stars, and even collecting the chippy order for the players as I joined them for a ride on the team bus back from London, I know I've enjoyed a unique life too.

I will always be grateful to Carl and Arnie as this book would not exist without them. I hope everyone enjoys reading my dad's story as much as I've enjoyed being a part of putting it together.

I'd like to thank the publishers, Trinity Mirror, for doing such a good job on the book, particularly Paul Dove, Roy Gilfoyle, Rick Cooke, Colin Sumpter, Chris Brereton and Claire Brown.

The family is also grateful for the full support of Liverpool Football Club, particularly Christina Kilkenny, Harriet Johnstone, Ailsa Gardner and the club's retail marketing and PR departments.

The whole process has given me the opportunity to realise what a lucky upbringing I had and how many fantastic memories I have had with my dad, all of which are now included in this book.

There are also a few gems we've managed to dig up from the archives in here, including a Melwood diary my dad and the staff recorded which kept track of training schedules, injuries and matches. They kept one every season for several decades and pages from the 1984/85 diary are used inside the front and back covers of this book.

Dad is now suffering from dementia, an illness he was diagnosed with in 2012. During the process of gathering memories and information for this book, his illness has worsened to such a degree that on November 8, 2016 the family took the heartbreaking decision to put my dad in a care home, where he now resides in Southport.

It's sad to see the dressing room sergeant major of so many past glories now struggling to recall the matches and the people that helped build his legacy.

Early in 2016 my dad and I got to visit Melwood just before the League Cup final at Wembley, which was to be on the same day as my dad's birthday, February 28. Jürgen Klopp walked by, nodded hello and a few seconds later he came in and asked my dad how he was and we talked about the upcoming final against Man City. Jürgen said the team would try and win the cup as a present and I got a picture of him with my dad.

A couple of months later at a legends dinner at the Hilton hotel in Liverpool city centre, my dad was able to attend with Anfield's stars of the past. One fan at the event asked my dad about his recent trip to Melwood but he couldn't remember it.

Even though his memories are fading I'm proud to be able to carry them on through this book.

"I remember my dad saying to me
once that it was a pity they never had
five-a-side teams in the late 1940s
because him and his four brothers
would have been unbeatable."

– Paul Moran

Chapter 1

1934-1954

RONNIE Moran is a Liverpool phenomenon. During his half-a-century at Liverpool Football Club, he served nine different managers; George Kay, Don Welsh, Phil Taylor, Bill Shankly, Bob Paisley, Joe Fagan, Kenny Dalglish, Graeme Souness and Roy Evans. For 49 years he served with distinction in roles as varied as youth-team player, reserve-team player, first-team player, reserve-team manager, physio, first-team trainer, chief coach and finally as first-team manager. Ronnie was taught by the best and he, in turn, produced the best.

Ronald Moran was born on February 28, 1934 and lived on Coronation Road in Crosby; a Merseyside town, situated just north of Bootle, south of Southport and Formby and west of Netherton.

The Moran name comes from Ireland but can be tracked all the way back to Spain due to Spanish sailors who were shipwrecked in Ireland from their fleet, the Armada, in the Anglo-Spanish War (1585–1604). The surname Morán is quite common in Spain as well as in South America where the Spanish also sailed centuries ago.

When Ronnie was five years old the family moved to a larger house in Alexandra Road, Crosby, which to this day is the home of his older sister, Margaret. The house on Coronation Road where he was born in L23 no longer exists. Ronnie was the youngest of five brothers and four sisters, born when mother Alice was 39 and father Joe was 40. His brothers were Joe, Ned, Billy and Tommy, who have all passed on. Of Ronnie's four sisters, Emily and Alice are no longer with us but Margaret and Hilda are still alive.

Margaret remembers Ronnie used to play football at the top of Alexandra Road by the old dairy building where workers had drawn a goal on the wall and allowed her brother to take part in their games. When Ronnie and his brothers were having a kick about in the yard at home one day, their ball went straight through the kitchen window and landed in a bowl of Scouse cooking on the stove.

Margaret says: "As our irate mother stormed out the house, Ronnie looked round for support from his brothers, but they were nowhere to be seen as they had all scarpered up the entry leaving the youngest to take the blame."

Being the youngest also had its perks as Ronnie's siblings would look out for him. Due to his footballing ability, Ronnie's time away from school revolved around the various teams in which he featured, giving him no scope to be led astray and get into real trouble.

Ronnie's mother, Alice, who passed away in 1981 aged 86, dedicated her life to her nine children as a housewife and to Ronnie's father, Joseph, "Joe" for short. Joe fought in the First World War and became a binman when he returned home, a profession he stayed in until his retirement, transporting rubbish around the borough by horse and cart. Ronnie would help his dad as he came into their street as he valued his dad's hard work. Ronnie's father never had any involvement in football other than being very proud of his son's achievements as a player. Joe attended Ronnie's football games while he was at school and kept track of the results in a scorebook but very rarely saw him play professionally. Joe died of a heart attack in 1970, aged 76.

During the Second World War, Joe assisted the Home Front by dealing with fires from incendiary bombs that had missed their main target, the docks, and landed around Crosby. His job was to ring the town siren from a nearby station to alert the residents when the bombs started dropping. "We'd hide under the stairs. It was a tight squeeze with a family of our size," Ronnie said, as that was the safest place in the home.

The German Luftwaffe attacked the Merseyside area for the first time on August 28, 1940 and made 80 air raids until January 10, 1942, the worst being the blitz that lasted eight successive nights from May 1, 1941 when Ronnie was only seven years old. 1,746 Merseysiders were killed during the May blitz and more than 90,000 homes destroyed or damaged. Ronnie's borough, Crosby, was hit on May 7 and 8 with high explosives, parachute mines and incendiaries killing 22 people. If five of the six parachute mines had landed in a residential area instead of the shoreline near Harbour Road, that would have resulted in a significantly greater loss of life in Crosby.

The Bryant and Mays match factory in Bootle was destroyed during these 48 hours as David Huxley, who lived in Crosby at the time, recalls in a WWII account named *A Young Family in Wartime at Crosby*: 'We were taken from our bunk beds and allowed to peep out of the shelter for a few brief moments to see the spectacle. The whole sky seemed ablaze, and all subsequent bonfire nights bear no comparison to the sight we beheld then. The factory was completely destroyed.'

He vividly remembers the landscape that the Moran family would have seen at this time. 'The shore at Crosby had many signs of coastal defences, including anti-tank traps, concrete pyramid-shaped pillars about three feet high and set in the sand at every few feet lined the area around the high tide marks, and there were miles of barbed wire and other defensive measures as well,' Huxley said. 'Often the sky was filled with large barrage balloons. On higher ground there were look-out posts, and beyond the shore the estuary was filled continually with shipping, convoys of naval vessels and even hospital ships bearing large red crosses, either leaving from, or returning to Liverpool.'

Crosby got off relatively easy compared to Bootle, only four miles away, as that was closest to the port's biggest docks. Two hundred and fifty people were killed in Bootle and only 15 per cent of its houses were left standing. In total the Germans' bombing killed around 4,000 people on Merseyside and Liverpool was the most heavily bombed city outside of London, due to having the biggest port on the west coast of England.

"The blitz had killed and injured many civilians, but the community spirit during the conflict had brought the people of Liverpool closer together," says Billy Howard, who was a junior player at Liverpool from 1955-1962. "Looking back, with my football head on, it reminds me of a footie team, all pulling for each other. Everything was rationed, some had very little and some had next to nothing. Some had not only lost all their possessions, but also their homes as a consequence of the bombings. Others had suffered the loss of husbands, sons, fathers, mothers and daughters who were sadly killed in action. Many more had suffered the loss of limbs."

Billy and other kids in Liverpool, Ronnie included, had to make do with their sometimes rudimentary surroundings when they wanted to play football. "Liverpool had been decimated by the bombing, leading to numerous 'ollers' close to where we lived on Sherdley Street by the city centre," Billy remembers. "The council demolished damaged buildings, levelled the ground and covered over it with cinders and these would become our footie pitches. We organised our own street versus street and school versus school games on the 'ollers' where we had coats or bricks for goals. There were no refs, but if someone cheated they were barred from playing again.

"Our mothers must have gone spare. The cinders would ruin our pumps, and our legs and elbows would be cut to ribbons. We wore kecks that were short trousers, until we were about 14 years old. However, we as kids didn't care and we would be back the next day playing footie."

Football was a favourite pastime in Liverpool. "Every bare wall had a goal chalked on it," Billy recollects. "We would bunk over school walls and play in the playgrounds. On Sundays the older teenagers and some men would organise games there. Balls were different then, made of thick rubber, so they would bounce all over the place.

"We soon realised that our first touch was vital and we learned also to keep the ball on the deck as if it hit anything sharp it would rip to pieces," Billy concludes in his vivid account of life in Liverpool at the time when Ronnie was growing up.

Ronnie attended Saints Peter and Paul Catholic Primary School on Liverpool Road in Crosby. This is where Ronnie first set his eyes on his future wife, Joyce Morley, who was in the year above. Joyce lived on York Road just half-a-mile away from Ronnie's family home on Alexandra Road. Ronnie and Joyce became good friends and spent a lot of time in Coronation Park, called 'The Rec', where there was a pond for model boats and bowling greens. They also played in a wooded area near Crosby called Sniggery Woods and took walks along a large estate on a path called the Wood Wall.

The Education Act of 1944 was an answer to surging social and educational demands created by the war. During the 1940s many church schools, including Saints Peter and Paul, could not afford to modernise on their own. The act opened new opportunities for working class children and one was providing the best pupils from the church schools' academic scholarships the chance to attend the best schools in the area.

In 1945, eleven-year-old Ronnie sat an exam with hope of achieving one of the newly introduced academic scholarships for maths, his favourite subject in school. Ronnie was successful and in September he attended secondary education at Bootle Technology College, which is still going today under the name of Hugh Baird College.

He played centre-forward for the school football team and the college offered him a better playing environment to blossom and increased his chances of being spotted by one of the area's bigger clubs. Ronnie eventually featured for Bootle Boys, who had a stronger team than Crosby Boys, and won the Merseyside Championship Cup with them in 1948. He went on to represent Lancashire Schoolboys from 1948-49.

"School football was really competitive in my era. There was a real sense of pride in beating the districts around you," Ronnie said. "I got a fair amount of stick from friends in Crosby for playing for Bootle. So whenever we beat them, I made sure I gave it back to them." Ronnie also used to turn out alongside his friends for Our Lady's, a youth club team.

Only a ten-minute walk away from Ronnie's home at Alexandra Road was Rossett Park on College Road, home of Marine Football Club. From an early age Ronnie attended Marine's home games in the Lancashire Combination League and witnessed the biggest football crowd in Crosby's history of 6,000 when the Nigerian national team visited College Road in August 1949 to play its first games outside of West Africa. The match organised by the newspaper, the *Sunday Dispatch*, finished 5-2 to the visitors, who notably played barefoot. The Nigerians played nine matches in five weeks in England against the top amateur sides of the country.

Like many Merseyside kids at the time, Ronnie went down the usual route of going to Anfield one week to watch Liverpool and Goodison Park the next to watch Everton, brought there by his brothers and brothers-in-law. Ronnie wasn't too bothered if the players wore red or blue. "If anyone, Formby was my team because two of my brothers, Ned and Billy, played for them as amateurs; one was a goalie and the other was a right-back," Ronnie explained.

Edward, or 'Ned' as he was to everyone, was the goalkeeper and was once described as a "Stone wall keeper" in a match report in the *Lancaster Guardian* when Formby drew 1-1 in a cup-tie versus Lancaster City at Giant Axe stadium. Ned Moran's agility surprised the crowd and some of his saves bordered on the miraculous. He repelled shots from all angles.

Ned and Billy were Ronnie's biggest early influences in football and gave him helpful advice. They would later take great pride in the achievements of their younger brother, who managed to make their pastime his profession. Ronnie benefited from attending Formby's matches as there were only a handful of people watching so he could hear all that was being said on the pitch. It taught him the importance of being able to get your message across to your teammates and what to say and, more importantly, what not to say.

Ronnie's son Paul recalls: "I remember my dad saying to me that it was a pity they never had five-a-side teams in the late 1940s because him and his four brothers would have been unbeatable."

The Football League started again in 1946, having been sus-pended during the war. The Liverpool team had gained strength in the US prior to the campaign away from the British austerity programme. Billy Liddell, aged 24, was finally unleashed on the First Division, having scored 82 goals in 152 games in the regional divisions of wartime football. Billy made his league debut in a 7-4 win against Chelsea, playing on the left wing in front of another debutant, left-half Bob Paisley, on an unbearably hot day when overcrowding forced hundreds of spectators at Anfield to seek refuge on the track around the pitch. A crowd of 49,995 were said to be in attendance, but several youths had bunked in over the walls of the Anfield Road end.

After a 5-0 defeat to Manchester United that followed the 11-goal Chelsea thriller, flame-haired forward Albert Stubbins was bought for a club record fee of £13,000 from Second Division Newcastle United, £1,000 less than the league record signing of Bryn Jones, who moved from Wolves to Arsenal. With their new number nine in their ranks Liverpool went on a rampage and won eight of their next twelve matches, drawing the other four. George Kay's men were top of the league and had captured Liverpudlians' imaginations, with Jack Balmer scoring hat-tricks in three successive First Division matches in November 1946, against Portsmouth, Derby and Arsenal.

The deafening Kop roar dominated the atmosphere at Anfield as well as the 'clacking' of the rattles, that had been used by air raid wardens in the war as a warning for gas attacks. Some fans would paint their rattle red and white and adorn it with a player's name on top. Singing wouldn't become prevalent at games until the 1960s but one ditty went…

After the ball was centred
after the whistle blew
Liddell got excited
and down the wing he flew

he crossed the ball to Stubbins
Stubbins scored a goal
and knocked the poor old goalie
sitting on his old banjo

Liverpool were ably assisted by the crowd that included Ronnie Moran and one particular part of the ground was the loudest, as it still is today.

"It was a wonderful experience just to play at Anfield, particularly when you played towards the Kop," Albert Stubbins said. "If you were losing 1-0 and you were playing into the Kop in the second half it was worth a goal. The enthusiasm, the wave of sound that came out of there was terrific. We always had our pre-match kick-ins down at the Kop end, like they do today. The energy that the crowd could put into it was amazing. We would thrive on it."

Liverpool were not only going strong in the league but also reached the semi-final of the FA Cup where they faced Burnley. Albert Stubbins and Jack Balmer used to sing popular folk-blues song 'Sitting on the Top of the World' before each round but forgot to do so against Burnley. Jinxed or not, Liverpool lost 1-0 in a replay. Liverpool had relinquished the number one spot after a 5-1 defeat to Wolves on December 7 but retrieved it in their penultimate game of the campaign. Liverpool beat Wolves 2-1 in a tremendous battle in their final match on May 31 and were two points ahead of Stoke, who had a superior goal average. The Potters still had one game left, against Sheffield United at Bramall Lane, which took place on June 14, kicking off fifteen minutes prior to the start of the Liverpool Senior Cup final between Liverpool and Everton at Anfield. Liverpool were winning 2-1 with ten minutes to go when club director George Richards announced over the loud-speakers that Stoke had been defeated.

"The crowd didn't care two straws what happened after that," Billy Liddell remembered. "All they wanted was the final whistle, so they could come swarming over the ground from the Kop and Kemlyn Road and carry us off the field. It was a scene of amazing enthusiasm." What a tremendous campaign for Ronnie Moran, who turned 13 during it, to be introduced to league football!

A postman, who was a good friend of one of Ronnie's brothers, used to deliver letters to the home of a Liverpool director by the name of Thomas Valentine 'TV' Williams, who in 1956 became chairman of the club. During one morning in 1949 the postman took it upon himself to recommend Ronnie to Williams. Subsequently, the postman made an unexpected delivery to the Moran household with Liverpool manager, George Kay, and TV Williams in tow.

"A week later, after I played one of my last games for Bootle Boys, the then manager of Everton, Cliff Britton, wanted me to sign for him," Ronnie said.

Ronnie thanked Everton for their kind offer but informed them that he had already agreed to sign amateur forms for Liverpool Football Club when he left Bootle Tech the previous week.

Ronnie trained twice a week at Liverpool, on Tuesday and Thursday evenings. He earned £5 in winter and £3 in summer. During the week Ronnie served an apprenticeship as an electrician at the Mersey Docks and Harbour Board, who own and administer the dock facilities of the Port of Liverpool. Ronnie travelled along the Liverpool Overhead Railway, known locally as the 'Dockers' Umbrella' which operated along the Liverpool docks.

His time working on the docks influenced his desire, passion and dedication for hard work and inspired him to greater deeds in a Liverpool shirt later on in life as he knew many of the fans who attended Anfield were dockers who worked a lot harder for less money than footballers. Ronnie felt the responsibility to give his all on the football pitch to the fans and ex-work colleagues as he knew first-hand the happiness football gave them.

"I stood on the Kop as a lad and the place was packed with humourists and enthusiasts; the right mix for football," Ronnie said in the match programme ahead of Liverpool's last game in front of the old Kop before its demolition in 1994. "Those fans had worked hard during the week and demanded the same effort from the players they supported. The noise they created was frightening, but players had nothing to fear provided they put 100 per cent into their game."

Ronnie enjoyed his time as an apprentice electrician but his heart was always set on being a professional footballer. He started out playing his career at Liverpool FC for the youngsters in the C team that would often face adult teams. Ronnie suffered plenty of knocks in these rough games that helped to form the philosophy that he would later pass on to the players that he coached. He learned that he had to look after himself as no-one was going to help him out. Ronnie was moved from striker to left-back simply because the left-back in the C team wasn't very good. Ronnie wasn't bothered about moving into defence and would have quite happily played in goal if he was asked to.

Soon after Moran joined, in 1950, the club purchased land from St Francis Xavier's School in West Derby on which a new training ground was built. It was named Melwood after two of the priests who taught at the school and had devoted a great deal of their time to coach students at football – Father Melling and Father Woodlock. "There would be a kick about going around on this rough patch. It was a bit of a mess," Moran said of the early days at Melwood.

When Moran started at the club as a junior, he trained at Anfield and out on the strip of land that later became the Main Stand car park. He ran around the perimeter of the ground and up and down the steps of the Kop. He also used a skipping rope, a punch ball and hung from the bars in the small gym. On his 17th birthday in 1951, Ronnie was given a part-time professional contract.

One of the moments that stands out for Ronnie during his time as a Liverpool youth took place on April 29, 1950. The Reds had beaten Everton in the semis to book their first FA Cup final appearance at Wembley. Liverpool had only played once in England's biggest showpiece when they lost to Burnley in 1914 at Crystal Palace. Ronnie had just turned 16 and the club took him and the other young apprentices down to London to watch their heroes play against Arsenal.

Unfortunately, Liverpool were beaten 2-0 on the day and talisman Billy Liddell was kicked to pieces. The Liverpool lads came home on Monday and got a tremendous reception when they came out on the balcony of the town hall where captain Phil Taylor held tight to their mascot, a teddy bear. Ronnie was very disappointed not to see his team lift the cup for the first time, but the whole experience and the occasion inspired him.

In 1951, after almost 15 years and 357 games in charge, manager George Kay left Liverpool and the jovial Mancunian Don Welsh took over. Liverpool persuaded Welsh to move north from the south-coast town of Brighton to replace Kay, who had retired for health reasons two months earlier in January. Welsh already had links to Merseyside because he had been a popular guest player for Liverpool during the Second World War, scoring 44 goals in 39 games, and had also been keen to join the club as a coach back then, but it was a move his employers, Charlton Athletic, refused to allow.

Mr Welsh must have seen potential in 17-year-old Moran's abilities. On December 29, 1951, Welsh wanted to see how he would perform at reserve team level. Ronnie's 18th birthday was looming. If players hadn't signed full-time professional forms by the age of 18, they were most likely destined to be released. Liverpool reserves hosted Bury on a Saturday afternoon at Anfield. The first-team was playing at Huddersfield Town so manager Welsh wasn't in attendance to see Ronnie's performance. However, reserve team manager Jimmy Seddon, a former England international, watched carefully.

Ronnie was in great company that day as three first-teamers coming to the end of their Liverpool careers turned out for the reserves; goalkeeper Cyril Sidlow, 36, who played 165 times for Liverpool's first-team, former captain, Jack Balmer, 35, a veteran of 309 matches in which he scored 110 goals, and striker Cyril Done, 31, who scored 36 goals in 110 appearances in a Liverpool shirt. Liverpool beat Bury 3-0 and a clean sheet for left-back Moran would have helped his cause.

CROSBY KID

On January 7, 1952, seven weeks before his 18th birthday, the hopeful Scouser signed full-time professional forms for his hometown club.

A week before the start of the 1952/53 season, on August 16, Moran came on as a second-half substitute for the reserves against the seniors in a training match set up to sharpen match fitness as well as give the second string a "chance to prove their worth." Come the first matchday of the campaign, veteran Ray Lambert was in his regular spot at left-back as Liverpool drew 1-1 at Preston North End, but Ronnie finally made his long-awaited first-team debut at Derby County on November 22. A scribe at the *Daily Mirror* took special notice of the debutant, whose discovery had been so unique: 'Don Welsh, the Liverpool manager, is hoping it is true that the postman always knocks twice. He might get another potential star footballer. For Ronnie Moran, 17 [he was 18], chosen yesterday to make his first league appearance at Derby on Saturday, was recommended to the club by a postman who delivers letters to a Liverpool director's house. That was three years ago and Ronnie, an apprentice electrician from Crosby, was signed as a part-time professional as soon as he was seventeen. He has been playing particularly well for the reserves.'

Moran featured at left-back in a makeshift defence as keeper Charlie Ashcroft and full-backs Eddie Spicer and Lambert were all out injured. It didn't make Moran's task any easier when right-back Steve Parr got injured after 15 minutes. Parr continued to play, but left the Reds effectively with only 10 fit players. Moran had difficulty in containing Derby's outside-right Reg Harrison but Bob Paisley, who was left-half, did his best to help Ronnie out on the flank.

According to the writer at the *Liverpool Echo*, Moran was obviously out of his depth in the first half and when he gave Harrison ample time to make a centre, the ball went right to the head of Jimmy Dunn, who cleverly turned it into the net, well out of Russell Crossley's reach. The home side was 1-0 in front after half an hour's play.

Ronnie played more confidently in the second half, having needed the first 45 minutes to settle down, but despite his and his teammates' efforts, they lost the game 3-2 to 20th-placed Derby County.

Liverpool were in the middle of a miserable spell, having now lost five out of the last six. One week later Ronnie made his Anfield debut against Blackpool. He breathed a huge sigh of relief as the great Stanley Matthews was missing. His stand-in, Albert Hobson, didn't prove as great a threat to the inexperienced Moran as Matthews would have done. The Anfield surface was icy and treacherous, but Ronnie did himself justice in a 2-2 draw. Ronnie kept his place for the following eight games, taking his first-team appearances into double figures before losing his position to Lambert. During his run in the side, Moran made his FA Cup debut for the Reds as they crashed out of the third round to Gateshead of the Third Division North.

Moran's boyhood hero at Liverpool was Billy Liddell, who, in the opinion of so many football supporters, and not just from Liverpool, was one of the greatest men ever to have played the game.

"Bill was so strong it was unbelievable," Bob Paisley, who

played behind him on the left, remembered. "You couldn't shake him off the ball. It didn't matter where he was playing, though I suppose his best position was outside-left. He could go round you, or past you, or even straight through you sometimes!"

Moran's other hero was Preston and England's Tom Finney, whose biggest fan was one Bill Shankly who played with him at Preston. "I've said that Tommy Finney was the best I've seen and I'd bracket Pele, Eusebio, Cruyff, Di Stefano and Puskas up there with him," Shankly claimed.

On December 20, 1952, Ronnie faced Finney in only his fourth game for Liverpool and if that wasn't enough of a thrill for Ronnie, he had Liddell as his teammate. Preston North End were seventh in the league while Liverpool were 11th. The main attraction was the use of a white ball that was still a novelty in the Football League. Preston went 1-0 up at Anfield after only eight minutes and could have scored another with Charlie Ashcroft well beaten if not for Moran who saved a certain goal by heading the ball off the line. After just over a half-hour gone Liddell equalised with a sublime free-kick cleverly lobbed over the wall. Liddell then delivered an accurate pass onto the head of Kevin Baron who ensured Liverpool's lead at half-time.

Preston came to life in the second half and Moran again came to Liverpool's rescue when Bill Jones meant to pass the ball back to Ashcroft, who was out of position. Moran rushed towards the empty goal and cleared off the line. Moran's never-say-die attitude was singled out for praise by the *Liverpool Echo* reporter: 'Moran was certainly earning his money. It is not given to every youngster to save twice in this fashion in one game.'

However, Finney, who struggled to make his mark on the

game in the first half, engineered a quick break that allowed Angus Morrison to equalise. Despite Moran's heroics the game ended 2-2.

Ronnie was perhaps grateful he wasn't involved in Preston's next visit to Anfield, on September 5, 1953, when Spicer was given a torrid time as Finney orchestrated a 5-1 victory, scoring a hat-trick as Liverpool suffered their biggest home defeat of the season.

The youngster, who was 'earning his money' according to the *Echo*, was on £8.10s-£9.10s a week, as stipulated in Ronnie's contract signed in March 1953. The maximum wage for players at the time in the Football League was £15, but there were all kinds of incentives on offer at the club to earn a few bob. The players got £2 for a win and £1 for a draw on top of their basic wage and were even once presented with a chicken each for beating Rotherham! The team was also rewarded for attendance figures as Ronnie's former teammate and England international, Alan A'Court, reveals. "For home games we got £1 for every 1,000 supporters over 28,000. For example, if 45,000 people turned up we got a £17 bonus and it would be carried over for the next week's away game. It wasn't about the money in those days, but it was a nice way for the club to reward you with that little bit extra. It was like dangling a carrot in front of you, because the more games you won, the more supporters would show up, the more you would get paid."

Ronnie made two further appearances during the 1952/53 campaign. The first came in a 3-0 defeat at Stamford Bridge against Chelsea in March, a game where Liddell played in almost every position except where he should have played, at centre-forward. His roaming around the ground confused his teammates more than his opponents. Ronnie's final game of this campaign was an eight-goal thriller in April at Highbury. Don Welsh's men lost 5-3, having been 4-0 down after 65 minutes.

The Reds ended up 17th during Ronnie's debut season with the first-team, their worst finish in 16 years. Relegation to the Second Division was narrowly avoided on the last day when the Reds roared to a 2-0 win over Chelsea in front of 47,000 at Anfield, relegating the west-Londoners. Although it was a valuable experience for the youngster, Ronnie failed to finish a game on the winning side, losing nine and drawing three.

Joyce Morley had left school in 1947 to become a shopkeeper at Maypole's Grocers in Crosby Village. Ronnie and Joyce, who had known each other from primary school, were dating by now and would frequent the Regent picture house on Liverpool Road in Crosby and the Plaza picture house in Waterloo.

As an established first-teamer, Ronnie had the privilege of travelling on close-season tours. Ronnie had never been abroad before so the trip to the USA and Canada in the summer of 1953 was extra special. He and the rest of his Liverpool team-mates embarked on a five-day voyage on the RMS Queen Mary from Southampton to New York. The whole group was dressed up in tailored grey club suits with the Liver Bird crest, although a group of elderly ladies mistook them for a fishing club!

The lads from Liverpool made good use of the ship's gym and swimming pool and there were several games on offer, but not snooker. Alan A'Court discovered this after being sent on a wild goose chase to find the ship's snooker table by none other than Bob Paisley, the practical joker of the Liverpool team.

The coaching staff tried to keep the players in shape by having them run around the top deck of the 181ft-high ship and kicking a ball back and forth but after one too many balls had gone overboard an end was put to that exercise.

From May 14 to June 14, 1953 Liverpool played 10 games, winning nine and drawing just one. The first game of the tour took place at Ebbets Field, the home of Jackie Robinson's Brooklyn Dodgers. Moran was called into action during the match due to Louis Bimpson breaking his ankle against the Irish All-stars, a team made up of players from Northern Ireland.

During the sixth game of the tour against the Toledo All-Stars in Ohio, Ronnie got his name on the scoresheet for the first time in his career for the first-team. Unfortunately, it was an own goal, but Liverpool ran out 10-3 winners so it had no real influence on the outcome of the match. Ronnie went on to only score two own goals in his lengthy career. He argues, however, that they were both unfortunate deflections.

The most gruelling match of the tour took place in St Louis as Louis Bimpson recollected in the *Football Monthly*. "It was tremendously hot, well over 90 degrees. I felt as if I was in a furnace merely sitting on the touchline. The 11 who were playing must have lost pounds in weight and they looked a sorry sight, hardly able to walk off the field when the final whistle blew. I let them get into the dressing room, then joined them. What a sight I saw! There were 11 red-shirted Liverpool players standing under ice-cold showers, in boots, stockings, shorts and jerseys! They were so hot and worn out that they just hadn't the strength to take off their kit."

The tour ended at the legendary Yankee Stadium in the Bronx, with a 1-1 draw against the Swiss side, Young Boys. The players had played another game against the Irish All-Stars in Toronto the day before and landed in New York at two o'clock in the morning before facing the Young Boys in the afternoon. Liddell rescued the Reds from defeat with his second-half finish.

This wasn't the only time the players got acquainted with the Yankee Stadium as they all had the privilege of watching the world famous New York Yankees in action, with Yogi Berra and Mickey Mantle as their biggest stars, during their visit Stateside. The Yankees were leading the American League with a 78 per cent winning percentage and went on to beat the Brooklyn Dodgers in the World Series for their fifth consecutive title, which is still a record, so this was Yankees' most successful side in their illustrious history. The most memorable incident in the game watched by Liverpool's squad was when manager Don Welsh showed remarkable agility to catch a home run ball that had been launched into the stands by Mantle himself.

In August, 19-year-old Ronnie swapped Crosby for Trenton, Somerset, to join the Army to do his National Service that had been put into effect on January 1, 1949 to extend the British conscription after World War II. All healthy males from 17 to 21 years old were required to serve their nation for two years and remain on the reserve list for three-and-a-half years. Ronnie joined the Royal Electrical and Mechanical Engineers, the corps in the British Army that services its equipment.

Just like any other serviceman, Ronnie was granted leave to visit family and friends, and made a couple of appearances for Liverpool reserves, but his football career was firmly on hold. Ronnie did manage to feature in one league game for the first-team during the 1953/54 season when he replaced the injured Ray Lambert at left-back in a 3-2 defeat at Anfield against Charlton on February 13. Ronnie also represented the first-team in a testimonial game a month later, in a 3-3 draw at Brunton Park against Carlisle United. The beneficiary was Billy Hogan and, although it was his testimonial, he failed to turn up as he missed his train on the way to the match!

The Liverpool players had certainly enjoyed themselves and put in hard work during their adventurous trip overseas in the summer, but that didn't pay off during the season as the club got relegated to the Second Division for the first time in fifty years and for only the third time in its entire history.

Liverpool finished rock bottom of the First Division, picking up 28 points and winning only nine games. They also conceded an incredible 97 goals, the worst tally in all four divisions. The two previous times Liverpool got relegated – in 1894/95 and 1903/1904 – they won the Second Division the following campaign, but this wasn't going to be the case this time.

Welsh had been unlucky in the respect that he inherited an ageing team with a lot of the players in their thirties, but luckily he was willing to inject a bit of youth into his squad that benefited Ronnie originally. Moran has fond memories of Welsh and liked his cheerful personality and great enthusiasm for the game. Welsh resembled the great Bill Shankly in one aspect, according to Ronnie, in that he played in practice games and wouldn't allow the final whistle until his team was in front.

Liverpool's relegation, only seven years after the league championship was won, was a huge disappointment. Billy Liddell was still a force to be reckoned with but as the *Liverpool Echo* pointed out: 'Liddell has suffered these last two years from lack of support. It has been disappointing to watch him so frequently forced to go chasing for the ball in order to get a kick at it. Liddell should always be well plied with passes of the type which enable him to make the most of his speed, strength and final shot. Where Liverpool would have been without him I hate to contemplate.'

Liddell tried to make sense of Liverpool's capitulation, saying: "After last season's close call when the lads beat Chelsea at Anfield in the last game and saved themselves from the big drop, many people said we had been taught our lesson and it would never happen again. The injury bogey has been the cause of most of the bother. Unfortunately for the balance of the team, the injuries have been sustained by the older and more experienced players."

The worst injury was suffered by left-back Eddie Spicer in December 1953 when he broke his leg for the second time in his career. Liverpool's goalkeeper, Dave Underwood, who was making his debut that day at Old Trafford, mistimed a clearance and shattered Spicer's leg. He had no less than 19 fractures and was in and out of hospital for the next 12 months. Spicer never played professional football again.

"I am not trying to dodge the issue or make alibis," Liddell continued. "Merely trying to show that events in the football world come in cycles. A team has a spell on top of the world and then it goes into the background for a while."

It took eight long years for Liverpool to get back to where they belonged.

"I never saw my dad play for Liverpool but I remember going to watch him in charity games and thinking how hard he used to strike the ball. One day my dad was hitting shots at me in the garden. I was about 10 and was stopping them all and told him he couldn't score past me. The next shot he smashed at me and nearly took my head off as it flew into the net. He said: 'You never stopped that one, son.'"

– Paul Moran

Chapter 2

DOWN BUT NOT OUT

1954-1959

THE Liverpool players were dealt a double blow at the end of the 1953/54 season. Not only were they coming to terms with life in the second tier of English football with their neighbours Everton going in the opposite direction, but they were also having to deal with the death of their former manager, George Kay. He had fought his continuing illness with strength and courage but he died in Liverpool on April 18, 1954.

The great Billy Liddell described Kay as a father figure and knew how much his job had taken out of him. "He told me often of the times he had lain in bed, unable to sleep, pondering over the manifold problems that beset every manager. If any man gave his life for a club, George Kay did so for Liverpool," said Liddell.

Bob Paisley was also full of praise for Kay and his importance in the club's history. "He took Liverpool through the War to come out a bit like West Ham did after the First War. He was one of the people who laid the foundations for the way Liverpool teams would play in the future, keeping the ball on the ground and passing it well, but being strong on the ball as well." Although Welsh gave Moran his debut in the first-team, it was Kay who was responsible for bringing the 15-year-old Crosby boy to Liverpool FC back in 1949.

After last year's gruelling post-season tour of America and Canada, some of the players got easily tired during the regular season that ended in such disaster. With the strains of the Second Division looming, it was decided a tour would not be organised, allowing the players to feel revitalised for the new season. In addition, a loss in gate revenue was forecast so a luxurious tour was not likely to be on the directors' list of priorities.

The average attendance at Anfield dropped 12 per cent from 40,979 to 36,150 in Liverpool's first season out of the top flight. Moreover, Liverpool lost three senior players in Phil Taylor, who stayed as part of the coaching staff, Bill Jones, who signed for Ellesmere Port Town, and Bob Paisley, who went on to study to be a physiotherapist and masseur. However, Bob promptly returned to the club by the start of the 1954/55 season as he was offered the job of reserve team manager and his expertise on how to use the new electrical medical equipment eventually made him the in-house physio.

DOWN BUT NOT OUT

Ronnie Moran made his debut in the Second Division on November 27, 1954 when he was granted leave to play at Elland Road against Leeds United. He came in for Frank Lock, who regained his place when Ronnie went back to the Army. Lock, who had been signed from Charlton, played in the following three games, among them a 9-1 drubbing at St Andrew's against Birmingham City, the club's record defeat.

"We went to Birmingham, had a pre-match meal of boiled potatoes, chicken and rice pudding. It was the middle of winter, the pitch was frozen, it was hard underneath and wet on top," Alan A'Court remembered.

"In those days, there were no rubber boots, so they came out with plimsolls on. They were five up in a quarter of an hour. We could not keep our feet! We lost another four in the second half and Billy Liddell's one goal was the best of the ten! He cut through the middle and blasted it right into the top corner of the net past the English goalkeeper Gill Merrick!"

A week later the Reds travelled to Belle Vue to face Doncaster Rovers with hope of bouncing back. Although the scoreline was more than halved, Liverpool crashed to a 4-1 defeat.

Two changes were made for the following game that took place on Christmas Day morning at Anfield against Ipswich Town. Eric Anderson lost his place to Louis Bimpson and Lock was replaced once again by Moran, who was back in Crosby on Christmas leave. The Reds finally stopped their slump with a 6-2 victory. This must have been a great Christmas present for Ronnie as he was now on the winning side for the first time after 14 attempts of trying with the first-team.

Two days later he was in the side when Liverpool played Ipswich again, but lost 2-0 this time around.

Ronnie stayed in the team as he was to be stationed from January onwards in Burscough, only 15 miles north of Liverpool. He was now able to feature for Liverpool regularly and made the left-back position his own during the latter part of the 1954/55 season. He also represented the Western Command XI and featured at centre-half for the Army team against Manchester United at Ashton United, on March 22. That evening under the newly-installed floodlights at Hurst Cross, Ronnie played alongside future England and Arsenal manager, West Brom's Don Howe, and Swansea City's Mel Charles, future Wales manager. In United's line-up were the likes of David Pegg, Liam Whelan and Geoff Bent, who all perished in the Munich air disaster on February 6, 1958 that devastated the great 'Busby Babes' team.

One game that stands out for Ronnie during this campaign was his first Merseyside derby, at Goodison Park on January 29, in the fourth round of the FA Cup. Ronnie was still very inexperienced and was treating every game like a big occasion, but this was extra special as the Reds were the underdogs and had lost 10 out of 13 away games that season and drawn the other three.

"I only gained a regular place just before Christmas 1954, replacing Frank Lock. Perhaps this saved me in a way from a really bad attack of nerves," Moran said.

Ronnie looked back to this game in a press article in 1967. "I can see that Liverpool team now. Remember it? Rudham, Lambert and myself, Saunders, Hughes, Twentyman, Jackson, Anderson, Liddell, Evans and A'Court. There were a few useful ones in the Everton team too. Peter Farrell, Tommy Eglington and Dave Hickson, just to mention a few."

DOWN BUT NOT OUT

Astoundingly Liverpool beat Everton, of the First Division, 4-0 in their cup duel. Liddell gave Liverpool a great start with a spectacular goal and A'Court made it two before half-time. Centre-back Laurie Hughes was struggling with injury and had to be moved to centre-forward in the second half, which forced Liddell to take his place in defence. Hughes was a virtual passenger for the rest of the match but this move didn't blunt the attacking force of the Reds and John Evans added a couple of goals to ensure a memorable victory.

The papers were full of praise for the red men, with one report saying: 'That deserves four exclamation marks...nay forty-four! This is why I call this affair the sensation of the season and probably the most dramatic day in the long history of the famous Merseyside football derby.'

Liddell revealed that Moran and his other teammates got an unexpected treat after the match. "Manager Don Welsh was so pleased he gave us 10 shillings each!"

Liverpool finished 11th in their first season in the Second Division and Ronnie, who was finally assured of a regular place in the first-team, had made 21 appearances.

Ronnie, who was discharged from the British Army on August 1, 1955, had enjoyed his National Service as he said it "really hammered home how important it was to work hard and be focused."

A testimonial in Moran's Army book, dated July 7, 1955, gives us a great insight into Ronnie's life at the time. He was employed as a vehicle mechanic and clerk during his service and was said to be a 'diligent, reliable and a conscientious tradesman.' His footballing skills hadn't gone unnoticed either: 'In addition he is a professional footballer, a calling to which he worked with extreme enthusiasm.' Ronnie's stay in the Army was said to have been of a 'high standard' and he was praised for being 'very smart and clean in appearance, sober of habits and most loyal and trustworthy.'

Moran went from strength to strength in the 1955/56 season as he could now fully concentrate on football. He played 44 games from a possible 47, 10 more appearances than he had made during his first three seasons. Although Liverpool managed to finish third, improving their league position by eight places, it was not enough for Welsh to keep his job as manager and he was sacked on May 4, 1956. It was felt that after two years of failing to get Liverpool out of the Second Division, Welsh had done all he could and a new direction needed to be taken.

Phil Taylor, club captain during Moran's debut season, had been on the coaching staff for two years and took over as care-taker-manager on May 15, 1956. The same day Taylor signed his contract he took the players on a five-game post-season tour of France. The first game was against Angers in north-western France. Liverpool only arrived in Angers three hours before kick-off, having endured a 28-hour journey by train and ferry. Their pre-match preparation was also disrupted when they were separated from their kit in Paris by officials who insisted that the skips were to be transported on a different train. Liverpool won two out of the five games, against Racing Club Franc-Comtois and Rouen, drew against Angers and Saint-Étienne, and only suffered defeat in the final game of the tour against Toulouse. Incidentally, Liverpool's preparations for this game were also hindered by being forced to leave their hotel rooms by noon even though the match was an evening kick-off.

Taylor's first official game was played on August 18, 1956, a 3-2 league defeat to Huddersfield Town at Anfield with Moran starting at left-back. The only joy Liverpool had during this campaign came on October 24, 1956 when they won the Lancashire Senior Cup for the eighth time in the club's history and for the first time in nine years. Liverpool beat Blackburn Rovers 2-0 at Anfield with goals from A'Court and Liddell. This local cup was Moran's first honour with the first-team since his debut in 1952. Two months later Ronnie made his 100th appearance for Liverpool in a home fixture against Bury.

On March 9, 1957, Ronnie married his beloved Joyce Morley at St Helens church in Crosby. Normally the bride and groom would go away to have some photos taken or simply rest before the reception. Not Ronnie Moran. Straight after they had signed their wedding papers, Ronnie had the small matter of playing for Liverpool at Anfield to take care of. That's right, on his wedding day Ronnie played in a 2-1 victory over Barnsley, with his new wife in the stands. Ronnie and fellow defender Laurie Hughes were picked out for praise by the *Liverpool Echo* for their 'defensive heroics' in this lively match in which Ronnie kept the diminutive right-winger Arthur Kaye fairly quiet. After the game had finished, Ronnie sharply got changed back into his wedding suit and carried on the celebrations with family and close friends at Rileys in Moor Lane, also in Crosby. The newlyweds spent their honeymoon in London where they enjoyed a show at the West End and took walks around the centre of the capital. Ronnie couldn't stay away too long as he had to play at Port Vale the following weekend.

Right-back John Molyneux attended Ronnie's wedding as well as their teammates Louis Bimpson and Alan A'Court, who both featured against Barnsley. "It was nice to be invited to share their special day," John says. "Ronnie and I enjoyed playing together but we didn't socialise much as I lived in Warrington and he was in Liverpool. I remember when we played away matches and stayed in hotels, I always shared a room with Dick White and Ronnie always shared with Alan A'Court. If walking around town, we were all together, along with Louis Bimpson."

Ronnie's daughter Janet was born on Christmas Day in 1957, roughly nine months after the wedding. By then Joyce and Ronnie had moved together into a club house in Broadgreen where Liverpool owned 10 properties in a small neighbourhood. Geoff Twentyman, Dick White, Alan Arnell and Louis Bimpson all lived next door to the Morans. The players would meet up before training and take the bus together to Anfield. Their families socialised frequently and generally stayed locally around Broadgreen, but when they did venture into the city centre, although the players would get recognised, there would hardly be any hassle like today's stars would get.

Albert Shelley, who had been George Kay's trainer at Southampton, went to Liverpool in March 1937, in Kay's first campaign at the club. Shelley was in charge of the players' training, assisted by Jimmy Seddon, and former Liverpool player, Tom Bush. The trainers either had a white or a brown coat on. The players usually got Sundays and Mondays off, trained at Melwood on Tuesdays, ran around the pitch at Anfield on Wednesdays and Thursdays and then returned to Melwood on Fridays where the focus was on quick sprints to loosen the limbs. The coaching staff withheld any organised ball practice as they believed that the players would then be much hungrier for the ball come matchday. Hardly any emphasis was put on individual skills or team tactics.

Life revolved around football for the Morans and Joyce's patience was sometimes wearing thin as Ronnie used to do exercises on a field close to their home after he came back from training. Ronnie wanted to be different to those he and Bob Paisley referred to as 'Fly-by-nights', footballers who wanted big recognition right away for how they were performing for the club, even though "that kind of recognition takes years," as Ronnie used to say. Joyce would usually only watch Ronnie play when Liverpool were at home. Initially she went with Ronnie's brothers or sisters until she got friendly with Bimpson and A'Court's wives.

For the second season in a row Liverpool finished third in the Second Division. Taylor had failed to deliver promotion but after serving his season-long apprenticeship as manager, this was reported on May 1, 1957: 'At their weekly board meeting last night Liverpool FC directors appointed Phil Taylor as manager. Hitherto he has been acting manager only.' Bob Paisley was promoted from reserve team manager to first-team trainer. On a personal level, however, Ronnie's career kept on improving. He played all 42 league games during the 1956/57 season and also featured in Liverpool's FA Cup third round defeat against Southend United at Roots Hall. He was the club's only ever present for that campaign.

Ronnie's attributes were described by the *Evening Express* on the day of his wedding. 'This season Moran has established himself as one of the leading full-backs in the Second Division and his improvement is such that Liverpool believe they have one of the best in the country. Already he has been tipped in many quarters for a place in a representative eleven, and it may come before the season is over. This season his distribution has shown marked improvement and the cross-field pass has been a feature of his play. All good full-backs can kick with either foot, and although Moran's 'natural' is his left, he is never at a loss with a ball coming to the other side. One look at Moran and his power is obvious. He tackles strongly and can offer speed as another challenge to any winger.'

The representative side mentioned was a select XI of the English Football League where the best players were chosen, regardless of their nationality, to face other national league select teams. For a long period, the yearly fixture between the English and Scottish leagues was only second in importance to the matches between the two national teams. These matches grew less important during the 1950s, particularly after regular European club competition was instituted.

Moran played for the representative eleven on two occasions, in both instances as a Second Division player. He featured against the League of Ireland on October 10, 1957 as the Football League XI celebrated a 3-1 victory at Elland Road. His other appearance came on March 23, 1960 at Highbury when the Scottish Football League was beaten 1-0.

"It has always puzzled me why no further honours have come his way," said Ronnie's football idol, Billy Liddell, in 1960 and went on to sing his praises, which must have been inspiring for Ronnie to read at the time. "He is an extremely sound and capable back, who covers his goalkeeper in the way that Dougie Gray of Rangers used to do when I watched him in the days of my youth. I should say that Ronnie has saved Liverpool more times than any back in my experience by his splendid anticipation. Many are the goals he has prevented by heading or kicking off the line when the goalkeeper has been beaten. If there is a better or stronger kicker of the dead ball than Moran I would like to see him."

Moran's ability with a dead ball was backed up by his son, Paul, who remembers how dangerous his dad could be, even in a back-garden kick about.

"I never saw my dad play for Liverpool but I remember going to watch him in charity games and thinking how hard he used to strike the ball," said Paul. "One day my dad was hitting shots at me in the garden. I was about 10 and was stopping them all and told him he couldn't score past me. The next shot he smashed at me and nearly took my head off as it flew into the net. He said: 'You never stopped that one, son.'"

Although Ronnie never received an England cap, he did represent his country on one occasion, in Dixie Dean's testimonial on April 7, 1964. Over 34,000 fans witnessed England take on Scotland at Goodison Park, with the English team selected from players from Everton and Liverpool. The Scots – with one Englishman in Peter Thompson and one Welshman in Roy Vernon – beat the English 3-1. Ronnie lined up against team-mates Ron Yeats, who captained the Scottish side, Ian St John, Tommy Lawrence, Willie Stevenson and Gordon Wallace.

The 1957/58 season started extremely well for Liverpool and by October 12 they found themselves at the top of the Second Division, after beating Swansea Town 4-0 at Anfield. However, Liverpool's lead at the top of the table was short-lived as Taylor's men travelled to Derby a week later. This match proved to be quite eventful for Ronnie. Goalkeeper Tommy

Younger dived at the feet of striker Darwin two minutes before half-time and there was cause for alarm as Younger lay motionless on the pitch. Younger had received a kick in the back and had to be stretchered off. Captain Billy Liddell asked forward Tony Rowley to go in goal, but he refused. Liddell then turned to Ronnie Moran, who he knew as a fine keeper in an emergency. Ronnie could not say no to his idol and went in goal as the first half drew to a close with Liverpool losing 1-0.

Younger hobbled back on for the second half but was ordered upfield with Liddell switching to left-back in place of Ronnie, who turned out to be impressive between the sticks and doing 'better than anyone had a right to expect,' according to the *Daily Post*. He got lucky twice as Derby missed easy chances, but 'the fortune which favoured him was no more than he deserved.' Meanwhile, Younger was in dire straits 'with the worst limp I have ever seen on a football field,' as described by the scribe of the *Liverpool Echo*.

Ronnie produced two saves that prevented certain goals, including a flying save from left-half Upton 'which Younger himself could hardly have bettered.' Liverpool equalised in the 64th minute but seven minutes from time a low cross-shot from the edge of the box beat Ronnie. Then, curiously enough, the crocked Younger went back in goal despite the fact that he could 'barely cover the width of the posts without stumbling,' as reported by the *Daily Post*. Moran lost his debut game in goal, 2-1, and Liverpool dropped to second in the league.

On October 30, 1957 Moran took part in a historic night at Anfield when the ground's floodlights were switched on for the first time. They were installed at a cost of £12,000 and the visiting team were neighbours Everton. There was also a trophy at stake, a cup provided by the Liverpool County FA to celebrate its 75th anniversary. The two sides were playing in different divisions so derby matches were now few and far between. 46,274 supporters turned out to witness the first night game at Anfield, which was nearly 8,000 more than the average home attendance during this particular season. Liverpool won 3-2 on the night, but lost the cup over two legs. This was the first of many special nights under the lights at Anfield for Ronnie Moran and the supporters of Liverpool.

Taylor's men ended fourth in the league and missed out on promotion by a mere three points. Although things seemed to be improving it was still deemed an unsuccessful season. Ronnie did, however, enjoy the best FA Cup run of his career by reaching the sixth round of the competition. Liverpool failed to qualify for the semi-finals for the seventh time in their history after losing 2-1 to John Carey's Blackburn Rovers. Around 51,000 football fans witnessed the occasion with Ewood Park full to the brim. During the second half a crush barrier broke and five people had to be treated for their injuries.

Liverpool went on a post-season tour of Spain and France where the Reds beat Real Sociedad, Osasuna and Perpignan and lost to Elche and Centre d'Esports L'Hospitalet. Among the perks of being a footballer for Ronnie were trips like these to foreign countries as Billy Liddell pointed out. "Only well-to-do people could travel in the manner we did on those trips, and all it cost the player was what we paid in duty on presents when passing through customs on our return. It becomes a holiday without worry. There are ample opportunities for sightseeing and entertainment as the games are usually so spaced out that there is a fair amount of free time," Liddell said.

The 1958/59 season also began with a game outside England. Liverpool travelled to Scotland to face an Edinburgh select team at Tynecastle, the home of Heart of Midlothian. It was the second time Liverpool participated in such an occasion as part of the City of Edinburgh's charity day.

Ronnie's only own goals in competitive matches came during this campaign. His first came at Ashton Gate against Bristol Rovers in September. Moran's misfortune was so described in the *Liverpool Echo*: 'Liverpool lost their lead on 21 minutes when Rovers' Hinshelwood let go what appeared to be a centre but Moran got his foot to the ball as it was rising and Younger was beaten.' His second came at The Valley against Charlton Athletic the following January and, as usual, the *Echo* was there to give us the details: 'Another blow to Liverpool with an own goal by Moran. The leading up work was by Sam Lawrie again who slipped through Liverpool's defence like quicksilver, crossed the ball low and Moran, running in to intercept, turned it into his own net.'

Another important date in Moran's playing career was November 15, 1958 when Liverpool travelled to the Baseball Ground to face Derby County. Captain Johnny Wheeler was absent that day so Ronnie took over the captaincy for the first time and led the team to a 3-2 victory over the Rams. Incidentally, Ronnie also made his first-team debut at Derby six years earlier.

Liverpool enjoyed a tremendous cup run in the previous campaign but this time around Moran was involved in the biggest cup upset in Liverpool's entire history. On January 15, 1959 Liverpool visited St. George's Lane to be hosted by non-league Worcester City. Despite their status, Phil Taylor didn't underestimate them: "I know Worcester aren't Second Division class, but they will be difficult to beat on their own ground."

Eight of Worcester City's starting eleven had been doing their day jobs that morning to earn an income. English football was in shock after Liverpool's 2-1 defeat. Despite his disappointment Taylor was noble towards the minnows: "Worcester deserved to win. They outfought us on a pitch that may have reduced the odds against them, but was still as good a playing surface as you can get in England right now. We lost because our forwards refused to fight."

On the back of this embarrassing third round cup exit, fans started to lose their patience with manager Taylor so perhaps Liverpool's rise to fame started on this freezing cold afternoon in Worcester. Moreover, Taylor could only manage another fourth-place league finish. After the league season ended, Ronnie added a second Lancashire Senior Cup medal to his collection on May 5, 1959 as Liverpool beat Everton to win the competition for the second time in four seasons.

Ronnie's career continued to flourish and he started the 1959/60 season as club captain. He was very proud to be bestowed with this honour, following in the footsteps of so many great players. When Ronnie started to attend matches after World War II, inside-left Willie Fagan was captain, sharing duties with goalscorer supreme Jack Balmer, who took over the armband formally from the injury-prone Fagan in the 1947/48 season. They were both part of a select few who had also featured in Liverpool's team in the 1938/39 season, the last before the war. Their highlight as captains was undoubtedly guiding the club to the 1947 league championship. Moran's then-manager, Phil Taylor, was captain for four years until 1953 and led Liverpool out at Wembley in the FA Cup final in 1950, the club's first for 36 years. Bill Jones, grandfather to Rob who played 243 matches for the Reds, was captain when the team got relegated in 1954, and was replaced by Laurie Hughes, who held on to the armband for one season before Billy Liddell was given the captaincy.

As the 1958/59 season started, right-half Johnny Wheeler had replaced the 36-year-old Liddell as captain. Wheeler, who was born in Crosby just like Ronnie, was, however, not too fond of this responsibility and pleaded with manager Taylor to relinquish the armband, but was persuaded to carry on for the rest of the campaign.

Ronnie Moran had been appointed in his place when Liverpool faced Cardiff City at Ninian Park in the opening game of the 1959/60 season. The home fixture that season against Cardiff on December 19, 1959 at Anfield is one game that Ronnie nor anybody connected with Liverpool Football Club will ever forget as it was the Monarch of Merseyside's first-ever game in charge. Ronnie Moran was his skipper.

"My dad said the first thing he realised about Bill Shankly was that the club was destined for greater things under his management and my dad wanted to be a part of it."

– Paul Moran

Chapter 3

MERSEYSIDE MONARCH

1959-1962

A THIRD-place finish in 1957, followed by two fourth-place finishes in 1958 and 1959 might have been satisfactory at some other clubs but not at Liverpool as chairman Thomas Valentine Williams' ambitions surpassed those of his predecessors.

Phil Taylor's last game in charge was a 4-2 defeat at Lincoln City on November 14. The following Tuesday, Taylor handed in his resignation after 23 years at the club. "We had a long chat and it was made clear they had a new man, Bill Shankly, in mind, so I took the hint and agreed to call it a day," Taylor said.

"I can't remember that the board actually stopped me signing anybody I specially wanted, but they were not generally happy to pay out large sums of money and we had very few scouts at the time to recommend outstanding prospects.

"I was pleased to see Liverpool do so well in the years that followed, but couldn't help wondering occasionally how I would have fared if I had been able to sign newcomers like Yeats and St John," Taylor revealed.

The players talked among themselves that Liverpool's lack of spending was a hindrance to progress, as Alan A'Court explained. "The board wouldn't give the manager any money to spend, but we were always third or fourth, there or thereabouts, but not quite capable of making the extra step. We felt that although we were getting 45-50,000 fans every week, where was that money going? It wasn't being spent on transfers!"

Taylor's successor, Mr William Shankly, agreed to join Liverpool on December 1, 1959. He stayed for two weeks more at Huddersfield Town while they got their affairs in order. Shankly watched Liverpool reserves play on December 12 while the first-team travelled to play Bristol Rovers. When the team arrived at Eastville Stadium there was a telegram waiting addressed to skipper Ronnie Moran. It simply said: "We still have a chance. Good luck. Bill Shankly," no doubt inferring that Liverpool could still get promoted.

Liverpool were in inspired mood against Rovers, none more so than the captain. Rovers lay siege to Liverpool's goal at times but found 'left-back Moran in Superman mood.' He twice kicked certain goals off the line with goalkeeper Bert Slater well beaten and when his defence seemed wide open and the route to goal was clear, Ronnie was time and again ready with a last-ditch tackle. Moran and his teammates kept a clean sheet and Jimmy Melia grabbed a couple of goals that guaranteed victory.

Shankly was officially presented at Anfield on Monday, December 14 and the *Liverpool Echo* scribe was happy with the appointment and had clearly done his homework.

'Shankly is a disciple of the game as played by the Continentals. The man out of possession, he believes, is just as important as the man with the ball at his feet. Shankly will aim at incisive forward moves by which Continentals streak through a defence when it is closed up by British standards. He will make his players learn to kill a ball and move it all in the same action,' the *Echo* said, giving a good account of what Shankly later preached at Liverpool.

The Scotsman's aura was overwhelming and he cast his spell on the press. His disciples would be next. 'If every Anfield fan could talk with Shankly as I did they could not help but be impressed by his sincerity, enthusiasm and burning desire to improve the side. And for sustenance in this task there will be no smoke, no hard drinks. Just plentiful supplies of the herbal tea from Brazil, which is where the other Knuts of soccer come from. Good luck to you, Mr Shankly!' the *Echo* concluded, referring to the foul-smelling herbal tea that Shankly used to drink.

Cardiff were Liverpool's first opponents under the management of Shankly on Saturday, December 19 and he set about preparing his team three days prior to the match.

Moran, rarely given to hyperbole, said: "The very first thing Bill said to me and the players was in a team meeting on the Wednesday morning after joining was that everyone had an equal chance and that he had no preconceived opinion about anyone at the club."

Alan A'Court remembered this meeting differently. "Typically Bill Shankly's introduction to his players was highly theatrical. He strode into the room where we sat waiting for him, then stood facing us, feet apart, body leaning slightly forward and his arms at half cock, like a Western gun fighter. We sat hypnotised as he barked: 'Some of you boys have been here too long.' Just the kind of encouragement us older hands needed!"

Ronnie's son Paul remembers his dad telling him about the inspiration of Shankly. "My dad said the first thing he realised about Bill Shankly was that the club was destined for greater things under his management and my dad wanted to be a part of it."

Shankly's first game in charge was less than inspirational though, as Ronnie recalled some years later. "How could I forget Bill's first game? It was Cardiff at home and we lost 4-0. Walking off at the end with Alan A'Court, I remember saying to him: 'I wonder what will happen now. I bet we get kiboshed!' But Bill wasn't like that; the only time I saw him get really angry was with one of the reporters who'd written something in the *Echo* that was incorrect. Shankly was in the Bootroom that day and, as he saw the reporter pass, he didn't half give him a rollicking. Bill never did it in the dressing rooms. He wasn't one of those 'tea cups at the wall' types. He'd have a cup in his hand but he'd be sipping hot water out of it. He'd take a sip, then spit it out of the corner of his mouth. You could see he may be angry but he'd never go for a player in that way."

Maybe Ronnie was just being protective of his old boss as Tommy Lawrence, who played in the first-team from 1962 onwards, remembers differently: "He was a funny fella, Shanks. He wouldn't let anybody else criticise you, but he would. After a game if you'd had a nightmare he'd come in and he'd railroad you, really hammer you, then he'd walk out and tell everyone, 'that lad had a great game.'"

Furthermore, future Liverpool captain Ron Yeats can remember Lawrence being a victim of a Shankly outburst after he let in an equaliser by Arsenal 20 minutes before time at Highbury on December 7, 1963. "Joe Baker hit the ball from 25 yards. I am not joking, but he stubbed his toe first and then hit the ball. It trickled by me and I went: 'It's yours, Tommy',", Yeats recalls.

"Tommy was on the line and opened his legs and the bloody ball went right through him. They put pressure on us for the last five minutes, but we held out. I am thinking to myself all this time, 'when we get into that dressing room I am going to get into the bath before Shanks comes in the door.' Little did I know that the ten players I was playing with thought the same thing. When the final whistle went... if we had sprinted that much during the game we would have won it easily. Everybody was trying to hurry into the dressing room but it wasn't quick enough. The door opened and in came Shanks. His face was blue and I am thinking, 'here it goes.' He went, 'where is he?' I didn't realise but big Tommy Lawrence was behind me. I was three inches bigger than him and didn't know where he was. His finger went up and he said, 'I am here, boss.' 'Where?' 'I am here, boss.' Tommy said, 'before you say anything, boss, I want to apologise to you and the lads. I should have never opened my legs to that ball.' Shankly went, 'it's not your fault. It's your mother who should have never opened her legs.'"

The 4-0 defeat to Cardiff was far from the ideal Anfield debut for Shanks whose team heavily underperformed in front of their new manager. Right from the start, Shankly was made to realise the tremendous task that lay ahead of him as his average Liverpool team was torn apart by Cardiff City. The final blow for Shankly that day was having to stand the jeers hurled at the directors' box from many sections of the crowd as the final whistle was blown. Nonetheless, Shankly had never been afraid of hard work and was optimistic after the game: "Naturally, I'm disappointed but it's just as well that I've seen the team give an off-form display in my first match. I've learned quite a few things this way."

A week later, on Boxing Day, Shankly and his inherited team travelled to the Valley to take on Charlton Athletic and were well beaten again, 3-0 this time. Two days later, the Addicks visited Anfield for Shankly's second game in front of the home crowd. After their team had failed to score in their previous two games and conceded seven goals, the 25,658 spectators who turned up probably weren't overly confident going into the game. This was proven by an unusually silent Kop until A'Court's goal in the 58th minute. Five minutes later Roger Hunt made sure of Shankly's first win in this otherwise colour-less match as described by the *News Chronicle and Daily Dispatch* whose reporter stated that 'Liverpool's forwards ran around like scalded cats, without understanding or method,' for the best part of an hour.

Next up for Shankly was the first game of what would become a highly successful decade for Liverpool. On January 2, 1960 Ronnie led his team out against bottom-of-the-league Hull City at Boothferry Park. Jimmy Melia scored the only goal of the game, taking Liverpool up to eighth in the table. Leyton Orient in the FA Cup and Sheffield United in the league were beaten at Anfield. Four wins in a row and Shankly had started to build up momentum and instil some well-needed belief back into the supporters. The scribes at the *Liverpool Echo* were certainly impressed: 'Bill Shankly's Liverpool are a changed side. They think more, thump less. Chase more, chance less.' The Sheffield United game also marked the reintroduction of left-back Gerry Byrne, who had only played a couple of games in two-and-a-half years and been on the transfer list prior to Shankly's arrival, as was reported on November 4, 1959: 'Byrne is being allowed to [go on the transfer list] because it is felt there will be little opportunity for him some seasons as deputy to the first-team back and captain, Ronnie Moran.'

Liverpool were heading for a fifth consecutive win when leading Middlesbrough 3-1 at half-time. Brian Clough, later a controversial manager at Derby, Leeds and Nottingham Forest, scored his second of the game and Boro got their equaliser from the penalty spot after Moran handled in the box eight minutes from time. Next up were Manchester United in the fourth round of the FA Cup on January 30. Liverpool could not contain Bobby Charlton, who scored two brilliant goals in a 3-1 win at a rainy, muddy Anfield.

Shankly's men responded by winning three out of the next four, scoring 12 goals in the process. Moran was an impressive performer and after a 2-2 draw against Shankly's former club, Huddersfield, on March 19, the *Echo*'s Jack Rowe felt international honours were within reach for Moran. 'Anfield followers, in the past couple of weeks, have had the opportunity of seeing two full-backs who have had claims to a place in the England team. Allen of Stoke was here a fortnight ago, and on Saturday it was Huddersfield's Wilson. I wonder how many would give either of them preferences over Moran.' He went on to claim Moran had an excellent chance of playing for his country as he was 'the outstanding full-back on Saturday.' Horace Yates at the *Post* agreed with Rowe's estimation: 'If one has to decide on this showing whether Moran or Wilson was better qualified for the left-back position in the England side, my vote unhesitatingly would go to Moran. He was so much tidier, more efficient looking and gave one a feeling of solid confidence.'

Unfortunately for Ronnie, the England selectors didn't agree with Liverpool's local papers and Ray Wilson made his debut for the England team three weeks later in a 1-1 draw with Scotland, and went on to get 68 caps for his country and become a World Cup winner.

Ronnie experienced something new during the 1959/60 season; scoring goals. His first-ever goal for Liverpool came in his 211th appearance on August 29, 1959 against Hull City at Anfield. Liverpool were 2-0 down until the 52nd minute when Jimmy Harrower went past three men before delivering a left-foot shot that sailed into the net. Jimmy Melia headed in an equaliser six minutes before Ronnie Moran took centre stage and completed Liverpool's comeback. His 65th-minute free-kick flew low and unerringly through the defensive wall. Alan A'Court and Billy Liddell added two more in the last 10 minutes and an unlikely 5-3 victory was guaranteed.

Less than a month later on September 26, Ronnie got on the scoresheet again from a free-kick. Liverpool were 3-1 up against Plymouth Argyle when their keeper, Geoff Barnsley, was caught out of the area with the ball. Ronnie's direct strike roared home and Liverpool celebrated amid protests from the Argyle players who thought that the referee had given an indirect free-kick.

Ronnie's first goal away from Anfield came in a nine-goal thriller at Vetch Park a week later. Swansea Town went 3-1 up in the middle of the first half but A'Court and Hunt had pulled the deficit back when Liverpool were awarded a free-kick in the 70th minute when centre-half Mel Nurse handled just outside the area. Ronnie spotted a narrow gap in the defenders' wall and struck the ball in off the foot of the post. Swansea netted their fourth through Reynolds, who scored again 60 seconds from the final whistle with a shot that was so tremendous that it was 'enough to turn the swerve-imparting Puskas of Real Madrid green with envy,' according to the *Liverpool Echo*.

Moran's fourth goal of the campaign was his first from open play, against Portsmouth at Anfield on October 24. Moran came up for a short A'Court corner in the fifth minute and smashed the ball first time in superb fashion past goalkeeper Dick Beattie.

Ronnie's fifth and final goal of the season was his first under Shankly and his first from the penalty spot, as Liverpool lost to Lincoln City at Anfield on April 2. The ball had merely bounced on Jeff Smith's shoulder as he was clearing but still a penalty was given. Moran banged the ball in to bring Lincoln's lead down to 2-1 after half an hour's play. Lincoln refused to be rattled and wore out Liverpool by a superb defensive display, winning the game 3-1. Incidentally, this was Shankly's first home defeat of 1960.

In the following match, Shankly tried to accommodate Byrne in the team. He hadn't figured since he made his sole appearance three months previously. Byrne came in at left-back in place of Moran, who was moved a bit further upfield to left-half. Liverpool's opponents were Derby County in a rear-ranged midweek game after play had been stopped after 71 minutes due to Anfield's 'swirling mist' in their original fixture two months earlier.

The weather was just fine this time around, but while Liverpool beat Derby 4-1, this change of position for Moran was not at all well received by Horace Yates of the *Liverpool Daily Post*, who reported: 'The experiment of playing Moran in the left half back line had shown no signs of working out well. It was a completely undistinguished try-out with appearances all against his making a success of the role. Now, if Liverpool had been trying to find a left-back instead of a left-half, there would have been every occasion for a rubbing of hands for Byrne scarcely put a foot wrong and acted with the assurance of a player very much his senior in experience.'

Shankly persevered three days later at Leyton Orient, but even though Moran played well, the *Daily Post* was still in disagreement. 'One could not be completely happy either about the defence, for it seems to me that Moran's solidity is missed when he is not at full-back. Byrne played coolly and with plenty of promise and it is a temptation to wonder whether there could not be a re-alignment at full-back without losing Moran's strength in the position.'

Shanks wasn't entirely convinced either and for the next game Moran was moved back to his original position and Byrne replaced John Molyneux on the right. This decision was met with universal approval but was far from the biggest talking point in Liverpool's 4-0 win over Bristol Rovers at Anfield.

As Moran reclaimed his left-back berth on April 16, 1960, a 17-year-old local boy by the name of Ian Callaghan was introduced into the side on the right wing. Cally had only signed professional forms six weeks earlier, but what a debut he had! So good, in fact, that at the final whistle Bristol Rovers' outside left Peter Hooper dashed up to shake Ian by the hand and referee Reg Leafe ran over to give the lad a word of praise. Callaghan deserved it as he'd had a part in three of the four goals. Moreover, the Anfield crowd stood up from their seats and cheered him back into the dressing room.

Cally was very grateful to Ronnie when he first started out in the first-team. He said: "I don't know how I would have managed without him. It was a big step up playing in the first-team and I don't know how I would have coped without someone keeping an eye on me and helping me out of difficult situations. I soon learned that at Liverpool, we were essentially part of a team and depended on each other."

Moran also held Cally in high regard: "I always used to accuse him of being injury prone and missing games. Cally always countered by telling me the exact number of games he had played." That argument would prove more difficult to uphold for Ronnie as Cally finally became Liverpool's record appearance holder, playing a total of 857 games.

Moran's milestone 250th appearance for Liverpool came against Rotherham United on April 19, 1960 on the dusty, iron-hard Millmoor pitch where the Liverpool defence was chopped wide open by long passes. Ronnie and centre-half Dick White both misjudged the bounce of the ball which allowed in firstly Alan Kirkman, and then Gordon Swann. However, Ronnie did redeem himself for previous errors by coolly clearing off his line from Ken Waterhouse in the last minute to save Liverpool a point in a 2-2 draw.

Ronnie captained all of Liverpool's league and cup games during the 1959/60 season, 44 in total, a feat only six other post-war captains have achieved: Jack Balmer, Dick White, Ron Yeats, Emlyn Hughes, Phil Thompson and Phil Neal.

Ronnie had a very humble attitude with regards to the captaincy: "It was an honour to be captain of Liverpool FC but it was always more of an honour to be playing for the team. Shanks always preached that we had eleven captains. He wanted to see players think things out and rectify things themselves if they were going wrong. You never got shouted at for trying to change something out on the pitch. You were always taught to work things out for yourself. Mind you, if you tried something stupid and it didn't come off, he had a saying that he would 'hit you on the head with a big stick from the touchline.'"

Liverpool employed a particular tactic at this time that would leave the full-backs in space for a shot or cross, put into effect when the team had a throw-in in the opponent's half. The wing-half would take the throw, the winger at that side of the field would go as close to the corner flag as possible to take the opposing full-back away, the centre-forward would move to the far side of the penalty box and the inside-forwards would take their markers into deep forward areas. This tactic benefited Ronnie especially as he had an extremely accurate shot and his crossing from deep positions was great for the strikers.

Billy Howard, who was in the Liverpool junior team at the

time, made a note of this tactic and used it later when he became an accomplished junior league coach. He often watched the games at Anfield from a little walled area behind the dugout where the club's junior players were allowed to stay.

"Ronnie would have got in the team in any era," Billy claims. "He was strong, a brilliant reader of the game and motivated all those around him. He had power and accuracy in that golden left foot and it was a joy to have watched a 'real pro' at work."

Liverpool ended the 1959/60 season third behind Aston Villa and Cardiff City, who were both promoted. Despite the disastrous start, Shanks finished the season with a 52 per cent winning record. Ronnie, now 26, had made 252 first-team appearances and had since 1955/56 played in 97 per cent of all of Liverpool's competitive matches, missing just six games in five seasons.

Ronnie, who was an experienced campaigner, was very impressed by the new boss. "I learned more in the first season with Bill than I'd done in the seven years that I'd been a pro. I wish I'd been five years younger."

Ronnie firmly agreed with the board's decision to replace Phil Taylor. "No disrespect to the previous management but when Shanks came he was like a breath of fresh air. He completely changed the club around and took it to where it is today, renowned all over the world," Moran said.

Once Shankly took over as manager he got rid of the dreaded long-distance running that had been prevalent during the reign of Don Welsh and Phil Taylor, especially at the start of the season. "We used to run down to Melwood from Anfield, which was about three-and-a-half-miles, do our training, and run back," Ronnie says. "Shanks did away with all that. He said:

'You don't run on the road in a match so we won't do it in training.'"

Goalkeeper Tommy Lawrence was glad to see the back of this exercise: "Roger Hunt and I used to travel by train from Warrington and after about three days, we couldn't even go down the steps, the backs of our calves were just gone."

Many of the players weren't too keen on the running, especially in the plimsolls they used to wear. The players were supposed to leave their cars at Anfield but some would cheat and park close to Melwood pretending they had run all the way, check in at the training ground and then jump into the car once they left to go back to Anfield.

Tom Bush, who was a jack of all trades at the club, cycled behind the players to make sure no-one cut any corners or hitched a ride. Moran hardly ever cheated as he believed simply that there were "no shortcuts to success."

Shankly had a different perspective on how to achieve that success. "Some people may say that we are lazy, but that's fine. What's the point of tearing players to pieces? We never bothered with sand dunes and hills and roads. We trained on grass where football is played."

First-team trainer Bob Paisley was inventive in his approach and introduced the gallows at Melwood. He tied a ball to the gallows and the players took turns leaping into the air to head it. Now and then Bob pulled the string a bit so the players had to adjust their leap, having to time it perfectly.

Scottish striker George Scott moved to Liverpool from Aberdeen in 1960 and has fond memories of Moran. "When I joined Liverpool, along with Gordon Wallace, Bobby Graham, Tommy Smith and Chris Lawler in early 1960, Ronnie had been a professional at the club for eight years and was club captain. We were young kids of 15 and in the case of Bobby, Gordon and myself we were hundreds of miles from home.

"Of all the people at the club who were on the playing staff Ronnie stood out as someone who took an interest in our progress and I would not be at all surprised if Shanks had not had a word in his ear, requesting that he looked after us. To us he looked a giant of a man with legs like tree trunks and a heart of a lion. He used to always be up at the front during training sessions, and along with Joe, Bob and Reuben, who were already our coaches, Ronnie instilled a self-belief and enthusiasm into our characters that was so very important for young players Shankly had such high hopes for."

There is no doubt that Ronnie Moran's coaching style was influenced by the 'Iron man of Anfield', Reuben Bennett, who was retained by Shankly as first-team coach, having joined one year before his compatriot's arrival. Reuben was ruthless in his approach, but he didn't ask of the players what he couldn't do himself. He was super fit and didn't tolerate any slacking.

"Reuben considered that any feeling of pain or hurt was soft," former player Willie Stevenson said, recollecting a memorable day in Blackpool. "We were on the beach playing in snow and the water was iced out to about 30 or 40 feet. One of us kicked the ball into the water and Reuben says, 'Go and get it.' We told him to bugger off. So he called us a load of wimps and promptly proceeded to run into the sea, swim out, get the ball and come back and carry on playing. He only had shorts and a T-shirt on. We all had balaclavas, hats, gloves, pullovers."

Like Ronnie, Reuben was a modest man who didn't seek the limelight. The tough Scot stayed on the coaching staff until 1971 when Joe Fagan took over his job and Ronnie was promoted in turn.

Moran was always picking up tips and techniques that he would later use in training routines. "I learned so much from Bob Paisley and Joe Fagan about how the game should be played, however, Shanks was my master. Shanks was very astute at picking out strengths and weaknesses of direct opponents and would always explain himself clearly to the lads during training," says Ronnie. "It was very much like his half-time team talks, which again were extremely clear and direct to the point and largely depended on the state of the game and whether the team had been following pre-match instructions and tactics or not."

The simplicity of the approach Shankly took to training led to much confusion and disbelief among his peers. As the trophies began to roll in, a growing band of onlookers would gather at Melwood to watch and learn. They would all go away muttering about how little Liverpool seem to do, completely missing the point of what was on display.

The infamous 'Sweat box' tested the stamina of the players to the maximum. Wooden boards were put up as walls of a house. "We used Roger Hunt as a guinea pig with the boards," Shankly said. "We placed them 15 yards apart, and told him to play the ball against one of the boards, take it, control it, turn and dribble up to the other board with just 10 touches. We wanted to know how long this function should last. We were probing. After 45 seconds, Roger, who was as strong as a bull, turned ashen and I said: 'That will do, son.' Later Roger could do that exercise for two minutes."

Another wooden board with numbers on tested accuracy

and awareness as the ball was thrown from all angles at the respective player who had to hit it first time at a certain number. "Look at that board," Shankly told reporters in 1964, "Roger Hunt can hit that with nine shots out of ten. This is where all his goals are made. I wouldn't be far wrong in saying that Hunt has had hundreds of thousands of shots at these targets."

Shankly and his trainers organised training to a tee. After about 30 minutes of warm-up the players were split into six groups; A, B, C, D, E and F. Group A did weight training, B focused on skipping, C on jumping, D on squats, E on abdominal exercises and F on sprints. The players were rotated until they completed all six. The group also did several drills that focused on how to chip, shoot, control and head the ball.

"We devised a system where the players went through the functions in two-minute sessions over a period of 15 to 17 minutes. Two minutes, then half-a-minute's rest, and so on," Shankly said.

"Footballers normally train for an hour-and-a-half, but it doesn't mean they work for an hour-and-a-half," Shankly explained in his final interview, published in the *Liverpool Echo* on July 13, 1981. "Some might be demonstrating a function while the others are watching. And then it's your turn. It's not how long you train, but what you put into it. If you train properly, 35 minutes a day might do. We built Liverpool's training on exhaustion and recovery with little areas of two-a-side, three-a-side and five-a-side in which you work like a boxer, twisting and turning. Training was based on basic skills, control, passing, vision, awareness."

This is the sort of organisation that Ronnie Moran was raised on at Liverpool that served him so well in his future role.

"People missed what it was all about," Moran said. "They would just see us doing a bit of jogging then go straight into games of five-a-side, or maybe a bit of ball work. They never saw the little things that we were doing, teaching the players when to pass, how to move into space and so on. Sometimes players would be corrected for passing to someone who was marked for instance. I was blessed as a player, I found it easy; but some didn't and they had to be taught."

"If Shanks looked at a couple of kids juggling a ball, it wouldn't matter to him which one was better. He would want to see how they played in a game situation," Ronnie added. "You don't get opportunities to juggle the ball in a match, so it was irrelevant. I'm not saying having great ball skills is wrong, but with Shanks it was not the most important thing."

These were lessons that Moran would take on board and develop as he spent year after year at Melwood. "When I was a player I had no real understanding of how teams were built. Then, when I started watching Shanks, I began to work it out. If he had a player who lacked a bit of pace but was a really good passer, he would play someone alongside him who could compensate. It was all about balancing out the shortcomings of one player with the strong points of another," Ronnie explains.

Shankly and his coaching staff always drummed into the players the notion that they had to control a game with their heads as well as their feet. "If you watched youngsters playing a game you might spot the one who gives you something extra, a bit of fight or determination for example. Shanks would want to see what the lad could do with his natural footballing brains," Ronnie says. "Does he know how to pass? Can he tackle? He would be looking to see if that lad had something about him."

Shankly felt he could better spot the youngsters' temperament by playing against them, but in truth it was just an excuse for a kick about. Shankly would immediately lose his focus as he was so competitive. "The lads used to joke about it because he'd be going around kicking anyone who wasn't quick enough to get out of his way, but before we knew it we became as competitive as he was," Ronnie remembered. "We went to the kids and had an eight-a-side and Shanks didn't like losing that.

"Bob always had his watch. One day we were losing two-none. Bob says: 'It's quarter past twelve, boss. Will you finish?' Shankly said: 'We won't finish until we get winning.' We played on and luckily we got two goals, but it was about twenty to one."

The 1960/61 season started off with a trip to France to take part in the Friendship Cup against Nantes. Liverpool won the first leg 2-0 with goals from Roger Hunt and new signing Kevin Lewis. Ronnie played in his normal left-back position; however, the captaincy had now been handed over to centre-half Dick White, an indication of what was to come for Ronnie.

Moran's 47 games as captain oversaw some legendary debuts for Liverpool. On September 9, 1959, due to an injury to Billy Liddell, 21-year-old Roger Hunt was called up to the first-team to face Scunthorpe United at Anfield. Liverpool won the game 2-0 and 'Sir Roger' scored his debut goal. Moran and Hunt were great friends. "It was an honour to have played in a team with a World Cup winner and I actually went to watch Roger play for Bolton a few times after he left Liverpool," says Ronnie.

Moran's captaincy also oversaw the debut of Dave Hickson,

who took the bold decision to cross Stanley Park from Everton on November 6, 1959. He got off to a great start against Aston Villa at Anfield as he scored twice to earn his new side a 2-1 victory. Moran was instrumental in helping to settle Hickson's nerves as the striker revealed in Ronnie's testimonial programme in 2000. "Ronnie was the club captain and he made me feel very welcome as I settled in. He was an inspiring captain and a great left-back. His dead ball kicks were awesome, both in power and accuracy. He developed from a fine player to a great coach which is why he is one of the most respected men in the business. I am very proud to know Ronnie and have him as a friend." He had never forgotten how well he was received by his former Liverpool captain 41 years previously.

In the fourth game of the 1960/61 season Billy Liddell made his last-ever appearance for Liverpool. At that time no other player had played more games for the club than King Billy, a total of 534, eclipsing Elisha Scott's 468. Ronnie lined up alongside his hero for the last time in a competitive match against Southampton at Anfield on August 31. Liverpool were unable to produce a winning performance, slumped to a 1-0 defeat and dropped down to 17th in the league.

Ronnie, as everyone else connected with the club, held Liddell in the highest regard, not only as a footballer but as a person too. When Liddell finally called it a day he was rewarded with a testimonial against a select side that included the likes of Bert Trautmann, Jimmy Armfield, Nat Lofthouse and Tom Finney. The game took place on September 21, 1960 at Anfield, three weeks after Liddell's final outing for the first-team. Liverpool had a strong line-up of Bert Slater, John Molyneux, Ronnie Moran, Johnny Wheeler, Dick White, Gordon Milne, Alan

A'Court, Roger Hunt, Dave Hickson, Jimmy Harrower and last, but not least, Billy Liddell. Six of those players had featured in Liverpool's 2-1 win over Derby County two days previously, so Shankly wasn't just sending out the reserves.

Stanley Matthews had been scheduled to play but did not show up. This was, in fact, something Matthews did regularly. He would be billed to play in testimonials and benefit games to increase the crowd and revenue for the player concerned as he was the major draw in English football. Prior to kick-off a telegram from Matthews was read out over the tannoy: "Sorry, Billy, indisposed, good luck, Stan Matthews."

His absence meant Tom Finney lined up at outside-right opposite Moran at left-back. Avid Red, Billy Howard, was at the game and remembers it well. "Because it was a friendly, Ronnie wasn't making heavy tackles on Tom, just mainly jockeying and trying to block or pinch the ball off him, without much success," Billy says. "Tom would just approach him, drop his shoulder and he was gone. Ronnie was having a terrible time trying to stop him. I was in the Annie Road, right in line with that wing. When Tom went past Ronnie for the umpteenth time, Ronnie just turned to us in the crowd with his arms outstretched as if to say, 'what do I have to do to stop this fella?' It was a compliment to the great player Tom was, but I don't think Tom would have got off so lightly in a league game."

A crowd of just under 39,000 gathered for this showpiece in which Liddell also played for the opposition and even scored against Liverpool. The referee added time to the 90 minutes in an effort to get Liddell to round the game off with another goal. Liverpool won 4-2, but the result wasn't of great importance. Liddell pocketed a tidy sum to go with the £2,500 he had earned in club benefits throughout the years. "When I called it a day I was on £20-a-week plus a win bonus, but money was worth a lot more then. The testimonial game netted me £6,000 and I was able to buy a house," Liddell said.

Ronnie was ever present at left-back during the first 10 games of the 1960/61 campaign, chipping in with two goals. The first came from the penalty spot against Luton at Anfield and the second one was a rebound from this own penalty kick, again against Luton Town, but this time at Kenilworth Road. On October 1, 1960, Liverpool beat Derby County at Anfield to leave them in ninth position. Moran got injured and when he was ready to play again after an absence of three weeks, he went into the reserves. Shankly had taken stock of the players he had inherited and felt Gerry Byrne's time in the first-team had come at Ronnie's expense.

The Scotsman said that Byrne, who was a Scouser like Ronnie, was the most courageous player he ever had on his books. Byrne's rough tackling soon earned him a fearsome reputation. "I was nicknamed the 'Crunch'," Byrne said. "I used to wait for the ball to come and then I was on my way. You hit someone when the ball was there and that was it. That's how I got the crunch."

Ian St John said that Byrne's tackles were so hard that he was the only player banned from making a challenge in the five-a-sides at Melwood as the coaching staff feared he would injure his teammates.

Moran had to settle for a place in the reserves for the rest of the season apart from one outing at Brighton on January 14 when John Molyneux was unavailable. Moran, who 'returned in the strange position of right-back,' was far from impressive as the *Daily Post* reported. 'I could not help feeling sorry for Ronnie Moran. He was so desperately keen to seize his opportunity to reclaim his first-team place, but the weeks of activity with the reserves appear to have slowed down his reactions alarmingly. This was only a shadow of the Moran we used to know,' the writer in the *Post* said and 'saddled him with the responsibility' for two of the goals in Liverpool's 3-1 defeat. As a result, Ronnie found himself out of the first-team for the next 12 months.

Shankly's Liverpool finished the 1960/61 season third for the second campaign in a row. They just couldn't get over the finish line to achieve promotion, but Shankly fully realised what was missing.

"We had a choice of A'Court, Lewis, Callaghan and Morrissey as wingers, and Melia, Hunt, Hickson and Harrower from which to choose for the inside positions. We had five men without a leader. What was lacking was a man of experience to occupy the centre forward position, a player who could play football, create openings, score goals, and at the same time hold the line together," Shankly said.

Ian St John was brought in from Motherwell on May 2, 1961. The Saint's first goal for his new club came a few weeks later in the opening game of Liverpool's post-season tour of Czechoslovakia, against Vodní Stavby Tábor. Moran travelled with the first-team for the four-game tour. Interestingly, the second game against Rudá Hvezda Brno was only 80 minutes long because the stadium was required for the finish of a big cycle race and cameras needed to be placed on the pitch!

Ronnie made his tour debut six days later in a 1-1 draw against Slovakian side Tatran Presov. Despite scoring Liverpool's only goal, new signing St John later got himself sent off for kicking out at an opponent. Moran also played in the final game of the tour in a 4-1 victory over Mesto Most. Jimmy Melia scored twice, as well as St John, who ended the tour scoring four goals in four games.

What stood out the most regarding this particular tour for Moran was the flight back home from Czechoslovakia, a life-threatening situation that Ronnie simply described as "bizarre". The Saint remembers this incident well:

"When we took off, heading back to Liverpool, I could see the ground below us and all of a sudden the main plane door flew open. The cabin crew forgot to lock the door before we took off and just closed it instead. It was the most harrowing experience of my life," St John admits.

"All the cabin crew worked between them for about two minutes to close it. However, due to the wind, it was difficult for the one who was actually trying to close it to stay on his feet. Therefore, in order for him to regain his balance another flight attendant grabbed him by the waist in order to shut and then lock the door. Although, we were only about 100 metres from the ground all the squad were terrified. When they managed to finally close the door we just carried on with our journey. There was no need to land or turn back as the door wasn't faulty at all, just that they had forgotten to lock the thing!"

Ian and Ronnie were never close off the field as they belonged to two different tribes at the club. "When I arrived in 1961, there weren't many other Scots there, apart from Bert Slater and Tommy Leishman, until Ron Yeats joined a couple of months later," the Saint says. "Therefore, most of the team had known each other for years as they played in the Second

Division together and were mostly Scousers. Ronnie wasn't a big drinker either, which I don't knock him for, as it contributed to him being a model professional. Ronnie, as a player, made the best of the abilities he had. He wasn't that fast but he would be the first to admit that. He was extremely reliable though, gave his absolute best during every game and would do absolutely anything to fight for the shirt. He had a great left foot on him and could hit a great free-kick with it. He was Liverpool through and through and loved the club."

Shankly had secured a new centre up front, but felt he also needed a leader in the centre of defence. After an unsuccessful attempt to secure Jackie Charlton from Leeds, the Scot turned his attentions north of the border to Ron Yeats at Dundee United, whose signature was secured on July 22.

"Big Ron was a fantastic looking man, with black hair," said Shankly. "The first time I saw him he was wearing a light-grey suit and I said, 'It should be Hollywood you're going to.' He looked as if he could outclass all the film stars."

Yeats became Shankly's long-term captain on Boxing Day in 1961. "A captain should be like a puppeteer, with the other players on his strings all the time. Yeats was a natural to be a captain; a big man who commanded respect and his position in the centre of defence meant that he could see everything going on in front of him," Shankly recalled.

Moran became great friends with Yeats, and said of him: "Ron was the player who made the difference to a side missing out on promotion to the team that did it."

Shankly had found out, just as Phil Taylor had before him, that money was not forthcoming from Liverpool's board in his first couple of years at the club, but that changed in 1961 with the arrival of Eric Sawyer, an accountant with Littlewoods Pools, who had been nominated by Littlewoods founder and Everton chairman, John Moores, for a place on the board. "When we discussed possible transfer moves at board meetings the tune was still: 'We can't afford them.' That's when Mr. Sawyer stepped in and said, 'We cannot afford NOT to buy them,'" Shankly said.

Without Sawyer, Liverpool probably wouldn't have signed the Scottish pair and could have even lost Shankly as he had initially been very frustrated with the board. Reuben Bennett had also been vital in recruiting the talents of the Scottish duo who invigorated Liverpool.

"Dad was Shankly's constant companion in these early years travelling with him to watch matches and players," Reuben's son Mike Bennett said. "They were like two peas in a pod, sharing the same love of the game and the same devotion to it, spending long hours travelling together with the many conversations and discussions this would entail. In fact, the first two critical signings made by Shankly were Ian St John, who had been under Dad's tutelage at Motherwell, and Ronnie Yeats, whose family in Aberdeen were known to Dad. I even knew Ronnie's wife, Maggie, when I was a wee boy."

Lifelong Liverpool fan, John Martin, attended his first game in 1948 and remembers well the historic 1961/62 season. He said: "The season got off to a fantastic start. After 11 games we had won 10 and drawn the other and conceded only four goals in the process.

"Roger Hunt was proving to be a striker who might one day play for England and St John was outstanding. Standing only 5ft 8ins he was extremely small for a striker but he had a remarkable ability in the air and was capable of outjumping defenders who were over 6ft.

"At the back Yeats seemed to be impassable. It should be remembered that this was before the advent of the flat back four that was subsequently introduced with great success by Alf Ramsey. The centre-half was protected by his two full-backs and, when the going got tough, by a defensive wing-half. Yeats was simply magnificent. He was supreme in the air and often headed the ball from inside his own penalty area beyond the halfway line."

Liverpool lost two games in a row 1-0 right before and after Christmas, but rebounded with a 4-3 victory over Chelsea in the third round of the cup and a 5-4 win against Norwich City in the league, but these only highlighted the cracks that were starting to appear in defence. The injury of Dick White, who had replaced John Molyneux at right-back and lost the captaincy to Ron Yeats five weeks earlier, gave Moran a chance to redeem himself, against Brighton at Anfield on February 3, 1962.

Byrne, who had made the left-back position his own, was moved to the right to accommodate Ronnie. He had hardly taken a breath before Brighton were 1-0 up after 15 seconds! Slater was clearly disgusted with himself to concede almost instantly after kick-off from an unexpected shot that was nothing special.

Brighton packed their area and defended valiantly but Liverpool's equaliser came in the 52nd minute from an unlikely source. Byrne scored his first goal for the club with a lob that deceived the goalkeeper. Gerry only scored four goals in his 333 games for the Reds.

Hunt scored his 26th goal of the season and St John finished the Seagulls off three minutes from time. The *Daily Post* highlighted Moran's performance: 'One of the biggest thrills of the afternoon was to see the way in which Ron Moran grabbed his comeback chance.'

Ronnie had returned to the team after almost one-and-a-half years out, with 15 league games to play and Liverpool three points clear at the top of the Second Division.

He may have been out of the team, but life has still been eventful for Ronnie. The Morans had left their club house in Broadgreen and bought their own house in Thornton, situated to the north east of Crosby, where they lived for over 40 years. They had a good reason to get a bigger house as on January 15, 1962, Joyce gave birth to their second child, Paul. Ronnie and Joyce lived in Thornton until their children, Janet and Paul, left to raise families of their own. They then downsized and bought an apartment in Birkdale, near Southport, on the Irish Sea coast.

Shankly was impressed by Moran's performance against Brighton and he featured in the following game against Bury. Former Liverpool striker, Dave Hickson, who led Bury's front line, lost this shoot-out to 'Sir Roger' who scored his fourth hat-trick of the season! The Preston fifth round cup tie was next, Liverpool's biggest game of the season so far. A mammoth 54,967 packed Anfield and saw Preston unlucky not to come away with a victory in a 'rip-roaring cup tie' in which Alex Dawson had two goals disallowed. Liverpool fans were excited to see the replay at Deepdale, leading to an exodus to Shankly's old ground. Liverpool arrived at Deepdale at 7.32pm, two minutes after the appointed kick-off time after being stuck in traffic despite a police escort and the game was delayed by 25 minutes. Neither side managed to score, even in extra-time, and a third game had to be played at a neutral Old Trafford.

Hunt added another hat-trick in the league against Middlesbrough before Preston and Liverpool met again in arctic conditions in Manchester. A promising Preston winger by the name of Peter Thompson scored the winning goal in the 55th minute after 265 minutes of deadlock and knocked Liverpool out of the cup.

"I was doubtful to play as I had trouble with my leg," Thompson reveals. "It was snowing. The ball came out of the sky, I just swung a foot and it went straight in. It could have gone anywhere. One of those nights."

The players had become so close after facing each other so often in such a short period of time that the prior adversaries ended up playing golf together in the months after.

Moran was pleased to be back in the first-team, but would have been exhausted by this tough schedule as he featured in all three Preston matches as well as the Middlesbrough game in between, a total of four matches in the space of nine days!

Liverpool were due to play Swansea away on April 14, but a smallpox outbreak in South Wales postponed the game. Meanwhile, Liverpool's closest rivals missed out on vital points and the Reds had to wait one week until Southampton arrived at Anfield to try to clinch the one point necessary for promotion. St John was suspended so Kevin Lewis played up front and A'Court was very close to scoring as early as the second minute against the Saints when his cross beat Godfrey and hit the inside of the far upright. Liverpool were in the ascendancy and got in front in the 19th minute when Lewis knocked in his own rebound, off the upright. The Ellesmere Port native added his second 10 minutes later with a beautiful header into the corner of the net.

Finally, after eight long seasons in the Second Division, Liverpool were promoted with five league games remaining.

Moran has fond memories of the Southampton game. "I was particularly proud because I'd played a lot of games for the club in Division Two and we had tried so hard for so long to get into the top league."

The scenes after the game were something to behold as Ron Yeats described in the *Echo* the following week: "As we were leaving the pitch one or two of our most ardent admirers managed to evade the police patrolling the Kop end. One of them had a white straw hat trimmed with red ribbon which he managed to put on my head. This part was not so bad, but I must say that I don't go for being kissed by our fans, or at all events by the male ones!"

A home game against Stoke City took place the following Monday evening at which the Second Division trophy was presented. Liverpool won the game 2-1 and, fittingly, it was Ronnie who scored Liverpool's first from the penalty spot. More pleasing still to the fans, Liverpool went the entire season unbeaten at home, scoring 68 league goals at Anfield, which to this day is a record.

The arrival of St John and Yeats had improved the team considerably and Shankly reflected: "The coaching and training staffs with the players, had spent a lot of time on tactical plans to suit the type of players we had, and this, together with the great physical fitness of the lads, added up to a feeling of optimism tinged with caution. I know everybody was looking forward to the start of the big effort which we had determined to make to win the prize which had been lost to us so often by such narrow margins."

Ronnie played each game since his return from his injury until the end of the campaign, bringing his tally up to 283 appearances. To top things off for Ronnie, four days after the season finished, on May 8, Liverpool travelled across Stanley Park to face Everton in the Liverpool Senior Cup semi-final. 46,521 turned out to see Ronnie score the only goal of the game. Ronnie rates this goal as one of the top two he has ever scored. "I'll always remember my goal against Everton at Goodison; it was a free-kick that flew past Gordon West and the ball got stuck in the stanchion."

The win rounded off a monumental season for Shankly's men and a memorable decade for Ronnie Moran in Liverpool's first-team.

"On the evening of the Swansea game an obviously disgruntled Liverpool 'fan' threw a lump of coal through our front room window, but luckily for him he had vanished before my dad got outside the house. My dad told me years later that when he'd scored the winner versus Burnley in an earlier cup tie, no-one posted pound notes through the front door."

– Paul Moran

Chapter 4

BACK IN THE BIG TIME

1962-1966

LIFE in the First Division didn't start ideally for Shankly as in the first 15 games of the season his disciples were given a reality check, winning just four, drawing three and losing eight.

Ronnie started the season as first-choice left-back and in only the second game against Manchester City at Maine Road, he scored Liverpool's first goal in a 2-2 draw from the penalty spot against the legendary Bert Trautmann. On November 10, 1962 Liverpool visited Old Trafford to face Manchester United for the first time since 1953. The game finished 3-3 with three of the goals coming in the last five minutes. Ronnie scored his second goal of the season with an 89th-minute free-kick which was so described by journalist James Holland: 'Not for a long time has one seen a ball hit with the power and pace with which he flashed it past a wall of defenders into the net.'

Along with his strike against Everton in the Liverpool Senior Cup, this goal stands out as the best in Ronnie's career. Moran must have thought he had won the game with only a minute to go but Johnny Giles equalised for United with almost the last kick of the game.

The raw power of Ronnie's shooting is mentioned frequently in press reports during his career. The accuracy of his shots would have improved considerably if the players had worn proper boots at the time.

"I think a modern player would have 10 fits wearing the kind of boots we wore," former Liverpool captain and manager, Phil Taylor, remembered. "Ours were so heavy, with solid toecaps that could murder you if you were kicked. I can remember sitting with my boots once in a tub of water so they would shrink to fit my feet."

Although Liverpool would have been disappointed not to have achieved what would have been their first away win of the season at Old Trafford, this result instilled belief into Shankly's team who went on an impressive nine-game winning streak in the league. Moreover, Ronnie added a third goal to his tally for the season, scoring from the spot four days later at Anfield in a 2-1 win over Billy Wright's Arsenal.

Shanks' team was on top form in the FA Cup and sailed past Third Division minors Wrexham 3-0 on a pitch a mixture of sand and snow at the Racecourse Ground.

BACK IN THE BIG TIME

The big freeze of winter 1962/63 blitzed the fixture list. Between December 22 and February 13, Liverpool didn't play a single home game with Anfield covered in a blanket of ice and snow.

Next up for Liverpool in the cup was Burnley away on January 26. Shanks was unable to conjure up a victory at Turf Moor against the Clarets and needed a replay at Anfield to secure their passage into the fifth round. It was a memorable occasion for Moran who took a penalty in the dying seconds of extra-time after St John had been fouled. All eyes were on Ronnie as he walked towards the Kop end.

"When I was putting the ball on the spot against Burnley I was suddenly conscious of the fact that there wasn't a sound to be heard in all Anfield," Ronnie told the press. "I never looked at opposing keepers. I would plant the ball on the spot, aim to the keeper's right and strike it with the outside of my left foot to find some swerve. On that occasion, I had some power in the shot, but it was only a yard wide of their keeper. He went down on one knee and pushed out an arm in the other direction. Seconds later, it was all over."

Captain Ron Yeats had turned away as Moran prepared to take the penalty, while getting a running commentary from Gerry Byrne. Ian St John recalled this immensely tense moment, in the *Football Monthly* a few months later: "We were 1-1 with thirty seconds to go when Adam Blacklaw drove his clearance against me and I was brought down going round him to push the ball into the empty net. It was a tragic finish for Adam who had been terrific that night. When Ronnie Moran came to take the penalty I just couldn't look. I had my eyes closed tight as he ran up. Silly, because a rebound might have come my way. The next thing I knew is that the heavens were bursting with sound; Moran's kick had gone home. I was just limp and not ashamed to admit that for once my nerves had got the better of me."

Liverpool's reserved hero was in the spotlight in the *Echo* with 'Merseyside's Man of the Moment' pictured on a settee at his home. The profile revealed Ronnie's low-key life. 'The new glamour has not gone to his head. Moran is essentially a family man, a man whose hobbies are pottering around the house and garden, cleaning the car and taking the two kiddies (a girl of five and a 13-month-old boy) out in the fresh air. He confesses: 'I'm a champion pram-pusher.'"

When West Brom visited Anfield on March 20, 1963, Ronnie was captain in Yeats' absence. The game ended 2-2 and Ronnie scored what would become his seventh and final goal of the season, again from the spot. More significantly, fresh-faced 19-year-old Chris Lawler made his first-team debut. Lawler and Moran became good friends and despite Chris being a defender he was also known for his goalscoring exploits, which Ronnie pointed out, "couldn't be coached".

Due to the cancellation of games over the bitter winter months, there was fixture congestion towards the end of the season with Liverpool playing five league games in just eight days. First up was Tottenham Hotspur's visit to Anfield on April 12. Liverpool were 2-0 down at half-time but won 5-2. Ron Yeats commented: "People wouldn't believe that we could be so bad and so good on the same day."

The next day, Matt Busby's Manchester United side took on Shankly's team. A St John goal secured a 1-0 win, Liverpool's second victory in just 24 hours in front of their home fans. Moran played in both games. Two days later Liverpool travelled to London to face Tottenham, where Nicholson's Spurs sought revenge for the drubbing they were given earlier. Not only did they achieve it, they increased the winning margin by two goals, running out 7-2 winners. Liverpool's defence was given a torrid time by Jimmy Greaves, who netted four goals. This was Shankly's biggest defeat as Liverpool manager.

On April 18, as Liverpool were preparing for their fourth game in six days, against Nottingham Forest at Anfield, Ronnie came down with the flu and was ruled out of action. Bobby Thomson deputised as Liverpool slumped to a 2-0 defeat.

Ronnie returned to Liverpool's starting line-up in the semi-final of the FA Cup at Hillsborough. Following cup wins against Arsenal at Highbury and West Ham at Anfield it was Leicester City who ended Liverpool's best cup run since 1950 and Ronnie's dream of playing at Wembley.

Two days later, in Yeats' absence, Moran was made captain again, this time in a 2-0 home defeat to Sheffield Wednesday. This was Ronnie's last appearance of the campaign. Shanks had to settle for eighth place in his first season in the top flight, taking 44 points from 42 games. The principal problem was Liverpool's away form as they only managed to achieve four league victories away from home all season. Ronnie made 39 appearances in all competitions during the 1962/63 season. This took his total to 322 competitive games in 11 campaigns with the first-team.

There was no post-season tour in 1963, but the first-team enjoyed a holiday in San Remo, Italy. Shanks took youngsters Bobby Graham, Gordon Wallace and George Scott with them as a treat for reaching the FA Youth Cup final. Captained by Tommy Smith, the young Reds narrowly lost to West Ham 6-5 over two legs in the final. George Scott recalls: "Ronnie and Alan A'Court took it upon themselves to virtually chaperone us young lads during the post-season holiday to Italy and stopped us from straying from the straight and narrow. It has always stuck with me what Ronnie said to us at the start of the trip: 'Lads, never forget you are always on duty when representing this club and there are standards to uphold, don't let us down!' We never did."

Scott recollects the last conversation he had with Moran as a Liverpool player: "I remember in 1965 when Shanks let me go by telling me I was the 'twelfth best player in the world' because the first-team at Anfield were the eleven best in the world and I was the leading scorer in the reserves. I told Ronnie what Bill had said before I left. I thought he would fall about laughing, but he didn't. He said to me: 'You know the boss tends to exaggerate, George, but I can tell you he wouldn't say that to just anyone, take it as a compliment.' He wished me good luck and told me I was one of the unluckiest players not to have broken into the first-team. Then he paused and said: 'Mind you, son, I think Pele might have struggled to get in.'"

Much discussion in the summer of 1963 was about the future of Bill Shankly as manager. He had worked without a contract for his first years at the helm as he'd done at his previous clubs. Liverpool wanted to tie him down, but Shankly had turned down their first offer. He told the *Liverpool Daily Post* he was in no hurry to sign his first managerial contract ever. "I considered the contract offer unsuitable. That's why I have not signed it. I am not tied to Liverpool, of course." Shankly's viewpoint was simple: "If Liverpool don't like me they can sack me and if I don't like them, I can go." The *Echo* could barely believe Shankly's stance: 'One wonders just how Mr. Shankly's refusal to sign a contract at Liverpool may affect his career. It's a brave man who does not want contract security in 1963.'

Everyone at the club was really relieved when the matter was finally put to bed just before the season started in August. "During the last four or five months it would be idle to pretend that there had not been some uneasy moments, but all that is a thing of the past and we move forward into a new era," Shankly told the *Daily Post* as it was announced he had signed a five-year contract.

"I believe that my job with Liverpool FC has only just started. A lot of work has been done, the spadework, but much more remains to be done. I am convinced that they will be one of the truly great clubs of our time."

Tommy Lawrence started the 1963/64 season as first-choice goalkeeper. He and Ronnie became firm friends. "I first met Ronnie when I was 16 during the summer of 1956," Lawrence says. "Liverpool would put on summer schools for the kids and Ronnie and Tommy Younger would be the only first-teamers who would come down and work with us. When I joined Liverpool as a professional in 1957, Ronnie was at the peak of his career. He had a great left peg on him and would hit all the shooting boards at Melwood with it. He looked after me when I first joined and continued to do so right throughout my career."

Ronnie was respected among his teammates and they trusted him implicitly.

"Ronnie worked his hardest for the team, the supporters and

everyone connected with the football club," Tommy recalls. "In 1960, after Shanks had joined, myself and Roger Hunt went to visit Ronnie to ask him for advice on asking for more money. 'Don't bother,' he told us, 'Shanks doesn't have much to do with the money side of things.'"

Gordon Wallace echoed his former teammate's sentiment. "Ronnie was always helping and advising you on what is expected of you on and off the field.

"Being one of the senior professionals I learned very quickly that here was someone you could go to and have a chat without having to go to the boss, Bob, Joe or Reuben."

Moran's advice was appreciated by his peers but his choice of automobile was seen as questionable, as Lawrence remembers. "Ronnie's first car was a yellow Morris Minor and he told all the lads he got it on the cheap because of its colour. Every time he parked up at Anfield there would be a bit of banter flying his way."

Liverpool's players reported back to training on July 25, 1963. Shankly held court at Melwood, addressing his team. "The early season drudgery has to be gone through. If you are asked by the staff to do something in the way of training, you can bet your boots that it has been well thought of, even though some of you may think it is hard or useless. Do it and we will get somewhere. A fit Liverpool team, and it will be fit, is equal to any team in this country."

Liverpool's cup slayer, 20-year-old Peter Thompson, was signed from Preston in August. Thompson had cemented a place in Preston's first-team, aged 17, in the 1960/61 season, taking over from the great Tom Finney, who had retired the previous season. Thompson scored seven goals in 38 league matches in his debut campaign, but the team still got relegated from the First Division.

"When I was at Preston I was a wonder boy. They said I was the new Tom Finney," Thompson recalls. "I was only 17. It was a lot to live up to. That put pressure on me. The fans said: 'He is okay, but he is not Tom Finney,' which I wasn't. He was magnificent. When I was twenty I was a has-been. We had got relegated and got beat every week. I couldn't get out of my own half, playing as a defender and was useless."

He was excited to join Liverpool as he felt that he wasn't progressing at Preston. Thompson yearned for success and came to the right club at the right time.

"Shankly used to prod you and say: 'Are you a winner? I'm talking to you! Are you a winner?' 'Yes, Mr Shankly.' 'I want winners. Second is no good to me. If you're second, I'll get rid of you. Simple as that,'" Thompson recalls.

Ronnie and his teammates learned to appreciate Thompson's talents immediately.

"Players would simply just pass the ball to Peter in order to have a rest while he beat the opposition players four or five times," Ronnie said.

Thompson made his debut in the first game of the season at Ewood Park against Blackburn Rovers. Ronnie missed a penalty in the 65th minute, but scored from the rebound to equalise before Ian Callaghan scored the winner to make it 2-1. Despite this away win Shanks failed to get his team off to a flying start as Liverpool lost their first three home games. The second of those came on August 31 against Blackpool when future Liverpool coach Tony Waiters saved Moran's penalty in the 63rd minute. The third straight home defeat was against

Ron Greenwood's West Ham and Ronnie was unsuccessful from the spot for the third time in the last seven games, denied by Hammers' Jim Standen. Shankly declared to the board after the game: "I assure you, gentlemen, that before the end of the season we will win a home game!"

Liverpool fans wished their team only played away and probably that Moran wouldn't take any more penalties!

It didn't take Shanks' assurances long to come off as just two days later, on September 16, his team went on to thump Wolves 6-0 at Anfield.

Liverpool lost 3-0 in the following match at Sheffield United with Byrne and Moran criticised for playing too wide, leaving centre-half Ron Yeats exposed. Shankly promptly addressed what he felt was the problem.

'Mr Shankly no doubt recognises the speed which Alex Scott can bring to bear on Everton's right wing and asks himself, will Ferns be better able to cope with such pace than Moran?' the *Liverpool Echo* reported.

Shankly dropped Ronnie, who was desperately unhappy as he had looked forward to featuring in the biggest game of the season so far, against Everton at Anfield. His replacement was utility player Phil Ferns, who had performed in four out of the nine league games that had already been completed, playing at left-half, deputising for Willie Stevenson.

Just before half-time Ian Callaghan put Liverpool ahead against Everton with a wonderful shot from 25 yards that had landed in the top right-hand corner when Gordon West made a move for it and added a second to clinch a 2-1 win at the beginning of the second half. Liverpool won the next four games, finally building some momentum after a less than convincing start that had left them in 10th place prior to the Merseyside derby.

Up next were bogey side Leicester, who Liverpool had lost three times to in the previous campaign, home and away in the league and in the semi-finals of the FA Cup, conceding six without reply. Gerry Byrne had been struggling with a knee injury in training during the week and faced a fitness test on the morning of the game with Ronnie Moran on standby. Byrne was passed fit to play, leaving Moran to face Manchester United for the reserves at Old Trafford where they won 2-0. Leicester proved invincible to Shankly's men again and celebrated a 1-0 win at Anfield with unprecedented vitriol showed towards the Leicester players by the home fans.

This game on November 2, 1963 has an added significance as it was the first time 'You'll Never Walk Alone' was played at Anfield as part of UK's Top Ten chart. The song had reached number seven a couple of weeks before, but this was the first match at Anfield that had taken place since then. Moreover, the song had just reached the number one spot, so when Anfield DJ, Stuart Bateman, did his rundown of the Top Ten, 'You'll Never Walk Alone' was the final song played before kick-off. Gerry and the Pacemakers' latest hit stayed at number one for four weeks before the Beatles' 'She Loves You' regained the top spot. YNWA remained in the Top Ten for a further four weeks and when the song had disappeared off the track list at Christmas time, the crowd demanded that it would still be featured. "When it went out of the Top Ten, the Kop were singing, 'Where's our song? Where's our song?'" Gerry Marsden said. As a result a tradition was born and Liverpool fans have embraced it ever since.

Byrne's knee had flared up again in the game against the Foxes, giving Ronnie another chance to impress. Ferns was moved to right-back in place of Byrne. Moran was praised for his performance in a 2-1 win over Bolton, while Ferns couldn't remember anything from the last part of the game after being struck in the face by one of Bolton's forwards.

Ron Yeats' goal against Manchester United on November 23, 1963 was a momentous occasion as his header put Liverpool on top of the First Division for the first time since 1947! The world was still in shock after John F Kennedy's assassination in Dallas the day before as Yeats headed his first goal for the club since he joined two-and-a-half years earlier. "Yeats is the greatest centre-half in the world today," Shankly declared outright after the match to the press.

The *Liverpool Echo* appropriately asked Billy Liddell, a key player in the club's last championship side, to evaluate their title credentials. "This side can win the championship on the strength of its defence. It is the secret of the team at present. It was the reason for our championship success in 1947. But I'd like to see a forward in the team slip defences with passes in the Johnny Haynes style. At times the attack plays too close," Liddell said. He also pointed out three obstacles to Liverpool's title charge: Lack of ability to beat a retreating defence, failure to attack quicker and lack of depth in the squad to cope with injuries that could be sustained on the approaching heavy grounds. Liddell believed, though, that the team had a better chance than anyone else to win the title for a simple reason. "I have been greatly impressed by the spirit. This is a price-less asset many other possibly more skilful teams would envy," Liddell concluded.

Next up were Burnley who visited Anfield on November 30. Liverpool were awarded a penalty in the 86th minute. Shanks was in need of a new penalty-taker after Moran's frequent misses. Until Roger Hunt went up to the spot, Shankly had declined to reveal who would be replacing Moran. Roger converted the spot-kick to make it 2-0. This was the only penalty he ever scored for Liverpool.

After Moran, Liverpool's second longest serving player at the time was Jimmy Melia, who got injured at Bloomfield Road on December 21. He had worn the number 10 shirt for the whole of the campaign. Alf Arrowsmith took over his position and Melia, a veteran of 286 games and 79 goals, only played three more games for Liverpool, his last being on February 8, 1964 at Goodison Park.

After his departure to Wolves, an irate Liverpool fan wrote to the *Echo*, complaining that the 'kick and rush boys have had their way', having failed to recognise the artistry of Melia.

Ronnie has fond memories of his fellow Liverpudlian teammate: "Jimmy was a player who could look after himself and score vital goals. I also remember my wife telling me once that during a game at Anfield a fan sitting by the wives had a go at Jimmy. Mrs Melia didn't take too kindly to this, leant forward and smashed the offender over the head with an umbrella. Nobody had a go at the players in the wives' earshot after that!"

Liverpool had won four games in row when they faced West Ham on January 18. Bobby Thomson, who had only played four games in the previous campaign, had in the match prior replaced Phil Ferns, who Shankly felt had been harshly criticised by the press.

Gerry Byrne was ready to return for the Hammers game and

Shankly decided to keep Thomson in the side and drop Ronnie. West Ham won 1-0 and Moran was absent again when Liverpool drew 1-1 with Port Vale in the fourth round of the cup. Shankly opted for Moran's experience in the replay two days later. The score was 1-1 with 60 seconds to go in extra-time when Peter Thompson hit an unstoppable drive that caused Liverpool fans to invade the field. The police had to rescue the goalscoring hero from the clutches of the travelling Kopites.

A cup and league double was still a possible target for Shankly's men. Liverpool were drawn against Arsenal in the fifth round, at Highbury. Moran and his teammates were still licking their wounds after a 3-1 defeat to reigning league champions Everton at Goodison Park. Ian St John nodded the Reds in front at Arsenal in the 15th minute. Arsenal had a huge penalty appeal turned down when Moran blocked a shot from Eastham with his arm, if Arsenal fans were to be believed, but photographs later showed that he'd headed away. All hell broke loose in the 38th minute when Joe Baker made a late challenge on Ron Yeats and then stamped on him that caused the big Scotsman to chase after him. Punches were thrown and both players got sent off. 'Rowdy' Yeats wasn't too pleased about his only sending-off in his Liverpool career as he spoke to the press after the game. "I have never struck a player in eight years and I never will. If I hit anyone I would expect to be sent off. But I swear I never hit him. I asked the referee if I had hit myself to get my cut and bleeding eye, but he would not listen." Yeats, who had returned to the ground after a brief walk around North London, was the first one on to the field to hug each of his teammates after the final whistle was blown.

Following a 2-2 draw with Aston Villa, Liverpool played their neighbours Birmingham in the league. Moran was inches away from giving Birmingham the lead when his miscalculated back pass went over Lawrence but thankfully just over the bar. In the 41st minute Liverpool got a free-kick just outside Birmingham's penalty area. Moran lined up the ball, facing the wind and the Kop and hit it so hard that despite a deflection off someone's head in the wall the ball 'travelled like a bullet' and ended in the net just under the bar. The experienced Moran celebrated, according the *Echo*'s Leslie Edwards, like a 'young player scoring on his debut.' Birmingham equalised seven minutes later before St John scored the winner 15 minutes before time.

On February 29, Liverpool played host to Swansea Town in the sixth round of the FA Cup. Four days earlier 22-year-old Cassius Clay, later Muhammad Ali, became the heavyweight champion of the world by conquering the seemingly indestructible Sonny Liston. Would there be another shock on the cards at Anfield? With the score at 2-1 to Swansea with 10 minutes to go, Liverpool were handed a lifeline when they were awarded a penalty in the 80th minute. Ronnie stepped up and unfortunately made it four penalty misses in a row by blasting the ball wide and Liverpool ended up getting knocked out. This was a harrowing experience for Moran who despaired: "That miss against Swansea was the most terrible moment of my life. I felt I had let Liverpool down." Tommy Lawrence remembers walking off the field with Ronnie after his infamous penalty miss. "I could tell Ron was devastated. As well as hating losing, he felt responsible for Liverpool's cup exit. I remember him saying to me: 'I think that's finished my contract!'"

Jack Rowe at the *Liverpool Echo* was convinced that it was Anfield's most vociferous fans who swayed Moran to take the all-important penalty. 'Poor Moran was the most reluctant taker of a penalty I have ever seen for many a seasons. Did he want to take it? This is the question which has raged and is still raging in Liverpool. Why did Moran finally step up and blast Liverpool's Cup hopes for another season high and wide? As the uncertainty was being played out on the field there came this chant from the Kop: 'Moran, Moran, Moran', indicating quite clearly the player they wanted to take the kick.'

Shankly revealed after the match that Moran was to be given the chance of taking a penalty against Swansea if such an instance occurred. If he didn't want to take it another player had been delegated (Ian Callaghan). Shankly didn't put any blame on Moran after the game, saying: "Unbelievable, unbelievable. I have never seen the boys play better. We could have scored 14 goals and yet here we are out of the Cup."

On the evening of the Swansea game, an obviously disgruntled Liverpool 'fan' threw a lump of coal through Ronnie's front room window, but luckily for him he had vanished before Ronnie got hold of him. Ronnie brushed this off and used to jokingly remark when telling this story, that after scoring the winner against Burnley in a cup tie the previous season, no-one had come and posted pound notes through the front door!

"It used to annoy me that despite the fact my dad spent 49 years at the club and all the trophies he won, people would often say to him: 'I remember you missing that penalty against Swansea Town,' and some said they were in the Kop that day and the ball came straight at them," Paul Moran says. "In the end we used to say: 'Well, you should have stood right behind the goal then, because if you had he would have scored.'"

Liverpool beat title rivals Tottenham and finally got rid of the

Leicester hoodoo in two successive away victories before facing Spurs on Easter Monday. Ron Yeats returned after missing three matches while serving a 14-day ban after his Arsenal dismissal. A promising centre-half by the name of Chris Lawler had performed admirably in his absence. Everton had a one-point lead on Liverpool, but had played two more games. The Blues were due to play on the Tuesday so the top spot was up for grabs. Ian St John, who was playing inside-left behind Roger Hunt and Alf Arrowsmith, netted two goals in a 3-1 victory. Everton lost 4-2 to West Bromwich Albion, leaving Liverpool in pole position.

Liverpool then faced third-placed Manchester United, managed by former Liverpool captain, Matt Busby. Alf Arrowsmith scored a brace after an Ian Callaghan opener in a convincing 3-0 win, making a giant stride to the title as they put United out of the race.

Ronnie recalled a hairy incident from this game. "George Best rolled the ball to Nobby Stiles but under-hit it and I got to the ball at the same time as Nobby and went straight through him. Stiles jumped up looking angry and I thought he was going to attack me but fortunately he just marched straight past me. I then remember shouting to George Best: 'Fuckin hell, George, you'll get me killed here!'"

Ronnie had the match of his life, keeping Bestie quiet and his name was chanted by the Kop in appreciation. After the match, boxing fan Shankly echoed Cassius Clay when praising his players: "They're lions that go out hungry. Nothing will stop them. They're the greatest."

A sixth consecutive win, achieved at Burnley, meant that Liverpool could seal the title against Arsenal at Anfield, with still three games left to play. Ian St John put Liverpool 1-0 up against the Gunners after seven minutes. Ron Yeats handled in the box at the half-hour mark, but Tommy Lawrence saved George Eastham's penalty. Arrowsmith added a second in the 38th minute. Three goals in an eight-minute spell at the start of the second half settled the match. Left-winger Peter Thompson scored from two thunderbolts before setting up Roger Hunt's 30th goal of the campaign. Ian Callaghan had the opportunity in the 64th minute to score Liverpool's sixth, from the spot, having been nominated as Ronnie Moran's successor in spot-kick duties. Jim Furnell, who had conquered Hunt from the spot in the FA Cup two months previously, saved superbly from Cally. A 5-0 win secured the championship for Shankly's men.

Roger Hunt had thrived on Thompson and Callaghan's service the whole season and the trio were unstoppable up front. Hunt might have even scored more goals if Thompson had been more of a team player. One Friday, the day before a league match, Liverpool had a team meeting.

"Roger (Hunt) never said anything," Thompson recalls. "Shankly said: 'Meeting finished', but Roger said: 'Actually, Peter beats his full-back about four or five times and we don't know where to run.' Roger turned to me: 'Why don't you just beat your man and cross it?' Shankly said: 'That is a good idea.' We played against West Brom at Anfield, I pushed it past the full-back, crossed it, Roger smashed it into the net. Roger said: 'That's what I want.' I said: 'That's boring. Let Ian Callaghan do that,'" Thompson recollects. "Ian and I were completely different. Ian was straightforward. The problem was when I got the ball I got my head down and off I went. We complemented each other perfectly. Some games one of us would be struggling, the defender facing Cally may have been faster than him or the right-back could handle a dribbler like myself, so we'd simply switch flanks and it'd work."

Once the title was claimed, Shankly revealed the secret of his side's success.

"We are a working-class team. We have no room for fancy footballers. Just workers who will respond to the demands I lay down," Shankly declared.

Anfield had rarely seen such an atmosphere like during the match against Arsenal, before or since. 'The famous Spion Kop became a small mountain of chanting, singing, swaying Merseyside madness as Arsenal became the fall guys amidst the most turbulent soccer scenes I have ever witnessed!' *Daily Mirror*'s Sam Leith reported. His colleague Frank McGhee went looking for the players after the final whistle. "I only wish the whole Kop could have been there with me afterwards when the final chorus was sung – by eleven men in a bath in the dressing-room. 'We're the champ-i-ons, we're the champ-i-ons. Ee, aye, addio, we're the champ-i-ons.'"

After joining as a 15-year-old apprentice in 1949, the Crosby lad had finally reached the highest level in domestic football. Thirty-year-old Ronnie Moran was now a league champion. The champagne was still fizzling when the *Liverpool Echo* approached Moran to comment on his prospects for the forth-coming season. Moran was the oldest player of the league champions, at 30 years of age. The *Echo* doubted that the 'balding, popular Moran' would be a serious part of Liverpool's venture into the European Cup. Modest Moran replied: "It's a great day for us all. I've been here over 12 years. I've been hearing for nearly four years that the club has been going to buy a replacement. I know some of the critics have been slating me this season, but if Liverpool do buy to replace me, what can I do about it? It's no use complaining. Bill Shankly can't just look ahead to the next match. He's got to look years ahead, and, with the European Cup coming up, it's understandable that he should want reinforcements."

Ronnie made 35 league appearances during this memorable campaign. Alf Ballard of the *Liverpool Echo* analysed his performance when the season had drawn to a close: 'He may not be the greatest footballer ever seen on Merseyside. But Ronnie Moran is packed with the stuff that has made Liverpool a soccer wonder team. And the stuff is a loyal affection for the club. He is as much a feature of the Anfield scene as the Liver Birds are of the Pier Head.'

Within days of been crowned champions, Liverpool travelled across the Atlantic for a post-season tour of America and Canada which consisted of 10 games from May 8 to June 10. This was Ronnie's second tour of those countries and he played in all 10 games.

Although Moran didn't know this at the time, during this tour he would score his last goal for the first-team, against a San Franciscan Select. Liverpool won 14-0 at the Kezar Stadium, which at the time was home to the San Francisco 49ers. Liverpool ended the tour winning seven games, drawing two and losing just one to German side Hamburg SV. This was the first time Liverpool had been beaten in 36 games played over four tours to America and Canada since the war.

BACK IN THE BIG TIME

Tommy Lawrence, who was also on the tour, recalls: "When we went to America in 1964, Ronnie was the oldest player and was in charge of us all as the senior man. I remember our youth goalkeeper at the time, Trevor Roberts, grew his hair like the Beatles and when we were out and about some Americans would ask us if we were actually the Beatles. Some of the lads used to go along with it, but Ronnie would say: 'I can't join in with this one, lads, not with my hair!'"

A real highlight for the lads was a visit to the Ed Sullivan Show on May 10. The Beatles had made their first live TV appearance in the States on the show in February earlier that year and wowed the American public with over 73 million tuning in. This time around another popular Liverpool band, Gerry and the Pacemakers, was on stage. The Pacemakers opened their set with the 1963 hit 'I Like It' and then performed 'Don't Let the Sun Catch You Crying', but was by no means the only musical talent on hand as violinist Izthak Perlman and Dusty Springfield performed as well. The Liverpool team was part of the audience and host Ed Sullivan asked chief coach Reuben Bennett and captain Ron Yeats to stand up during the show and they, in turn, asked the rest of the players to stand. The team proved to be very popular among other audience members and had to sign quite a few autographs.

Ian St John remembers, above anything else, that Ronnie was very thrifty on the American tour. "We all got 10 dollars a day subsistence money from which you had to buy your lunch and dinner. It soon went on this, that and another, on a few jars. We were skint. All the dollars had well gone and we were looking for handouts at the end of it. When we got back Ronnie Moran was the only player who still had dollars. That was the joke for

111

years. When we were on a trip all the lads would go: 'Ronnie, spent any dollars yet?' He was more like a Scotsman than a Scotsman for keeping hold of his money."

Liverpool started the 1964/65 season against West Ham in the Charity Shield at Anfield. The game finished 2-2 and the trophy was shared. The following day Bill Shankly's men travelled to Iceland to face KR Reykjavík in the European Cup. It was a remarkable occasion for Liverpool Football Club; their first official European game. As the airplane carrying the squad approached Iceland, a frantic Ron Yeats, who was scared of flying, burst out of his seat, claiming the plane was on fire. He had, in fact, seen out of his window the volcanic eruption that created the island, Surtsey, off the south coast of Iceland. The plane circled the eruption three times while an annoyed Shankly told his captain off for creating panic on board.

Liverpool beat their hosts 5-0, while 'the Icelandic crowd and the players of KR watched like good students at a school,' according to a reporter from *Morgunbladid*. The local writer claimed that Liverpool could have won 15-0 if their players had applied themselves fully instead of focusing on entertaining the crowd and none more so than Peter Thompson.

"I was an individualist. I tried not to be like that but I couldn't change," Thompson admits. "In Reykjavík, I got the ball in their half and I set off. I didn't know where I was going. I kept beating player after player. Eventually I passed it. Billy Stevenson said: 'It was fabulous, you beat six players.' I went: 'Yeah, it must have been about six.' He said: 'You beat Ron Yeats twice and you beat me twice, went through my legs.'"

KR Reykjavík did come close to scoring, just after half-time, with the score at 2-0. Ellert Schram's header beat Lawrence but

Moran was on hand to clear on the goal line, preventing what was previously thought an unlikely goal.

Twenty-year-old Gordon Wallace scored two goals in Reykjavík during what proved to be his most successful season. "I played on the left wing in front of Ronnie," he said. "He was always encouraging you, shouting and I know this helped my progress at the club. He always gave 100 per cent and if you were not giving the same Ronnie would let you know in no uncertain terms. And quite rightly so. He had a tremendous left foot. You didn't want to be in the wall of a free-kick outside the box; you could imagine what you were holding!"

Liverpool beat Arsenal 3-2 in their first league game of the 64/65 season, Wallace scoring the winner three minutes from time. The defending champions lost, however, the next two, against Leeds United and Blackburn, having conceded nine goals in three league games. Liverpool faced Leeds again in the next match, this time at Anfield. Peter Thompson scored the first goal in the middle of the second half before young wing-half, Tommy Smith, who was deputising for injured Ian St John at inside-left, hit a tremendous shot from 30 yards that ricocheted from inside of one post on to the other before nestling in the net. Liverpool's failure to follow this victory in the next three matches set alarm bells ringing with the champions in 17th place with five points. Many champions had suffered a similar title hangover, but this was reaching catastrophic proportions.

One would have thought the Anfield faithful had waited long enough to be able to cheer on their team against European opposition at Anfield, but that wasn't apparent on September 14. The Kop knew the amateurs from Reykjavík were well beaten before the game had started; therefore, they did their best to make sure they weren't humiliated. Liverpool were already 2-0 up after 23 minutes when Willie Stevenson was booed by his own fans for breaking up a rare Reykjavík attack in the first half. Shortly afterwards, the Kop angrily roared at Moran for simply passing the ball back to Lawrence.

The biggest cheer of the game came in the 35th minute when Reykjavík's Gunnar Felixson cut Liverpool's lead in half and made it 2-1 on the night. Liverpool won 6-1 and for once had to receive what many teams had taken on when visiting Anfield, the full Kop treatment!

Moran's good friend, Alan A'Court, who was the only player in the squad beside Moran who had been relegated with the Liverpool side in 1954, made his farewell appearance in this historic match at Anfield.

Ronnie remembered A'Court in the *Liverpool Echo* after his passing in 2009: "Alan was a great teammate and even better friend. We used to room together on away trips and there were always laughs and jokes. Our families used to go on holiday together. I played left-back and he was just in front of me and I always said that when he went to the World Cup in 1958 with England that they had got us confused!"

A'Court recognised Ronnie wasn't "the classiest full-back of all time nor the fastest", but certainly appreciated Moran's commitment as a player "who played every game as though it was going to be his last" and his dry sense of humour. "He used to joke that he became bald through all the crosses and the shots he headed off the line," A'Court said.

Everton were next to visit Anfield after its European debut. A 4-0 defeat to their neighbours left Liverpool second from bottom. Ronnie Moran and Gordon Wallace were promptly dropped for Chris Lawler and Bobby Graham respectively. Lawler impressed in a 5-1 win over Aston Villa as well as Graham, who scored a hat-trick on his debut! Moran featured in three of the next five matches but only due to Ron Yeats' absence. The writing was on the wall for Moran.

From October onwards, 21-year-old Lawler established himself as the club's right-back. Lawler's career could have taken a completely different direction as he had come close to leaving the champions after featuring in only six games in their championship season.

"I was a centre-back then in the second team. And I only played if Ron Yeats, the club captain, was injured," Lawler says. "I thought there was no future for me at Liverpool. So I went to see Bill Shankly and said I wanted a transfer. He didn't expect that. Tommy Smith had seen I had gone in and then he went in. It was in the papers that Matt Busby would take us both. We wanted to stay at Liverpool, but there was an offer there to go to Manchester United."

It was United's loss and Liverpool's gain that Shankly realised he had to blood his youngsters. He calmed Lawler's nerves inside his office and convinced him to stay.

"Shankly said: 'I've got an idea. Leave it with me,'" Lawler remembers. "In the next few weeks Ronnie Moran was coming to the end of his career and Gerry Byrne was playing right-back. So he moved Gerry Byrne over to left-back and tried me at right-back. I played nearly every game after that." In fact, from October 2, 1964 to November 24, 1973 Lawler missed only five out of the 467 games Liverpool played.

When Ronnie had been out of the team for a while, he would

have a quiet word with Shankly. "Many a time I'd go and knock on Bill's door. He'd always be the same. 'Come in son and sit down,' he'd say. I'd tell him that I wasn't there to complain about the team. How could I? They were always winning," Ronnie recalled. "'Keep going, son, you'll have another chance,' he'd tell me. I eventually got back in for a few games but even when I was playing in the reserves I was enjoying it."

Moran made a brief return to the first-team at the end of this historic campaign, but missed out on a place in Liverpool's 1965 cup-winning team at Wembley.

Shankly tried to take his and his teammates' minds off the final by organising a competitive match-up, which Ronnie was part of, shortly before the final as the *Echo*'s Michael Charters remembers. "I acted as referee and timekeeper for a four-a-side session with four reserves, Arrowsmith, Chisnall, Moran and Molyneux, facing the executive department of Bill Shankly, Reuben Bennett, Bob Paisley and Joe Fagan. This was really a light-hearted frolic, but they put a good deal into it and the score, for the record, was a win for Arrowsmith and the boys by a hotly-disputed 3-1 margin."

Moran had played for the first-team in a league game a few days before the final, but so did many of the club's reserves as Shankly didn't want to risk any of his stars. Liverpool still beat Wolves 3-1. In a brochure called *Into Europe*, published at the start of the campaign, Moran revealed what his greatest ambition was; "I'd like to play at Wembley in an FA Cup final." Ronnie got to travel to London with the team, but his biggest dream was about to be shattered.

"I was in the squad for the final," Ronnie explained in 1994. "Gerry broke his collar bone in the first few minutes and he stayed on. He managed to play the whole game and even extra-time. If there had been substitutes in 1965, I would have been on. That's the only regret I had in my career, not playing in that FA Cup final at Wembley." Gerry's performance in the 2-1 win over Leeds is seen as one of the most heroic in the history of the club.

Liverpool's sensational victory over the European champions of Inter Milan at Anfield in the European Cup semi-final first leg in May is remembered as one of the best games in the history of the club, a match that Moran must have been proud of playing his part in, even though he missed out on the cup win three days previously.

Liverpool brushed Inter away 3-1 in such a manner that Shankly asked the press afterwards, "Have you seen anything like it?"

The Argentinian coach of the 'Grande Inter', Helenio Herrera, was impressed: "The Liverpool team is tremendously strong, fit and fast, the best we have ever played. The crowd was fantastic and played as big a part in this victory as the team."

The noise and fervour generated that night has become part of Anfield folklore, as well as the ingenious parade of the FA Cup by injured duo Gordon Milne and Gerry Byrne prior to the match that stoked the red hot atmosphere.

As glorious an occasion as this was, there was great disappointment in the second leg and Ronnie was rightfully frustrated with his last hurrah for Liverpool's first-team. Ronnie knew the Italians were pulling out all the stops to make sure Liverpool were not sufficiently prepared. The hotel that the team stayed in in Italy was by Lake Como, just by a church.

"The church bell was going all the while and we couldn't

sleep," Ronnie said. Shankly tried to rectify the situation. "Bob Paisley and I went to see the Monsignor about it. We tried to get him to stop the bells ringing for the night so the players could sleep. 'It's not very fair', I said to him through an interpreter. He was sympathetic towards us, but he said he could not do what we asked. So I said, 'Well, could you let Bob here go up and put a bandage on them and maybe kind of dull them a bit?' Bob was killing himself laughing. That would have been one of the funniest things Bob had ever done, one of his greatest cures as a trainer, creeping up the aisle with cotton-wool and bandages!"

"The following day, we wanted to move and the Italians put us in a hotel in Milan," Ronnie says, as he picks up the story. "The hotel was in the middle of the city, it was noisy, lots of traffic all the time. We couldn't rest. We got beat 3-0, but two of the goals were blatant cheats."

Liverpool were 2-0 down after nine minutes. Inter scored their first straight from an indirect free-kick and Shankly was particularly incensed by Inter's second. "The ball was kicked out of our goalkeeper's hands. It was dreadful," he told the press afterwards, although replays suggest Lawrence was dribbling the ball when Joaquín Peiró nicked the ball from him.

Inter were awarded 20 free-kicks to Liverpool's three, a fact that also incensed the Liverpool press. 'Senor Mendibil could only lean one way, like the tower of Pisa, in the direction of Milan,' the *Echo* reported, slamming the Spanish referee. A superb goal by legendary defender Giacinto Fachetti, future president of the club, put Inter 4-3 up on aggregate after an hour's play at the San Siro where the scene had been equally frightening for the away team as Anfield had been for Inter eight days before.

Ronnie Moran finished his Liverpool playing career in these controversial circumstances where everything was done to ensure a victory for the home side. "I don't think we would have got out of the stadium if we had beat them," Ian Callaghan claims.

Tommy Smith's career was just beginning when Ronnie Moran's was coming to a close. The Anfield Iron became a regular in Shankly's Liverpool side during the 1964/65 season. The *Sunday Mirror* had already predicted big things for Tommy in a feature published in November 10, 1963.

'He has developed physique and talent and at 5ft. 10½ins. and 13st. 5lb. he will take some shifting once he gets a chance in the Liverpool first-team.' When enquired of him Bill Shankly was very enthusiastic as well: "He is a natural player in every respect, a big lad with a strong tackle and a flair for attacking. He shows great promise."

Ronnie and Tommy played together on just seven occasions, two of which were the semis against Inter, but they got to know each other well in the ensuing years. Ronnie praised his fellow Scouser, whose false teeth he used to look after during matches: "He was a man when he joined the club from school. He never shirked a duty or a tackle. His approach was the same all through his years of development. He wanted to dominate play on every ground in the land. He would gee up players around him, too. That habit was there from a very early age," Ronnie remarked.

When Ronnie became a coach, their relationship became a little more tempestuous.

"Some people might call Ronnie Moran an Anfield phenomenon," Smith said. "I've called him other things at times, both as a player and a fellow member of the Anfield backroom team. But it's all water off a duck's back, or should it be the bald pate, of one of the game's most unusual characters. Ronnie was never satisfied with a performance, no matter how impressive. He got on my nerves, but then he also got on the nerves of every other player on the staff."

Smithy joined Liverpool's coaching staff in 1979 before moving on to his business interests. He'd had a hard time getting along with Ronnie at Melwood and complained to Paisley, who made him realise how important Ronnie was to the cause. "Bob looked at me and said: 'Smithy, a football club is like a jigsaw with many different pieces. Ronnie is an important piece. If we have a problem, we load the gun and he shoots it. His heart is in the right place. Like everybody else, he loves the club.'"

Those words resonated with Smith: "I will never forget what Bob Paisley said. Yes, Ronnie Moran can moan for England. He can wind you up and annoy you to the point where you could throttle him. But he is Liverpool through and through and in the final reckoning that will do for me."

Ronnie Moran could look back with pride on his playing career with Liverpool. He made a grand total of 379 appearances for the club with a 49.34 per cent win rate; winning 187, drawing 79 and losing 113 games. He made 342 league appearances and scored 15 league goals and 17 in total, many of which were from set-pieces. He captained Liverpool 47 times and his honours included winning the Second Division title in 1962 and the First Division title two years later. Ronnie spent 17 years as a Liverpool player.

During the 1965/66 season Moran played for the entire season in the reserves, finishing sixth in the Central League while Liverpool's first-team won another league title. Ronnie never ever gave less than 100 per cent in Joe Fagan's reserve team and woe betide any of the younger players if he thought they were slacking.

He did go overboard once when he was sent off for the only time in his career. Ronnie put in what he deemed a fair but tough challenge right in front of the linesman, who flagged for an aggressive foul. Ronnie reacted by using abusive language towards the linesman. Ronnie would recall this incident in years to come and always referred to the match official by the same dirty word that he used on that very day.

Moran was clearly frustrated not to be part of the champion-ship team, but he had to be realistic as he was now 32 years of age. Usually when a player reaches his early thirties and is only offered reserve team football, it would be time to move on. For Ronnie Moran this wasn't going to be the case.

"I really enjoyed going to Anfield on a
Sunday morning after match days. While
my dad was nursing an injured player
or sorting out bits of kit, he handed me
a ball and I'd be out on the pitch having
a kick around, usually re-enacting the
goals I had witnessed the day before."

– Paul Moran

Chapter 5

ON THE STAFF

1966-1977

RONNIE Moran attended all the World Cup games that took place at Goodison Park during the summer of 1966, the highlight being when Brazil and Portugal met on July 19 in the third and final round of their group. Pele was kicked left, right and centre by the Portuguese and Eusebio's goal ensured Brazil didn't progress any further in the competition.

Moran's qualities as a player had ensured a long stay for him at Liverpool and it hadn't gone unnoticed that his enthusiasm for the game had always spread around the teams he played in.

Ronnie was totally committed to his profession, a quality that prompted Shankly to offer him a new opportunity prior to the 1966/67 season.

Players received contract offers every 12 months and after each season they worried about getting the customary letter from the club in their mailbox, informing them that they were no longer needed. Moran knew that a couple of lower league clubs were after his services, Third Division Brighton & Hove Albion being one, so he was startled when Shankly called him over at Melwood. "I thought, 'this is it', he's going to tell me another club has come in for me,'" Ronnie remembered, "and he said to me: 'Ronnie, how would you like to join the backroom staff?'" Ronnie asked him what he would do with no coaching experience whatsoever and Shankly suggested he could be in charge of the kids. Ronnie asked Shankly if he could contemplate the offer overnight.

"I went off and discussed it with my wife," Ronnie said. "We are both from Liverpool and didn't want to leave, and the next day I said yes to Bill. I guess Shanks and Bob Paisley had seen me shouting and talking a lot when I was playing and liked what they saw."

Shankly's decision to offer Ronnie the job didn't surprise Ian St John. "Shanks thought Moran was the ultimate player and the perfect professional who always put the club first. This was the reason why he offered him a role on his staff. He was a local lad who always gave his all and Shanks admired him for that. Ronnie was able to carry on going to Anfield in the morning. He was lucky in that respect as his life was sorted. Many players after their playing days had ended, found it difficult to find work after retiring as a player. However, Ronnie deserved it and went on to become part of one of the best coaching teams of all time."

Ronnie was given freedom and left to his own devices when embarking on his new coaching role. Ronnie was only 32 years old and still playing for the Central League side while doing his duties as part of Shankly's staff. Ronnie obtained a preliminary coaching badge from the FA but that wasn't valued highly at the club.

"Nobody at Liverpool Football Club bothered about obtaining their coaching badges, so they never pursued any other levels," Roy Evans explains. "I had no training in my roles; I just learned my trade as a coach and eventually as a manager on the job with some great colleagues around me.

"Bill Shankly never understood the concept of coaching badges anyway. I remember after Ian St John retired, Shanks found out he was going to do his badges. Shanks told him before he left: 'Tell them nothing, son.'"

Even the term 'coach' wasn't welcome at Anfield, as St John explained. "Liverpool never had coaches back in them days, they had staff. They hated the word coaching and would never mention that word."

Ronnie had an interesting take on coaching, as he revealed towards the end of his Anfield career: "Just because someone has a full badge doesn't mean they're going to be a good coach, and vice versa. Certain things happen on coaching courses that aren't anything to do with the game as it's played. Bill Shankly never had a coaching badge. Bob Paisley only had a preliminary badge like myself and I think Roy has only got a similar qualification. I'm only quoting those names because they've had a bit of success."

Moran shaped his ideas early as he coached the youngsters. "When I first started with the kids this was one of my guiding philosophies: 'You get on with the game. If you give a bad pass you get ready to give a good one next time.' I've seen players who have come off the pitch thinking they've done well because they've scored a goal or they might have kicked a ball off the line. They've forgotten the other 89 minutes of the game. I had that philosophy as a young kid. I don't know where I got it from, but luckily I had it."

When Ronnie first started as a coach he remembered one occasion when Shanks called him into his office to give him some advice on coaching a youngster. This single piece of advice would shape the Ronnie Moran legacy. "I knocked on the door. 'Come in, son! What do you want?' I said: 'You want to see me?' He says, 'Christ, yes.' That was a favourite word of his. 'You're not doing it properly; kick him up the backside if he's not doing it right.' And it just went on from there."

From 1966 to 1968 Ronnie enjoyed a dual role at the club; working with the youngsters during the week and playing for the reserves in the Central League as well as helping Joe Fagan with coaching. He was able to develop his coaching and motivational skills with his teammates.

Ronnie had been a left-back ever since he had been changed from a centre-forward as an adolescent but was now moved to an altogether different position to become a more central figure. Moran was as shocked as anyone by this development.

"In those 18 months Joe Fagan kept playing me in the reserves in midfield. Me in midfield! As time went on I realised Joe Fagan knew what effort I put in. I was a shouter and could transmit things to players on the pitch," Moran said.

ON THE STAFF

The youngsters who were fortunate enough to get a game for the reserves hugely benefited from having their mentor playing alongside them as Roy Evans could testify. In 1963 Roy played in the A and B teams under the guidance of Tom Bush, before progressing into Joe Fagan's reserves. "I was only 18, so it was great to be playing alongside Ronnie who was in his early thirties," said Evans. "I remember him being very vocal during these games and he would talk the young players through the entire game."

Ronnie took good notice of Roy, as he later revealed. "I remember Roy well in that first season in the reserves. He used to turn up at the ground with a Ronnie Moran rosette on his jacket," Ronnie quipped. "I used to drive past his house on the way to training and I'd pick him up as he didn't drive then. We worked well together in the reserves and with Roy behind me at left-back, it didn't matter that I wasn't the quickest player in the world."

Probably the most notable player that Ronnie played with during his final stint in the reserves was an 18-year-old goalkeeper called Ray Clemence. "Ray was giving off all the right signals," Ronnie recalled. "Tommy Lawrence was first choice at that time, a great keeper too. But age was in Ray's favour. Ray had very special talents, he was prepared to work hard and wanted to be a winner."

In Ronnie's absence, Shankly's Liverpool were getting stronger and stronger. After winning the First Division title in 1964 and the FA Cup in 1965, not forgetting that very same year Liverpool were cruelly denied reaching the European Cup final, the next challenge on the agenda for Shanks' men was the European Cup Winners' Cup final against Borussia Dortmund on May 5, 1966 at Hampden Park in Glasgow. Ronnie travelled to the game with the other fringe players to witness Liverpool's first European final. Unfortunately, Ron Yeats' 107th-minute own goal proved to be the difference between the two sides.

By then Shanks had won his second league championship, clinching the title on April 30 against Chelsea at Anfield. Although Ronnie wasn't involved with the first-team, he would always try to attend their games. The youngsters played on Saturday mornings which was ideal as everyone was able to go to Anfield and watch the first-team in the afternoon. Ronnie was in charge of the A, B and C youth teams and always had the final say on who played for which side at the weekend. He was aware of the strengths of all the youngsters from working with the apprentices on a daily basis and coaching at Melwood on Tuesday and Thursday evenings.

Although Ronnie enjoyed his new role, the youth setup wasn't how it used to be when he started out as he pointed out in a news article in 1967: "When I look at all the youngsters coming up I marvel at the changes. When I first came into the game the maximum wage was £14 and there were very few young-sters on the staff. Because wages were so low, clubs could afford many more professionals than now. I remember playing in a Liverpool 'A' side which included nine full-time professionals. Now it's different. The game is much faster, the training far better organised, with new techniques and more attention paid to tactics. But one basic rule still applies, you've still got to be able to play the game. You can't manufacture footballers."

Ronnie loved working with the youngsters. He would always encourage them to enjoy playing, work hard, listen to advice and also to stand up for themselves and constantly try to improve.

Start of the journey: Ronnie in the early 1950s as his playing career was beginning to take off

Proud poses: With army pals (left) in 1953 and Bootle Boys a few years earlier (front, centre)

Last line of defence: In the right place to protect his goal as a Plymouth shot flies wide in 1960

Red alert: Ronnie takes charge during an FA Cup tie with Northampton Town in 1958, and (right) pictured a few years earlier

All aboard: Ronnie (third from the right) and the squad set sail for the USA in 1953

Doing it for the team: Ronnie replaced the injured Tommy Younger in goal as the Reds lost 2-1 at Derby in 1957, and scored his first goal away from Anfield at Swansea in 1959 (below)

Out cold: Even tough guys get hurt!

Leader of men: Ronnie runs out as skipper against Hull at Anfield in August 1959 and scored his first league goal in a 5-3 win

Fully committed: Ronnie gets to the ball first in a league game with Barnsley in 1955

Perfect platform: Part of Liverpool's travelling party (fourth from left) in 1958

At home with the Morans: Ronnie gave the cameras a glimpse of his home life in 1955 with his mother Alice, girlfriend Joyce, sisters Dixie and Peggy, brother Tom...and a canary

Big day: Ronnie married Joyce in March 1957, with teammates Louis Bimpson, Alan A'Court and John Molyneux in attendance, before nipping to Anfield to play in the Reds' 2-1 win over Barnsley. Roughly nine months later, daughter Janet was born

Liverpool leap: A towering header clears the danger during a 4-0 win over Swansea in 1959

Feet up: Ronnie has a well-earned rest after his last-gasp penalty saw the Reds past Burnley in the FA Cup in 1963

On duty: Shepherding the ball out of play against Spurs in 1964

I didn't do it!: Sheffield United's Len Allchurch is on the wrong end of a crunching challenge in 1963

American dream: Alan A'Court, Ian Callaghan and Gerry Byrne join Ronnie in a New York deli and on the Manhattan streets on a post-season tour to the USA in May 1964

Five-star travel: A handful of Liverpool greats take a first-class train journey in April 1965

Sheer frustration: Ronnie can't hide his anger as Fred Pickering scores a derby goal for Everton

Penalty king: One of eight spot-kicks Ronnie scored, this one against Manchester City in 1962

Mentor Moran: Youngsters Bobby Graham and Tommy Smith with Ronnie in 1965

Champions: Ronnie helped Bill Shankly's Reds claim the First Division title in 1964

Ronnie's coaching generally followed on from what Shanks was doing with the first-team in case players were needed at the next level so they could fit in straight away.

Ronnie's son, Paul, attended his first Liverpool game on February 15, 1969 against Nottingham Forest on a snowbound Anfield. "We lost the game 2-0 to Matthew Gillies' side and I watched it with my dad from the press box," Paul says. "I was also lucky enough to watch two games from the dugout against Leeds and West Brom in the early 1970s. Looking back, at the time I was just at a game with my dad but if you think about it, I was watching the first-team from the dugout with Bill Shankly, Bob Paisley and Joe Fagan. It makes me think what other people would give to be able to say that. When I think about it now I realise how lucky I am."

Paul enjoyed going with his dad to Melwood to watch the youth teams play as well as attending reserve games with him because he was allowed in the dressing room and could watch from the dugout.

"I also really enjoyed going to Anfield on a Sunday morning after match days," Paul says. "My dad would take me down and while he was either nursing an injured player or sorting out bits of the kit, he handed me a ball and I'd be out on the pitch having a kick around, usually re-enacting the goals I had witnessed the day before. Usually Roy Evans' son, Stephen, would be there and we would always have to pick him up to send him into the Kop for the ball, which in them days wasn't particularly easy.

"On first-team match days at Anfield I used to get to the ground at 11:15 and go to the players' entrance where Fred and John, who looked after that area, would let me in. I would hang around waiting for the opposition to arrive. When they got off the bus, I looked at the players to try to see who looked nervous or injured or whether I could overhear anything they were saying, possibly about tactics or injuries, so I could relate this to my dad, who listened to the results of my 'investigations' but I realise now he was just playing along with me so I could feel part of the club. To be honest, after doing this for a few years some players said hello to me and shook my hand as they recognised me from previous games at Anfield."

"I started going to away games regularly in 1977, aged 15," Paul adds. "Sometimes I'd have to meet the team coach as it arrived at the ground and get tickets off my dad. The players used to see me and make a big effort to wave and shout hello, then laugh as they went into the ground leaving me outside with the tickets being glared at and threatened by the home fans. I suppose this doesn't sound too much of a problem but try doing it at Birmingham or in London!"

Melwood was in a state of disrepair in 1959 when Shankly took over Liverpool. "It was a sorry wilderness," the Scot said. "One pitch looked as if a couple of bombs had been dropped on it. 'The Germans were over here, were they?' I asked."

Shankly set about fixing it from that moment on as he felt that the state of the training facilities reflected the club as a whole and would contribute to the team's success.

Harold Cartwright, chairman of Liverpool, told the *Liverpool Echo*, prior to the 1968/69 season, that Moran and the rest of the Liverpool personnel had a lot to look forward to working at

Melwood in the future. "To the manager, the training facilities for senior and junior players at Melwood are the most important part of Liverpool FC," Cartwright said. "We have made a hard all-weather pitch that has cost £12,000 which means that players can train in any weather during both the day and the evening. We've improved the floodlighting on one of the grass training areas and on the hard area. New sumptuous dressing rooms have been built with sauna baths, heat baths and normal baths. Everything has been done to make it among the top flight of training grounds in the country." Gone were the days when Melwood's head groundsman, Eli Wass, used a scythe, and even horses and sheep, to keep the grass trim.

One of those lucky enough to benefit from the new setup at Melwood was Steve Heighway, who arrived at the start of the 70s from the amateur game. He took up extensive running as he braced himself for the rigours ahead at a professional club, but he turned out to be ill prepared. "There were different functions during a training session: you might do six 440-yard runs, then six 220s, then six 100s and all the while you were being timed," Steve said.

Peter Thompson seemed to savour any challenge, whether it was skipping rope, racing over hurdles, lifting weights or his particular favourite, any kind of ball work. Other players had got used to the training regime at Liverpool that maybe looked easy on the surface, but was, in fact, not for the faint-hearted. Liverpool had one of the fittest teams in the country for a good reason.

One day Steve hit a brick wall as he tried to keep up with the lads. "I began to find that during a week's training session, you reached a peak on a couple of days, then it would taper off again," Steve said. "On one of those peak days, I found myself pushing really hard to stay in front of Peter Thompson all the way. At the end I simply collapsed and lay, retching on the ground. Ronnie Moran came across to give me a hand, and as he helped me to my feet, my legs buckled and buckled again when I made another heaving effort to stand up straight. Naturally, the rest of the players had a good laugh at my expense, and even today they will remind me of the occasion I flaked out."

Heighway was an immediate success at Liverpool and helped the team reach the FA Cup final in 1971. Ronnie was on the bench and can be seen on TV massaging the players' legs at the end of the 90 minutes, along with his ex-teammates Ron Yeats and Tommy Lawrence, as the game against Arsenal went into extra-time. Ronnie made sure the players were in prime condition but he was clearly not allowed to scream any instructions to the team on the field. Unfortunately, Charlie George's strike in the 111th minute gave the Gunners a 2-1 victory after Heighway had put the Reds in front a couple of minutes into extra-time.

Following the 1970/71 season, changes were made to the training staff as announced by Shankly at a press conference in July 1971. Paisley became assistant manager, Shankly's right-hand man instead of chief coach Reuben Bennett, who was assigned to 'special duties' such as building dossiers on Liverpool's opponents both in England and abroad. Ronnie took charge of the reserve team from Joe Fagan, who was promoted to the first-team and Tom Saunders was now in charge of the youth teams.

Shankly had signed a new contract, due to expire in three

years, having refused a five-year deal. Shankly was in a typically buoyant mood and as he left the press conference he declared: "Now, we are going for the big stuff. The league, the European Cup and the FA Cup will do for a start."

A young midfielder by the name of Kevin Keegan, who had been purchased from Scunthorpe at the end of the previous season, was now under Moran's tutelage at Melwood as the players reported back for training in the second week of July.

The reserves played their first practice match prior to the forthcoming campaign at Prenton Park against Tranmere's first-team. As the players came in at half-time Keegan thought he had done himself justice, but soon got a rude awakening.

"Ronnie Moran immediately started on me," Keegan recollects. 'What the hell do you think you're doing? You're not playing like a Liverpool player.' 'What do you mean?' I said, completely taken aback. 'You're just free and easy. You're just charging about the midfield. You're nearly playing up front. You're a midfield player, you've got responsibilities defensively as well as in attack!'"

Keegan had, until then, modelled his midfield play on West Ham's Trevor Brooking, who just floated around midfield without worrying about his defending and always wanted to go forward.

Liverpool's winner against Tranmere came from a penalty after Keegan had been chopped down, so clearly his forward play was paying off. After Keegan scored in the next game against New Brighton, changes were made for the following match against Southport on August 6. The first-team had just come back from drawing 4-4 with Hamburg SV in a friendly in Germany and Shankly was this time in attendance. This was the first time Shankly saw Keegan play in a Liverpool shirt. Keegan had already impressed during the end of the 1970/71 season tour in Scandinavia, but Shankly had not gone on the trip as these tours were not taken very seriously.

"Ronnie must have told Bill Shankly his feelings about my midfield play and suggested that I should be given a game in the attack," Keegan said. He scored Liverpool's goals in a 2-1 win at Southport. Shankly clearly liked what he saw as only four days later Keegan played up front for the first-team in its annual game with the reserves in pre-season.

The first-teamers beat the reserves 7-1 in a farcical match where Keegan was giggling half the time as he was just getting used to Shankly's sayings. 'Our Jeanette could kick a ball further than that!' was not an uncommon cry by Bill, referring to his daughter. Keegan was rampant and scored a hat-trick, spurred on by one thought above anything else.

"One of the reasons I played so well was that I wanted to make Ronnie Moran eat his words. I wanted to show him that I could play, because I did not think he rated me," the Reds' former number seven said.

Shankly was ready to fast-track Keegan straight to the first-team, but as he told the press that was "largely up to the lad himself. If he shows up well, he could force his way into the first-team reckoning this season, but we are quite happy to wait. Keegan is quick and enthusiastic and he has a great chance of doing something special in the game."

Come the first game in the league, against Nottingham Forest, Keegan was number seven in Liverpool's attack. He scored after 12 minutes and was hailed as the new hero of the fans, who loved his enthusiastic performance. Shankly was delighted:

"What a performance by Keegan. This lad has got all the confidence in the world!"

Keegan came to appreciate what Ronnie did to inspire him and sang his praises as he looked back. "Ronnie became the foundation the club was built on," Keegan says. "He was there as a player before Shanks came in. He was there with Shanks. He was there with Bob Paisley. He helped when Joe took over for a while. He was there with Roy Evans. If you think about it, he was the one link to it all."

The Liverpool training staff worked superbly together to keep everyone on their toes and Ronnie was undoubtedly the enforcer of the group, but he was a multifaceted character.

"There was a very humorous side to Ronnie and then there was another side," Keegan says. "You thought, 'what happened?' If you got him mad you knew about it. He had all these characters. He could slip into them. If things got really tough he would sometimes be the guy to say, 'come on, guys. It's only one game we've lost.' He would pick you back up and the next time, it might be Joe Fagan, or maybe even the boss himself or Bob Paisley. They all took it in turns. They were a foursome in the way they worked.

"Bob used to come in and tell players they were not playing. Shanks didn't do that. No-one really liked Bob coming over to them. 'Don't come near me, Bob.' Joe and Ronnie were almost like a double act, one worth listening to. Ronnie was the verbal one. You could hear him all over Melwood. His voice echoed with those walls around."

Moran had lost 'Mighty Mouse' to the first-team after having been in charge of him for only six weeks. He could have done with him up front for the reserves as they struggled for goals in the first couple of months of the Central League, apart from a 6-3 drubbing of Newcastle where Alun Evans scored two. Moran's reserves were made up of first-team players who fell out of contention or were coming back from injury and youngsters who were promoted from the A and B teams in order to prove themselves.

During Ronnie's first term as sole manager of the reserves, his team included ex-teammates such as Tommy Lawrence and Peter Thompson and budding youngsters Phil Thompson and Phil Boersma. Liverpool's second string ended up fourth in Ronnie's first season.

Bootle-born Hughie McAuley, who like Ronnie had featured for Bootle Boys, was a regular in the reserves. He went on to play seven games in the Lancashire Senior Cup for Liverpool and became a coach at the club's Academy.

"I remember watching one reserve team game with my dad and Hughie got kicked, but the cut was underneath his sock so therefore wasn't visible," Paul Moran recalls. "My dad and Roy were shouting to Hughie to run it off while he was limping around in pain. After the game we saw a deep gash on his shin. He was subsequently sent to hospital and ended up needing 14 stitches. There was no way Hughie could have run that one off!

"Hughie was a good lad and I will never forget the time I was at Leicester, again for a reserve team game with my dad. When Hughie ran out of the tunnel he was looking around for his dad and collided with Filbert the Fox and knocked his head off. The mascot wasn't amused and told Hughie exactly what he thought of him."

The reconstruction of Liverpool's Main Stand was completed during the 1971/72 season, which was pleasing to the training staff who had been "pushed around, forced to improvise and slum it" as Shankly described it, in the previous campaign when Melwood was the team's base instead of Anfield, thus unsettling the normal routine of the players. Liverpool hadn't won the league since 1966. That sped up Shankly's revamp of the side with Ray Clemence, Alec Lindsay, Larry Lloyd, Brian Hall, Steve Heighway and John Toshack joining the side in place of old servants like Tommy Lawrence, Ron Yeats, Roger Hunt, Bobby Graham, Peter Thompson and Ian St John. With the inspirational Kevin Keegan coming into the side as well, Liverpool finally clicked in the second part of the 1971/72 campaign, scoring 34 goals while conceding two during 13 league wins and one draw which left Anfield in the grip of title-chasing fever. Liverpool failed to score in their last two matches and finished the season within a point of the title.

Liverpool made a much better start in the following campaign and stayed the course right until the end, finishing three points ahead of Arsenal and thus equalling the Gunners' record of eight league titles. Shankly was relieved, having waited seven years for his third league championship. His second batch of champions had outdone the first in his mind.

"This is the happiest day of my life," Shankly said. "I have known nothing like it as a player or manager. This title gave me greater pleasure than the previous two, simply because here we had a rebuilt side. I wanted that title more than at any time in my life."

Liverpool were also unstoppable in the UEFA Cup. Due to Moran's commitments with the reserves, he never travelled away with the first-team to European games apart from the second leg of the UEFA Cup final against Borussia Mönchengladbach. Ronnie sat on the bench next to Shankly in the Bökelberg stadium in Germany. Liverpool lost 2-0 on the night, but won their first European trophy as they had beaten the Germans 3-0 in the first leg at Anfield. According to Paul Moran, this game in Germany was the first time his dad was seen and heard on TV shouting instructions at the players. Little by little Moran was developing as a coach and having more influence over the first-team. He still had time to coach his son though.

"When I used to play football with my dad, looking back on it now I realise how he was toughening me up for playing later," said Paul. "He would occasionally foul me or accidentally cause me to crash into the garden wall or a bush. It made me want to learn more how to get past him without being flattened, but that never really happened."

Despite the all-consuming nature of top-flight football, Ronnie kept his work and home life totally separate, at least most of the time.

"We would be able to feel if he was a bit tense or uptight if Liverpool were going through a bad patch, which wasn't very often," said Paul. "There was no real difference in my dad before big finals or important league games, although I do remember getting bollocked for asking him about final tickets prior to the semi-final of that tournament. 'Why? We're not in the final,' was my dad's terse reply. There was never the feeling that I couldn't go and ask him things about his day at Melwood.

"My dad didn't need to instil football into me. Everything I did with my dad revolved around football. I would really look forward to our talks about football and enjoyed discussing the opposition players and teams with him. Sometimes I'd say I thought an opponent was good and my dad would look at me and shake his head. My ambition was always to recommend a player to my dad who would then eventually sign for us but I never got it right. I remember insisting we should sign George McCluskey from Celtic in 1980; he eventually went to Leeds and played in the First Division."

"In a nutshell, it was really just a normal family life," Paul continues. "My dad was always interested in our days and how we were getting on at school. Wherever my dad lived he was never seen as a local celebrity and people used to treat him no differently to anyone else, which is exactly how my dad wanted it. People would obviously ask for autographs, which was never really a problem, and occasionally when Liverpool got to a final or before a derby game people who we didn't know would randomly knock on the door and ask for any spares. He always treated them extremely politely but obviously let them know there was little to no chance of a ticket."

Ronnie's daughter Janet had no real interest in football when she was younger and never went to any matches with Paul or her dad. She wasn't into sports in general, but enjoyed listening to music and her favourite artist was David Bowie. There was always a lot of football talk in the Moran household, which Janet and Joyce wouldn't always approve of. Janet tried to divert the conversation away from football, but Paul and Ronnie enjoyed turning any subject she had brought up back to football. If she mentioned a pop star of the day, the Moran boys would say: "Yeah, I've heard of him, he supports Arsenal," and then proceed to discuss that team.

While football was everything to Ronnie, he enjoyed taking the family on holiday while Janet and Paul were kids. They would often take Ronnie's sister, Margaret (known as Aunty Peggy) with them. June was the ideal time to go away as Ronnie had then finished with his post-season duties and July was the start of pre-season.

Ronnie and Joyce had two favourite holiday destinations, which they would drive to on alternate years to spend a week there. One was Paignton, a seaside town in south Devon. The other was Ilfracombe, a resort on the north Devon coast.

In Paignton the Morans would always stay at the Devon Country Club, a holiday complex that had been a prisoner of war camp during World War II. There were various activities on offer for children such as play parks, a paddling pool, and Paul's favourite, the grassy areas, where he could play football in front of the coloured chalets where they used to stay.

"I remember at the Country Club they organised a football match; holiday makers against the staff," Paul says. "I scored a 20-yarder into the top corner, looked round at my dad to see what his reaction was only to find he had his back to me signing an autograph. I've learned many things from my dad over the years but one piece of advice that always sticks with me is that you have to work hard for anything you want from life and if you think something needs to be done, don't stand by waiting for someone else to sort it, get it done yourself."

As well as enjoying the tranquility of the country club they would also venture out on day trips to Paignton Zoo and Babbacombe Model Village in Torquay.

In Ilfracombe, the Morans would always stay at the same bed & breakfast called the Sherbourne Lodge and spend a lot of time at one of England's best beaches, Woolacombe Beach. Janet and Paul would play with their bucket and spades in the sand and paddle in the sea, while Ronnie and Joyce relaxed in their deck chairs and enjoyed the occasional paddle themselves. Ronnie was rarely recognised in these parts, apart from by the holidaymakers who had also come down from Merseyside. The Morans were able to spend some quality time together away from the hustle and bustle of football, but in a way it wasn't a case of Ronnie wanting the opportunity of a break from football; it was more as if football was having a break from Ronnie, simply because there wasn't anything to watch on the television apart from the odd international game.

During his three-year tenure as the reserve team manager, attending first-team games proved difficult for Ronnie. When the first-team was at home, the reserves would be away and vice versa. The Central League covered the whole of England from Birmingham upwards, so some Saturdays he wouldn't get home until 11pm at night from Newcastle or Sunderland. Dinner was served at the Moran household with the master of the house absent. He instead enjoyed his meal on the team bus on the way back. Dinner came wrapped in tinfoil and would include chicken and a cold sausage with a bottle of lemonade to gulp down.

When Ronnie arrived home, he was unaware of how success-ful Shankly's boys had been in their match that particular day. Ronnie and his son, Paul, used to have a system in place where he would wait for his dad to knock on the door when he reached the house and let him know of the score before he walked in. "Thumbs up would mean we had won. That was usually the case when the reserves played away because the first-team was then at home. A horizontal thumb would mean a draw and thumbs down would mean we had got beat," Paul explains. "I would then open the door. He would clench both his fists if he was informed that the first-team had won."

Ronnie's reserve side was crowned Central League champions in 1973 and, better still, won the same competition by eight points the following season. Ronnie's success with the reserves was certainly impressive, but would it stand him in good stead after Shankly's unexpected departure in July 1974?

During the FA Cup final victory against Newcastle at Wembley in 1974, Ronnie was again on the bench as he was in the 1971 final, but this time around he had much more of an input and there were hints he might soon climb further up the ladder.

"I never went to the final in 1974 but I can remember my dad telling me I would be going to a lot more games the following season," Paul says. Paul was only 12 at the time and knew it was no use to ask his dad any further about the matter. "I've always wondered if he had an idea that Shanks would be going or he'd been dropping hints behind the scenes. My dad has never confirmed this to me though."

After Shankly left Liverpool, Ronnie would only see his former boss when he visited Anfield or Melwood as they never maintained a relationship outside of football. Ronnie related to his son that Shankly kept on visiting Melwood after he had formally relinquished the reins and offered advice to the players and staff. The main problem was that certain players were still treating Bill as though he was in charge, one of them being captain Emlyn Hughes, who insisted on calling him 'boss'.

It was evident that Shankly still wanted to be involved in the club in some capacity and help out with the transition of management, but the fact was that his presence at Melwood, just down the road from where he lived, was making it more difficult for Paisley to get from under Bill's shadow. Shankly was not exactly a quiet and an unassuming person, so he would attract a lot of attention while at the training ground and Bob felt this undermined his authority. This caused friction between Bill and the club.

"I went to the training ground at Melwood for a while," Shankly said. "But then I got the impression that it would perhaps be better if I stopped going. I felt there was some resentment. 'What the hell is he still doing here?' I packed up going to Melwood and I also stopped going to the directors' box at Anfield."

Paisley needed to stand on his own two feet and even though Shankly was ready and able to advise him, Bob explained: "If Bill advised you, you had to take his advice. His words were law, not advice."

Before Paisley's appointment, Shankly's former captain, Ron Yeats, said: "There will never be another Shankly and, in a way, I feel sorry for the man who has to replace him at Anfield."

On July 20, six days before Bob was offically given the job, the *Liverpool Daily Post* reported: 'Bob Paisley is to take over as manager of Liverpool Football Club from Bill Shankly. To my knowledge, Paisley has been the only name given any serious consideration.' Paisley professed complete surprise as his reaction was sought and his response must have been a relief for Ronnie Moran. "If I am asked to take over, the routine of the club would not change one iota."

Moran, though, couldn't be sure what his own position would be until Paisley had been officially appointed. The day after

Paisley had been formally hired as manager he declared his trust in the coaching staff at the club. "Bill has always been a boss who believed in allowing his staff to use their own talents," Bob told the *Liverpool Daily Post*. "He has interfered only rarely and quite honestly I don't think he has had much to complain about.

"We have always had a great team behind the team at Anfield. That's the way I shall try to keep it. You don't play around with ideas that have proved to work. You just feed and water them."

Bob Paisley's wife, Jessie, later recalled: "The persuasion was that he did it for the sake of the others there because he was afraid that when another manager came they'd bring in their own staff with them. So he took it for the sake of everybody else as well as himself."

Paisley gave Moran a glimpse of what he should expect as trainer of Liverpool Football Club in the *Liverpool Echo* in 1969. "A trainer's life is one of the busiest of all the jobs associated with running a football club. It is a seven-day-a-week affair. I have to go back a long, long time since I last remember a day when I didn't set foot in Anfield and that includes Sundays.

"A trainer is a combination of everything. He has to have expert medical knowledge, immense football experience, be quick and alert in summing up any conceivable situation both on and off the field, and when it comes to an injury he must, into the bargain, be something of a psychologist. You have to know your players inside out. Some need encouragement, others need bullying; and you've got to know which are which, otherwise results can be disastrous."

Now it was time for Shankly's disciples to take their next step into a potentially bright future.

Ronnie Moran had been at the club for 25 years. After Shankly left in 1974, everyone else simply moved up a position. Bob Paisley took over from Shankly, Joe Fagan became chief coach, Ronnie Moran first-team trainer and Roy Evans took over from Moran as manager of the reserves. As Ronnie was now the lowest ranked trainer in the first-team, he took over physio duties that on match day meant taking his magic sponge from his white bucket by the bench and running on to the pitch to treat the injured. While Ronnie was a player, Albert Shelley had been the in-house physio, whose healing ways were often quite rudimentary, as Ian St John remembers. "The remedy for bad knees most favoured by Albert was hot and cold towels. He would have the towels in two buckets, one red hot and the other one filled with ice.

"First he would reach into the hot bucket with his tweezers and slap a steaming towel on to the offending knee, quickly followed by a cold one. Often you would cry out, but Albert said it was the only way to do it," St John said.

Depending on the level of the injury, Moran and the coaching staff would attend to the injured in the treatment room at Anfield. This would usually happen on a Sunday morning where they would assess and treat the players who picked up injuries on a Saturday. Moran could tell if injuries were serious or not and the more serious ones were sent to hospital. There was also a club doctor on hand to do stitches for cuts, head injuries and similar cases. There was no treatment room at Melwood other than a room with a medical table in case anyone got injured in a training session or during a youth team game. Anyone already injured would still travel to Melwood on the bus with the rest of the squad to do some light training or to use the gym.

Paul Walsh, who joined Liverpool in the 1984/85 season, recollects how this system worked. "For physios you had Roy Evans and Ronnie Moran. If you had an infection of any sort, you got red or black penicillin. If you got any sort of knock, you got an anti-inflammatory. But if you had anything worse than that, they'd just treat it without knowing what it was. If they thought it was maybe something worse they'd send you to the surgeon and he'd try and work out what it was."

An amazing run of 18 goals in 25 matches in the 1985/86 season was a testament to Walsh's ability, but then disaster struck. "There's a picture of me on my wall at home of me in the dressing room with Roy Evans dabbing my ankle with a sponge," Walsh explains. "I've ruptured my ligaments and I've got Roy giving it a dab and wiggling it about saying: 'It'll be alright!' I was hobbling around for months. I didn't even know I'd ruptured my ligaments."

Roy Evans joined Liverpool in 1963 and played through the youth levels to the first-team before impressing so much as a member of the coaching staff that he was given the keys to the kingdom in 1994, the hot-seat of Liverpool FC.

Roy and Ronnie worked hand in hand on Liverpool's coaching staff for 24 years. During this time from 1974 to 1998 Liverpool won 23 major honours, including 10 First Division titles and four European Cups. The pair contributed massively to a golden era of success for Liverpool.

"I obviously knew about Ronnie before I joined Liverpool," Roy recalls. "When I was about nine, around 1957, my dad would leave me in the Boys' Pen and he would go into the Kop. Billy Liddell, Tony Rowley and Jimmy Melia were knocking the goals in then and the Reds were still in the Second Division. Ronnie was a solid full-back and had a great left foot on him."

Ronnie had also gained Roy's respect as a coach who showed such a genuine interest in the welfare of the youngsters. Roy played alongside him with the reserves but they were also on opposite sides, as he remembers fondly. "On a Monday morning it was a ritual to play five-a-side football in the Main Stand car park, the coaching staff versus the amateurs. We used two pumps (training shoes) for goal posts at one end and the wall at the other. Shanks, Reuben, Bob, Joe and Ronnie were very competitive and these guys would have played until dark to win."

Roy got to know Ronnie better when he joined the coaching staff, although it wasn't an easy decision for Roy to give up his footballing career.

"I was still only 25 and could have continued my playing career for a few more years," Roy says. "However, that would have meant moving away from Liverpool again after just coming back from playing in America. I had long chats with Joe Fagan, Tommy Smith, Bob and Ronnie, whose advice was really helpful. I decided to accept the role and never really looked back nor regretted having ended my playing career so prematurely. I was given full control of the reserve team, unless of course Bob wanted to give a first-team player, coming back from injury, a run out. This was great, as unlike the current under-23 setup, the lads would get inspired by playing alongside some of the best players in Europe. In them days you mostly learned your trade from players older than yourself."

Roy Evans had become a part of the Bootroom boys, an elite group of men who knew all the ins and outs of the game. During Shankly's reign trainers Fagan, Bennett and Paisley spent a lot of their time together in a small room at the top of a long corridor that ran at ground level in the old Main Stand. This was essentially a storage room where skips with the kit for the reserves and the first-team were kept as well as the boots for the players. Ronnie Moran had become part of the Bootroom legend from 1966 onwards when he joined the coaching staff.

Once the new Main Stand had been built in 1973 the storage room was moved to the centre of the stand and that became the famous Bootroom. "There was a double door which was the drying room; all the kit was hung up in there. The small door adjacent to this led to the boot room," Ronnie explained. "At first it was just one big room. On the left was a bench where the kids cleaned all the match boots. We had hooks put up at the end and boots would be put on them after the kids had cleaned them. After a while we had the room halved so that it would be a bit more private for us."

This room became an informal place where the coaching staff discussed matches past and present, players, tactics and anything to do with the club really. The Bootroom was a place where all men were equal and everybody's input was appreciated, whether the discussion revolved around the senior team, the reserves or the youth teams.

Shankly was never part of the Bootroom boys as he had his own office. He stayed well away from the Bootroom after games, finished off his press duties and hurried home to his wife and kids, leaving his coaching staff to its own devices. Paisley, who had been a part of the original Bootroom, would no longer hang up his coat there after he took over as boss, but was in there way more frequently than Shankly had ever been during his reign.

"Myself, Joe and Roy would always be in there though, even during the week after training," Ronnie explained in 2009. "You'd have your lunch and do a bit of work, sorting the kits or whatever. Then we'd sit down and have a natter. 'It's the officers' mess,' Peter Robinson once said to Kenny Dalglish. Kenny replied: 'Peter, they're generals, not officers.'"

Evans had his own take on the essence of the Bootroom. "It was a pooling of resources and a mixture of ideas from experienced football men who only ever wanted the best for the football club they worked for," he said. "We would gather informally to analyse matches, assess players' abilities and talk about the opposition and the latest gossip. Visiting managers and coaches would be invited in after games for a drink; some would have a whisky or just a cup of tea. However, once I remember Elton John coming in trying to give me a kiss and asking Ronnie for a Pink Gin."

Roy enjoyed the camaraderie. "Apart from Brian Clough and his assistant Peter Taylor, who were always a bit funny about coming in, opposition managers and staff would look forward to their invite into the Bootroom. Not only would they go over the game with us but would also be interested in how we did things at Liverpool. They would also admire the naked photos of women on the wall, which were my contribution. For that reason, most of the photos taken in the Bootroom are taken from the same angle!"

Ronnie decorated a Bootroom wall with a Liverpool team picture from 1955, in which he was standing in the back row, but to Ronnie's dismay someone had decided to draw horns on his head!

"All the important talking was done in the Bootroom," Roy reveals. "Whenever I wasn't involved with the reserves I used to get invited along with the first-team and when the first-team weren't in action, Bob, Joe and Ronnie would come down to watch my lads. They would never interfere during the game and any advice was given to me in the Bootroom usually on a Friday night and nearly always over a bottle of Bell's whisky that Bob had won for being manager of the month.

"We would discuss what had happened over the week and I would get asked about the progress of my players with regards to if they were ready for the first-team or not. Bob would also give me the freedom to comment on what I thought could be improved regarding the first-team as well. Our conversations were always in good spirit, never critical, just helping each other out as friends."

Dusty cupboards on the walls kept the secrets of the Bootroom boys in the form of A4-sized books. Joe Fagan started this documentation in the 60s and Ronnie took over in the 70s. Everything that was considered of some importance was jotted down; what the weather was like, who was injured, the results for the first-team and the reserves with ratings of the first teamers' performances, the setup for each training session, how the players warmed up, the length of sprints, the essence of each exercise and how many were involved in the small-sided matches on a pitch that varied in length and breadth. The 'Bootroom Bibles' became an important reference tool to the coaches, a database long before the daily use of computers.

Although Ronnie's role changed in 1974, he already knew the

players' weaknesses and strengths as his reserve side had often trained with the first-team. Training took a familiar pattern under Paisley, focusing mainly on the small-sided games. However, there were variations such as one or two-touch games or 10 passes equals a goal. Nevertheless, everything was always geared towards passing and movement and making sure that, as a player, you were available to receive the ball. What was done in the training sessions was discussed between the training staff, but Moran would then carry out the sessions alone while Joe and Bob stood back and watched.

Back in those days the players met at Anfield before leaving on a coach for Melwood. On a typical day of training Moran would leave his house around 8:30 and drive to Anfield. He would always get there early before the players were due at 9:30. Ronnie would stay in the Bootroom and sort out the training kit while the players had a chance to chat and relax prior to training, without the staff being around. The coach with the staff and the players, including the youth teams, would leave Anfield for Melwood at 10:15 with the drive lasting 15 minutes. "Bill liked the banter on the coach. He thought it was good for morale and for bonding," former secretary and chief executive of Liverpool FC, Peter Robinson, said.

Training at Melwood would usually last until 13:00, after which the players would go back to Anfield for a bath and get changed before having lunch, which more often than not consisted of soup, steak pie and a dessert. Moran was in charge of the players' meals at Anfield, making sure the canteen prepared enough of what they wanted when they returned from Melwood. Ronnie wasn't used to having his lunch with the players and would instead sort out all the training kit and get it to the laundry room. He would then have a chat with the rest of the coaching staff before heading back home at around 15:00.

Jimmy Case remembers snapping his laces on his boots one morning as he was preparing to get on the bus from Anfield to train at Melwood. Case hurried down to the Bootroom and knocked on the door.

"It was a toss-up as to who would open the door, but I was hoping it would be Joe Fagan," Case recollects. "In my eyes Ronnie Moran was bad cop and Joe was the good cop. You can guess who opened the door… Ronnie."

Case hesitantly asked Ronnie for a new pair of bootlaces. Ronnie's reply startled Case. "Have you signed your new contract yet?"

"Yes, I signed an extension last week," Case responded.

Ronnie replied: "In that case, you can have a pair then. There you go, son."

"In his next breath Ronnie shouted at the top of his voice, 'Right, let's get on the bus, you lot!' and away we went to training. Talk about not getting ahead of yourself. That was the atmosphere around the club with Joe, Ronnie and Bob," Case reflected.

On August 10, 1974 probably the nastiest Charity Shield match ever was played. Kevin Keegan and Leeds United's Billy Bremner were dismissed early in the second half for fighting and it was a surprise that more players didn't join them for an early bath! Liverpool secured the shield on penalties after Ian Callaghan scored from the deciding spot-kick. The Charity Shield proved to be the only piece of silverware Liverpool would win that season as they narrowly missed out on the league title to Derby County.

However, that wasn't the case during the 1975/76 season when Paisley won his first league title as manager, finishing one point above QPR. Liverpool also faced Club Bruges in a two-legged final in the UEFA Cup. The Reds were 2-0 down in the first leg against Bruges at Anfield but won 3-2 in a sensational finish. Four days before the second leg in Belgium, Ray Clemence conceded a terrible goal for England against Scotland when Kenny Dalglish slotted a shot through his legs.

"Ray had a hatred of mistakes, to such a degree that he would take them to heart for a while," said Ronnie. "And he was still in a bit of a state with himself when we went to Bruges to protect that 3-2 lead. I took him for training. We wanted him livening up again and concentrating on the immediate job in hand. And what happened? Against all the odds he allowed one of my shots to slip through his legs and a couple of supporters gave him some good natured banter."

Despite his recent misfortunes Clemence was his usual self as Liverpool drew 1-1 in Belgium and Bob Paisley came back with his first European prize as a manager.

During the following season, 1976/77, Liverpool went from strength to strength and enjoyed more success. Although they narrowly failed to achieve a historic treble, losing to Manchester United in the FA Cup final at Wembley, they clinched the league title for the second season in a row and also won the European Cup for the first time in the club's history. Of the 2,000-plus games that Ronnie Moran was involved in during his time at Liverpool, the 3-1 win in Rome against Borussia Mönchengladbach stands out as his favourite. "When we first won the European Cup in 1977, it was one of the biggest things that had happened to the club and everyone connected with it."

Ronnie's son Paul has his own memories. "I remember going with my dad to Anfield the Monday before the 1977 European Cup final and helping him clean the boots from the FA Cup final on the Saturday and paint the white stripes on the boots so they stood out more. I always used to claim I'd done Terry McDermott's boots, so that's why he scored but I hadn't any idea whose I'd done."

Paul was fortunate enough to attend the game at the Stadio Olimpico and has fond memories of that night. "I ended up in the players' hotel after the game. The bit I remember best was being on Joey Jones' shoulders carrying the European Cup around the banqueting room. It was a brilliant night and as I was only 15, I wasn't drinking. The next day we flew home before the team and we were in our house at 4pm. When my dad returned later that night I opened the front door, ran out and saw he had the European Cup with him as they had decided not to leave it at Anfield. It stayed in my bedroom overnight, which was another fantastic memory of mine."

Emlyn Hughes lifted the European Cup that night. Paul recalls what his dad told him about their all-important skipper: "My dad was always positive about Emlyn's ability and enthusiasm. But I also remember him saying that if we were losing it was always important to make sure Emlyn wasn't charging around the pitch trying to save the day instead of carrying on in his designated role."

Three weeks prior to Liverpool's victory in Rome, Alan Hansen was signed from Partick Thistle for £100,000. Hansen recalls joining the soon-to-be champions of Europe: "When I came to Liverpool all the coaching staff was very welcoming. My first impressions of Ronnie were very good, simply because he was very friendly, especially considering they were preparing to go and play in a European Cup final in Rome."

Liverpool were now not only the champions of England but also the kings of European football. Shankly's bold statement had certainly come true: "My idea was to build Liverpool up and up until eventually everyone would have to submit and give in. I want to build a team that's invincible, so that they have to send a team from bloody Mars to beat us!"

"I went to away games with a lad called Ashy who would always shout 'Dad' as loud as he could when my dad was walking in front of the Liverpool fans after treating an injured player. I told my dad loads of times not to look up because it wouldn't be me shouting, but occasionally he did and the lads around us would take the piss out of me because he thought I was trying to get his attention."

– Paul Moran

Chapter 6

TOUGH BUT FAIR

1977-1983

DURING the summer before the 1977/78 season, Liverpool needed a replacement for Kevin Keegan, who had departed the club for Hamburg SV. Clemence's old nemesis, Kenny Dalglish, was Bob Paisley's choice to fill Keegan's boots.

Paisley had been in contact with Celtic manager Jock Stein since the previous season when he heard that Dalglish wanted to move on. Stein stated that Kenny was going nowhere for a while, but promised Paisley he would be the first person he would contact if he couldn't talk him out of leaving.

"While he was at Celtic we kept him in mind and watched him in televised club and international games," Moran explained. "The time came when we could make a positive move and it was one we never regretted."

Ronnie never really spoke about his admiration for players, but Kenny was different. "The one who's been really outstanding for me was Kenny Dalglish," Ronnie said some years ago. "Kenny took to the place immediately. It didn't take him six months to settle in, more like six minutes. He was the near-perfect professional. He was a winner."

Ronnie valued above everything else that players had to hate to lose and Kenny would even get angry if he lost in a practice match.

Liverpool started the season extremely well, taking 12 points from a possible 14 in their opening seven games and a future stalwart for the club, Alan Hansen, made his first-team debut at Anfield on September 24, 1977.

"Before my debut against Derby I remember Ronnie just coming up to me: 'Look, son, you've got no problems here whatsoever' and just walked away," Hansen recalls. "These short and simple words made me feel a lot better as I was a nervous wreck before he said that to me."

Moran later admitted that he had become a big fan of the Scotsman's playing skills, which he believed were unique for a centre-half.

"I have long admired Alan Hansen for the things he doesn't do. A lot of people have a fixed idea in their minds about what a centre-half should look like and how he should play. They want them big and tough and aggressive and they think their job is to be dominant in the air and strong in the tackle and little else," Moran said. "But Alan is a defender who has never found it necessary to launch himself at everything above head-height or go sliding around on his backside into every challenge. He used his head for thinking, not as a battering ram. Because he is so much more intelligent and knowledgeable than the average player, he sees the play developing and steps in to break up attacks long before they become dangerous to us. His skill in possession allows him twice as much time as most defenders."

Hansen was aware of the special status he had at the club.

"When a new player would arrive at Liverpool, especially a defender, Ronnie Moran would point at me and say: 'Don't watch Big Al play, don't try to do what he does, because he's a one-off," Hansen remembers.

Anfield was also a host to a World Cup qualifier between Wales and Scotland that season as the Football Association of Wales decided to play their home game at a bigger venue than Wrexham in order to sell more tickets. This match, on October 12, proved to be very controversial. Eleven minutes before time, with the game goalless, a throw-in was launched into the penalty area where Joe Jordan jumped up with Welsh defender David Jones and punched the ball to further its flight into the box. French referee Robert Wurtz thought it was the Welshman who had handled and awarded a hotly-contested penalty. Don Masson scored from the spot and Kenny Dalglish secured a 2-0 victory in the 87th minute.

"I went with my dad to the game and we watched it from the Main Stand," Paul Moran recollects. "After the game we went down to the Bootroom and Bill Shankly came in with Jock Stein, who was Celtic's manager at the time. The discussion turned to the handball incident that earned Scotland their penalty in the game. It seemed to me at the time that Joe Jordan had handled the ball. I was sitting quietly, when Jock Stein turned to me and said: 'Who do you think handled it?' 'I thought Joe Jordan had handled the ball, Mr. Stein.' At this point Bill Shankly interrupted me and said: 'It was the defender who handled the ball, son!' I again said I thought it was Jordan so Shanks said to me: 'It's nice to see you're honest, son, you're completely wrong, but at least you're honest!'

"The conversation then ended. As a 15-year-old I was hardly in any position to have a disagreement with Mr Shankly!"

Liverpool made a monumental signing on January 10, 1978 when Graeme Souness arrived from Middlesbrough for £352,000. The sum Liverpool paid for him was a transfer record between English clubs, £2,000 more than Manchester United paid for Leeds' Joe Jordan a week earlier.

"Graeme was a brilliant leader on the pitch and could be relied upon to get the team out of difficult situations. I wasn't surprised when he went into management due to the organisation qualities he showed on the pitch," Ronnie said.

Souness did, on occasion, need a little shout or two from Ronnie to fix something on the field, but as the Scot later revealed, he paid no attention to those instructions.

"The touchline ranters are kidding themselves if they think the players can hear them," Souness said. "It's only a release for themselves because as a player I know I didn't take any notice of Ronnie Moran during play. I'd just give him the thumbs up and carry on!"

Souness was an immensely strong character and didn't take too well to Moran's aggression. "I must be honest and say that when I contemplate this part of my life, I did not plan to be particularly benevolent to Ronnie 'Bugsy' Moran. I have had more rows with Bugsy than anyone in football," Souness said. "He is deliberately antagonistic, a personal device used only to motivate players. There are no pats on the back, no congratulations. In fact, in the end you feel that you have done it yourself in spite of him rather than because of him."

Souness did, though, admit that after having several run-ins with him, he realised how Ronnie was doing this for the benefit of the player and to keep the club's phenomenal success going. "He gets everyone working, not just the players I played with at Liverpool but those who went before. It cannot be a coincidence he has overseen all those great teams. Every club could do with a 'Bugsy'."

Welshman Joey Jones, who arrived from Wrexham in 1975, proved quite a handful at times for the coaching staff at Anfield. He was a fiery character who had his limitations but gave his all. He was a hard nut to crack for Moran, but his enthusiasm was certainly to Ronnie's liking, even though he sometimes went overboard.

Joey made his final appearance for Liverpool in the 1977/78 season and during that campaign he managed to stop training at Melwood because of his antics.

The team was preparing for a match at Manchester City. Joey was fooling around, shadow boxing with Kenny Dalglish, when he accidentally stepped on Ray Kennedy's foot.

"Ray was built like a heavyweight and I was built like a bantamweight," Joey recollects. "I remember I said: 'Sorry', but Ray said: 'I warned you before.' I thought: 'I know what's coming now.' Being brought up where I was, I had always been told, the only wrong advice my dad ever gave me: 'If you think somebody is going to hit you, don't hang around, belt him.' I used to take that sometimes on to the pitch. So I banged him. I hit him twice and we ended up in this brawl. I remember Bob Paisley saying: 'Both of you can leave the club.'"

Ray didn't quieten down at Melwood, threatening what he was going to do to Joey. Once it was time for the team to play a small-sided match in full view of the supporters at open training, all hell broke loose between the pair.

"They put me and Ray on the opposite team," Joey recollects. "You've got to bear in mind all the supporters are there at Melwood. Ray Kennedy has got the ball and as I close him down he hooked me right across the nose. I jumped on his back. You have got to picture this [Joey jumps up to show this to one of the authors of this book]. I have got one arm around his neck and I am punching him but he's swinging me around and my legs are going around. Apparently that is the only time that training got stopped at Liverpool.

"We had dinner and I know it sounds stupid but I did say: 'I'll just stab you, mate' to Ray. It was stupid. They had to take the knife off me. It was a blunt one, anyway."

Joey then went home to pack an overnight bag as the team was going to stay at a hotel before the game at City. Joey's next stop was Anfield where the team was gathering.

"I've gone into the Bootroom and Joe Fagan and Ronnie Moran were there," continues Joey. "I remember them saying: 'Have you calmed down now?' 'I went: 'no, if it carries on, I'm going to finish it off.' The door opens at the players' entrance and it is Ray Kennedy walking towards me. I thought, 'I better put the bag in the left hand because I know I am going to smack him with my right one.' He puts his bag down and I threw mine down and he went: 'Listen Joey, I am sorry.' He apologised and we didn't have any problems after that. It happens at all clubs all over the country."

As a left-back, Joey was followed more closely by Ronnie as it had been his position as a player. Joey was a bit of a hellraiser, but he was a funny character, who entertained the lads with his 'horrible jokes' as Ray Clemence called them.

When Joey left the club in October 1978, he was sent a farewell gift by Ronnie. "It was an Adidas shoebox and with it came a message from Ronnie Moran: 'You've forgot your boots,'" said Jones.

"When I opened the box, I found a pair of dirty, ankle-high hobnailed boots with leather studs, the kind they used in the 1930s. I've still got them at home, but that was the Liverpool sense of humour. It was either that or the way I played and they really thought these were what I should wear!"

The Reds finished the 1977/78 campaign seven points behind Brian Clough's Nottingham Forest, but retained the European Cup on home soil.

"I played in the European Cup final against Bruges at Wembley and Ronnie said exactly the same thing to me as on my debut: 'This isn't going to be a problem for you, son,'" Alan Hansen recalls. "He never would talk to me before a game saying: 'You've got to do this and you've got to do that.' What he could do is say the right things at the right time to lift you; he was a master of doing this."

Paul Moran was at Wembley too. "1978 versus Bruges was

a funny game because with the final being at Wembley it was more like a domestic cup final in the build-up," he said. "The club followed the usual procedure for a Wembley game, staying at the same hotel and doing everything in a familiar way. I went to the game with my sister and brother-in-law. It was one of those games where people would knock at the door of the house asking for tickets. I always remember my dad saying: 'Don't be nasty to anyone in case they did anything to the house if they never got a ticket.' For the second year on the trot he brought the cup home and we had it in the house.

"Because of my dad's position at the club I was lucky enough from the age of 15 to go training at Melwood on a Tuesday and Thursday night where my dad, Roy Evans, John Bennison and Tom Saunders would take the sessions," Paul says. "Possibly through a shortage of right-backs, I managed to play about 25 games for the Liverpool B team in the Lancashire League. My highlights were playing in a 3-2 win against Everton and scoring my one and only goal for Liverpool against Tranmere Rovers at The Oval in Bebington.

"One time at Melwood we were playing an 11-a-side game on the B team pitch and the rule was that the last man was in goal, meaning only the defender nearest the goal could use his hands. I was on the other team to my dad. As luck would have it, a clearance fell to me about 30 yards out and I hit it cleanly without noticing my dad was effectively in goal. The ball flew past him and into the net. I ran off celebrating, which annoyed my dad so much he made all the players on both teams do five laps of the pitch before the game could continue, which of course led to everyone blaming me for having scored. As we lined back up to carry on with the game there was a sudden announcement from Roy Evans that despite there not being any offsides in the game we were playing, someone had apparently been offside and my 'goal' was disallowed!"

Paul's visits to Melwood would leave him with other lasting memories.

"One night the floodlights weren't on when we got there. As we entered the changing rooms, Eli Wass, the head groundsman, said they couldn't put the floodlights on yet because Graeme Souness was in the sauna and the generator wouldn't power the lights and the sauna at the same time. We were moaning when Souness suddenly appeared from the sauna to get changed. As he sat down, my dad stuck his head into the room and said to me: 'Don't be messing around after training, I need to get off sharpish.' I said: 'Okay, dad' and Graeme turned to me and asked: 'Is that your dad?' I replied: 'Yes, he is' and Souness' reply was: 'Christ, that's unfortunate for you!' He was smiling when he said it, but I also remember him breaking a Dinamo Bucharest player's jaw and he was smiling after that too!"

Such regular contact with the Liverpool players at Melwood had Paul Moran believing he might make it himself. Those thoughts didn't last forever.

"I remember the moment I realised I was never going to be a professional footballer when Ronnie Whelan, who had just come over from Ireland, in 1979, joined in one night at Melwood and was on my side," Paul says.

"We cleared a corner and I set off and Ronnie, who had been about five yards behind me, overtook me before the halfway line and arrived in the opposition penalty area and scored with a volley while I was still about 15 yards outside the area.

"My dad told me I was too slow to make it at Liverpool but

I was never sure if he meant running wise or mentally and I never had the nerve to ask him! My dad did offer to try and find me another club at a high level, but if I couldn't play for Liverpool, I wasn't really interested in playing for anyone else."

Paul ended up in the Crosby and Southport and District Sunday Leagues and remembers once asking his dad why he never used to watch him play. "I'm watching racehorses all week so why would I come and watch donkeys on a Sunday?" was his blunt reply. Paul never asked him again!

Two days before the European transfer deadline of August 15, 1978, Bob Paisley made a signing he had huge confidence in – Alan Kennedy. "If this lad doesn't play for England I'll throw myself in the Mersey... when the tide is out," Paisley famously declared about his left-back.

Kennedy didn't find it easy to adapt to his new club. "When I arrived, Terry McDermott, Phil Thompson, David Fairclough and David Johnson told me: 'Don't get Ronnie annoyed, just do things exactly how he tells you to,'" Kennedy recalls. "It was nerve-racking stuff when Ronnie came up to me before my debut against QPR and said: 'This is what Liverpool Football Club is all about, son. Don't give the ball away, pass it to a red shirt and get forward if you can.'

"It was my first game in competitive football for Liverpool and in some ways it was too much for me. I was still in Newcastle mode who were long-ball specialists. This meant when I would receive the ball, my first reaction was to look up and look long rather than short. This obviously annoyed Ronnie, a former full-back himself, who always tried to play it simple. When half-time came, I saw Ronnie looking at me, shaking his head. I bet he was thinking to himself: 'What have we bought here?'"

Ronnie tried to iron out Kennedy's problems. "'Keep your eye on the ball and give it easy,' is what he would continuously drum into me," Kennedy recalls. "I could hear him bellowing at me from the dugout at the other side of the pitch: 'Alan, keep it simple!' He also would tell me to make myself available even if the ball was on the right hand side of the field, 'Stick a hand up, give someone a shout and give the players an extra option. When Ray Kennedy gets the ball, let him know you are there, but make sure you go around the outside,' Ronnie would also say to me."

Kennedy listened to Moran's advice but had difficulty in adjusting to the club's playing style. "David Johnson suited my game as he liked receiving the ball slightly over the top or sometimes on his head and chest. However, Ray Kennedy wanted it to feet; Graeme Souness wanted it to feet and I just couldn't get the balance right and Ronnie kept on picking at me," Kennedy says. "Once they started to trust me then the shouting would stop, however it was very difficult for me to learn what they called 'The Liverpool Way'. I played 43 games in my first season for Liverpool and every game Ronnie would pick up on one particular fault. He would say: 'You played well, son, but you could have done this better.' My career went from being an average player to a much better player and I owe all of this to Ronnie."

Only a couple of players had the nerve to stand up to Ronnie and former amateur footballer Jimmy Case was not known to back down to anyone. Case and Moran went for a 50-50 ball during a game in training and clashed shin to shin. Neither had shin pads on and Ronnie was clearly in pain. Case recalls: "Ronnie jumped up and we were eyeball to eyeball. Ronnie shouts: 'You're not playing alehouse football now, you know!' I just turned away and walked off hoping he wouldn't have it in for me. This was the mental strength the coaches at Liverpool wanted you to have. You had to take the criticism, shrug off the bollockings and carry on."

Howard Gayle struggled for the most part in his endeavours to break into Liverpool's first-team during his six years at the club, 1977-1983, and didn't escape a harsh word or two from the club's tough taskmaster. "Ronnie was old school," said Gayle. "If you didn't do it his way, it was the wrong way. Possession was key. If you would give the ball away or were sloppy with your pass he'd be on you. He hated that with a vengeance, Ronnie. If you go back to the games in the 70s to late 80s and listen in, you will hear his voice shouting instructions to our team and our players: 'Pass it.' 'Man on.' 'Move!'"

Liverpool were experiencing unprecedented success in the history of the club and Ronnie was the designated person to keep everyone grounded. "I'd bump into a lot of ex-players who moved elsewhere and they'd come up to me and say: 'Ronnie, you were a bastard to us. I wish I listened as I'm getting chased out of my club for not working hard enough.'"

Ronnie had to be vigilant to keep Liverpool's success going, as he explained to the *Sunday Express* in 1979: "The players make it easy for us. One or two float in the clouds, but we knock them on the head. At training sessions, we say: 'Look, there's Big-head from Saturday over here.' They know who they are and walk over with a laugh. It's the same with the training staff. Joe Fagan and I have a weekly joke. If we win we say: 'Okay for another week.' If we lose: 'We could be out of a job now.' There's no way you can afford to sit back."

There was no sitting back in the 1978/79 season. Many believe that the Liverpool team that won the league by a record total of 68 points (two points for a win) and only conceded 16 goals in a 42-game season, is the best-ever in the club's history. Liverpool went through the whole season unbeaten at home, winning 19 out of 21 games. Future captain Graeme Souness led by example.

"The 1978/79 season was sensational and I am tempted to say that the team was the best I have ever played in, even though five years later we won the lot with the exception of the FA Cup," Souness said. "It was not a case of winning games but a question of how many we were going to win by. We were knocking the ball about and enjoying so much possession it was almost boring."

The ever-present Ray Clemence kept 17 clean sheets and conceded only four goals at Anfield. Right-back was Phil Neal, who played 417 games in a row for Liverpool between October 23, 1976 and September 24, 1983, a Liverpool record.

Left-back was Alan Kennedy, who was on the end of one of the biggest Paisley tantrums ever seen when Liverpool were beaten 3-1 by Villa on April 16, 1979. Kennedy had said in a newspaper interview before the game that Liverpool were virtually guaranteed to win the title. When the players entered the dressing room 2-0 down, Paisley blamed Alan for Villa's determination and Liverpool's lethargic display. "It's all your fault! Never, ever say you've won something until you have the medal in your hand," Paisley screamed at him.

The boss had every right to be angry as Liverpool had only conceded three goals in the last 15 league games and now conceded the same total in a single match.

Phil Thompson had a new partner in the middle of defence in Alan Hansen who emerged as a force to be reckoned with in place of Emlyn Hughes. Tommo and Hansen were not the most physical specimens ever seen and the other players joked that Liverpool must be the only team in the world with central defenders who couldn't tackle. The pair more than made up for that in their ability to read the game and how confident they were in bringing the ball out of defence to set up another attacking wave.

The intimidating midfield quartet of Ray Kennedy, Graeme Souness, Jimmy Case and Terry McDermott took no prisoners, although Terry was maybe the odd man out in that respect. His strengths were his vision, tactical awareness, long-range shooting and an ability to run until the cows came home. He also became a supreme finisher. Terry only scored eight goals in the 1978/79 campaign but scored 58 over the next three seasons. David Johnson and Steve Heighway shared the number nine shirt and Kenny reigned supreme and was voted Football Writers' Footballer of the Year. Liverpool finished eight points ahead of Nottingham Forest, who had won the league by seven points the previous season.

Despite the local success, Liverpool's stranglehold on the European Cup was broken in September 1978, due to an unfortunate pairing of the European champions and the English champions in the first round.

Bob Paisley had been in his office at Melwood when he got a call telling him about the draw. Paisley's mood would invariably be measured by his stride. Dalglish and Ronnie looked on as Bob came out of his office, walking across to the training pitch. Big steps meant it was a draw he relished, but small steps meant that he was the bearer of bad news. "Big steps," Ronnie said to Kenny, before changing his tune, "Oh, no, wait, small steps."

This wasn't an ideal situation for either side as this was Forest's debut in Europe's premier competition and they would face Liverpool, who had won the trophy two years running.

In the first leg at the City Ground, Garry Birtles' single goal wouldn't have been a mountain to climb, but another Forest goal three minutes from time gave Clough's team a two-goal cushion. Souness was well out of position for the second goal, which taught him a valuable lesson of not straying too far. Joe Fagan told him off for this error in the dressing room. Ronnie reminded Souness regularly of where he should ideally place himself, as the Scot recalled.

"Ronnie Moran would come out of the dugout and draw a circle with his index finger, meaning the centre circle, and then point right in the middle of it and that meant: 'Stand there and don't move.' That was his signal," Souness said. Forest held on for a goalless draw at Anfield in the second leg two weeks later and Liverpool were out of Europe.

In the summer of 1979, Fagan and Moran gained new titles. Joe was now assistant manager and Ronnie was promoted from first-team trainer to chief coach, with Roy Evans taking over his prior duties. Ronnie also acquired the new title of grandfather on June 13, 1979 when his daughter, Janet, and her husband, Chris Johnson, had a girl, who they named Christine. They had a son, Ian, four years later, on March 7, 1983.

A typical week at Melwood hadn't changed much for the

past 20 years. If there was no midweek game, players were not required for training on Sundays and Mondays. The players assembled on the Tuesday with a gentle warm-up to loosen the muscles and when the body was wide awake, hard half-laps of the training tracks were on offer to open up the lungs. Training throughout the week would always end with a small-sided practice match between the staff and the players, where Ronnie was dominant.

He would stir things up by telling the players he could still beat them, even at his age. "Some of you think we've never played," he said to remind them that the staff had been half-decent players. He would claim that Liverpool teams of old would have wiped the floor with the current batch wearing the red shirt.

If he detected a lack of enthusiasm during a practice match, he would simply say: "Right, if you don't want to play, we can just set the cones out and go for a run. It's up to yourselves." That threat would instantly get the game going again. Ronnie picked the staff team that had to be strengthened by a couple of players and more often than not he chose Jimmy Case, Ray Kennedy, Kenny Dalglish, Graeme Souness or Phil Neal to be on his side.

The Wednesday was the most demanding day. The real killer for the players were the shuttles where poles were put in the ground in a straight line, five yards apart with the furthest being 25 yards away. Two players run at the same time to the first pole, then return and keep on going until they've reached every pole. The reason behind this exercise is not only to increase stamina, but to practise twisting and turning at top speed.

Possession football was practised by having 12 players operate in threes from bases in the corners of a square. The target for the players was to get across the diagonal without losing the ball, while those at the diagonally opposite corner tried to dispossess them. The square was small so the players got used to trying to retain possession in a confined space.

Emphasis was put on ball work and tactics on Thursday after the heavy physical activity of the Wednesday. Clemence was bombarded with all kinds of crosses and shots and some of the players were given special advice depending on the opposition by Paisley, who had been fed reports from his scouts.

Phil Neal remembers a typical training ground conversation between staff and players: "'Ray, I want you to pick up 'Y' wherever he goes for corners. Usually he only acts as a decoy, but he once stuck one in against 'A' three weeks ago because they left him, thinking he was still only the decoy. Some decoy when he sticks the winner in.' This is the sort of precise detailing that takes place. Players were given names, faces and jobs to do."

Friday was less hectic as there was a game on the Saturday and there was no use in having worn-out players, but the small-sided games got extra competitive and Neal often sensed in those Friday matches how well the team would play the following day in the league. The starting line-up was announced, unless someone needed a late fitness test, and the players were raring to go.

The four men that kept the players hungry for success at that time were an ideal blend, according to Roy Evans.

"I was never going to be a Ronnie Moran, someone whose work can't be underestimated," Roy said. "He made sure everyone fell in line and gets called the 'sergeant-major', but he was much more than that. Joe was the glue. Bob wasn't great at speaking in front of a crowd but everyone on the staff knew what he meant. Then I was the fella that put the arm around a few, hence the reputation as Mr Nice Guy. There was a great balance, all good people, nobody went after anyone else."

When Liverpool played at Anfield in the league, the routine would be the same. The team stayed the Friday night at Lord Daresbury Hotel, near Warrington. As the team bus drove down Utting Avenue on a match day, the players tried to guess by the number of cars parked by the road how many spectators would be in the stands. Despite the fact that Liverpool were flush with success, the stadium was often not full to its capacity. When the attendance figure was announced, the players conferred among themselves who had been the closest. More often than not, Ronnie would guess the right figure.

In the dressing room, Ronnie massaged the legs of the players and gave them final instructions before they headed out of the tunnel, telling them who to mark or look out for.

During the match, Ronnie would bark orders as well as whistle to grab the attention of players who were not doing their job. He would also have to resort to using hand signals, especially for the likes of Jimmy Case, who is deaf in his right ear.

If the ball went out of play while Liverpool were leading in the game and it would land near Ronnie, he was in no hurry to give it back, as Kenny Dalglish recollects. "He'd either knock it down the track or jam his fingers into it, checking the pressure before passing it back, just wasting time. If Ronnie picked up the ball, he'd throw it against the wooden edging of the pitch so it bounced back into the crowd, killing a few more precious seconds."

Ronnie would also drum into his players never to argue with the referee because that meant they were not concentrating on the game, but he was, of course, allowed to influence the officials. George Courtney, who refereed at least 14 matches at Anfield, often came across Ronnie during his career.

The first Liverpool game that Courtney refereed was when the Reds beat Wolves 3-1 to seal the league championship at Molineux on May 4, 1976. After that he officiated 35 Liverpool matches over the next 16 years and among them were many historic ones such as three FA Cup semi-finals; 2-2 against Manchester United in 1985, a 2-1 win over Nottingham Forest at Hillsborough in 1988 and the 4-3 defeat to Crystal Palace in 1990. The most high profile match was the League Cup win against Manchester United in 1982 when many argued Bruce Grobbelaar should have been sent off for fouling Gordon McQueen outside the penalty area.

For Courtney there was nothing bigger in club football than to referee at Liverpool. "I would never let the Kop sway me, although I have to admit it's difficult to gauge how much they can influence you subconsciously," Courtney said. "Anfield for me was Ronnie Moran and Roy Evans, whom I've known for years. I didn't look at the Kop, I looked at the dugout. And, of course, they were never short of a bit of advice. I always allowed Ronnie to have his say, and I never had to talk to him once. I would just smile across at him, and that seemed to placate him. He was always good humoured and a good barometer of my performance. At the end of the game, I always got a good slap of the hand from him."

During half-time, Ronnie would reinforce his instructions if he felt anything was going awry.

After the game, Ronnie left the players with his usual message, as remembered by Dalglish. "Any injuries, see you tomorrow. Straight home. Don't go boozing or gallivanting with girls. Rest up, no messing about."

Liverpool beat Arsenal 3-1 in the Charity Shield in the opening game of the 1979/80 season with the same starting eleven that had finished the previous campaign. The team looked far less impressive though and only reached the summit of the league in its 15th game following a 2-1 win over Tottenham. The Reds won six out of their next seven games, including a top-of-the-table clash against Manchester United. The top two had a six-point lead on their rivals, but United didn't stand a chance in a one-sided game at Anfield where Alan Hansen opened the scoring with David Johnson adding a second five minutes before time.

'Seldom can a match between runaway league leaders have produced such one-sided football. United scarcely had an attack worthy of description, never mind a shot,' reported the *Daily Record*. Liverpool lost the reverse fixture 2-1 at Old Trafford, but kept on going and clinched the title with a 4-1 win over Aston Villa in their penultimate game.

David Johnson scored two goals against Villa and thanked 'Bugsy' for inspiring him to greater deeds. "Ronnie Moran had a go at me for not scoring enough goals with my left foot. I lashed one and it hit the post and shot across into the net."

Terry McDermott had the best season of his career and became the first Liverpool player to be voted Player of the Year by both press and players.

Liverpool ended the 1980/81 season in fifth, their worst finish since 1970/71. This was a downfall of epic proportions.

Paisley blamed Liverpool's poor league form on a catalogue of injuries. "I have been at Anfield in various capacities since 1939 and I can never recall a season so plagued by injuries as the 1980/81 campaign," he said. "Players went down like ninepins and hardly a game went by without our suffering another casualty or injury worry."

Paisley's men might have struggled in the league but were on a roll in the knockout competitions and put the League Cup in the trophy cabinet for the first time in their history. It took Liverpool two games to defeat West Ham, as the original final finished 1-1 after extra-time at Wembley. The Reds defeated the Hammers 2-1 in the replay at Villa Park. Liverpool were heading for Bayern's Olympic Stadium in the semi-finals of the European Cup after the first leg at Anfield had been goalless.

To make matters worse Liverpool had been decimated by injuries. Phil Thompson was out with a knee injury with Colin Irwin taking his place and Richard Money filled the void left by Alan Kennedy. Kenny Dalglish was touch and go and in the end declared fit, but only lasted seven minutes and was replaced by Howard Gayle, another player from the reserves.

On the positive side, Graeme Souness and David Johnson returned after having missed the first leg. Everyone had basically written Liverpool off, except for 'Bugsy'.

"Ronnie was so uplifting when players had any doubts," Hansen says. "Never more so than when we played in Munich during the European Cup semi-final and we had half a team. Ronnie was telling us we can do this and to go out there and give a performance. His simple words dragged us through."

David Johnson defied the odds and set up Ray Kennedy's goal in the 83rd minute. Karl-Heinz Rummenigge equalised four minutes later but Liverpool survived on the away-goals rule to reach their first European final in three years where they faced Spanish champions, Real Madrid.

"Ronnie reminded me of the guy who I would be marking, an English lad called Laurie Cunningham, but he also told me that he wanted me to get forward too," Alan Kennedy remembers from the build-up to the Real final at Parc des Princes. "Ronnie wouldn't change his advice just because it was a European Cup final. He would still say: 'Do the simple things, don't give the ball away and you will be alright.'"

Kennedy ended up scoring the winner in the 81st minute.

Hansen and others credit Ronnie Moran with being the inspiration they needed when the going got tough, but that wasn't necessarily known outside the club.

"Ronnie is quite unlucky that he isn't better known for his contribution to the success of Liverpool Football Club," Hansen says. "But in all honesty, he probably wouldn't have wanted it; he was quite happy just to sit in the background and do his stuff. The people who knew best were the players who were there.

"He never gave long speeches, just sharp reminders of what we had to do to get the job done for Liverpool Football Club. Throughout my career, he was in that dressing room and on the training field, a massive figurehead."

While Ronnie's interaction was mostly with the players and he liked to keep himself in the background, he was also noticed by other employees of the club who had a different perspective.

Linda Robinson worked for Liverpool Football Club from 1975 until 1982, mainly in the club's souvenir shop under the Kop. "Most people think of Ronnie Moran as the 'tough guy', but I was lucky enough to see a softer side," she said.

"One morning Ray Kennedy arrived at the club, but when he got out of the car he couldn't move. He asked me to help him get to the entrance.

"We managed to almost get there when Ronnie spotted us and came out to help him. Kopites were moaning because he was having an 'off day', only a minority, but they didn't know how Ray was earlier in the day. Being in a position of trust I couldn't say anything.

"It is a lesson I have learned, that if you see a player having a bad day, it could be because he has physical problems or something isn't right in his private life so I always give him the benefit of the doubt. No player wants to play badly. A lot of fans don't realise this.

"Ronnie's magic sponge would work wonders, but I would say that a lot of players played with injuries back then which they wouldn't be allowed to do today."

Linda got the impression that Ronnie was a caring person. "I used to take my disabled nephew and his family to Melwood when they came to visit us. We would watch the training and Ronnie always found time to talk to them."

Linda remembers the Bootroom boys as a lively bunch who were prone to the odd practical joke on each other. In the dining hall at Anfield, they always had their own table.

One day when Linda walked in she noticed a life-size blow-up doll that had been planted at their table. It was a birthday present from one Bootroom boy to another. Linda isn't sure whether Ronnie was the recipient of the gift, but Paul Moran doesn't remember seeing any blow-up doll at his family's home!

Ronnie was the watchdog at the club, a modern-day CCTV at Melwood and hotels where the team stayed overnight.

"Ronnie always had this way of looking at you that made you feel guilty," Linda says. "It's a similar feeling to when you go through the 'Nothing to declare' channel at customs.

"Working at the club, I often used to answer the phone in the players' lounge. I got to know one particular lady quite well. No names here but she was friendly with one of the players. The lads were playing near London and it just so happened that she would be visiting this one player.

"We arranged to meet at the team hotel, Selsdon Park Hotel, which wasn't very far from where my parents lived. The lady and I met for the first time in the grounds of the hotel and as we walked around, Ronnie saw us. He didn't appear too pleased, but then I always felt guilty when Ronnie looked at me even though I had done nothing wrong!

"I think he was aware of the lady I was with and why she was there. I went home and fetched my mum and took her for a walk around the grounds so that Ronnie knew that I was not there for the same reason as this lady! She told me that every night Ronnie would go around the rooms and check the lads were all tucked up in bed without any company around. She hid in the bath one night to avoid Ronnie seeing her."

Linda stopped working at the club when her husband's job took them to Hong Kong. She met Ronnie again at an event in 2016 where he greeted her with a beaming smile. "Ronnie had been poorly but he posed for a photograph with me," Linda says. "It was the first time I hadn't felt guilty when I saw Ronnie. A lovely man."

In the summer of 1981, Bob Paisley lost his goalkeeper, Ray Clemence, to Spurs, with Bruce Grobbelaar having to assume the responsibility of guarding the goal of the European champions far sooner than expected. Fans had difficulty coming to terms with the newcomer, who made a series of errors.

"One old man wrote to me regularly," Grobbelaar recalls. "He said that he had been watching top-class football for 32 years and if Tommy Smith had still been captain he would have already broken my legs three times. That was one of the more pleasant letters.

"I also began to hear the obscenities yelled from certain sections of the crowd and I took them to heart. It hurt that they were from our own supporters," Grobbelaar says.

Mark Lawrenson, who was brought in for a record fee for a defender from Brighton & Hove Albion, was still bedding in as well as the Reds continued to struggle in the first part of the 1981/82 season.

Everything that was going on at Anfield was set aside on Tuesday, September 29, 1981, an extremely sorrowful day for everyone connected with Liverpool Football Club. Bill Shankly sadly passed away at the age of 68. The front page of the *Echo* read: SHANKLY IS DEAD. It recorded the official hospital statement: 'Mr Shankly suffered a cardiac arrest at 12.30am and was certified dead at 1.20. Shanks had been battling for life since he suffered a heart attack early on Saturday morning. He had been making good progress until his condition deteriorated yesterday morning and he was transferred to the Intensive Care Unit. His wife Nessie was by his side when he died.'

Moran went to his funeral at St Mary's Church in West Derby and the memorial service, at Liverpool's Anglican Cathedral, was broadcast on BBC Radio Merseyside on November 22, 1981. Moran will be eternally grateful for everything Bill did for him.

"There were never any fall-outs with the manager and the trainers," Ronnie told the *Liverpool Echo*. "Bill wasn't that kind of bloke. Don't get me wrong, he ran the show. We'd always have meetings, Bill, Bob, Joe and me. Shanks would always listen but always make the final decision too. You'd tell the truth about certain players and how they were doing in the team but the buck stopped with the manager."

Ronnie always missed Bill's company after they finished working together.

"I wish he was still around," Moran said to *The Times* in 2013. "He wasn't just a great manager, he was also a good fella and obviously everyone who was lucky enough to know someone like that is going to miss him. That goes without saying. There was just something about him, something unique."

Shanks impressed Ronnie from the first day he arrived. "He got rid of a lot of players early on, then he brought players in who were like-minded in their thinking about the game," Ronnie said. "If he didn't get what he wanted from them, they too would be away.

"Shanks loved the supporters as much as they loved him. All he wanted to do was give them a team to be proud of and he did that. I was lucky to be a part of it all but I do miss him. When Shanks arrived we were in the Second Division. Without him we might still be there."

Following a 3-1 defeat to Manchester City on December 26, Liverpool were sitting 12th in the table and the Bootroom boys were fed up.

"Bob Paisley pulled me into the bath area in the dressing room and he just said to me: 'How do you think your first six months have gone?'" Grobbelaar reveals. "I said: 'It could have been better.' And he said: 'Yes, you're right. If you don't stop all these antics you'll find yourself playing for Crewe again.'"

Grobbelaar wasn't the only one taken to task over their below par performances. As players arrived at Anfield prior to training, Joe Fagan told Paisley to drive down to Melwood. "I'm going to have the lads," he said.

Fagan sat everyone down and had a go at everyone in sight, complaining that the coaching staff had more meetings in the last month at this club than he'd had in 17 years. His finishing words were: "I've said my piece. I want a high tempo in training. At the end of the day we're getting out of this. You're all playing as individuals; start playing as a team. I'm not having another meeting from now until the end of the season.'"

Phil Thompson was removed as captain and the armband handed to Souness as the coaches felt the extra responsibility was affecting Thompson's performance. Paisley was adamant that this was the right decision: "I'm convinced that Graeme Souness will respond to the added responsibilities. He has the make-up to develop into a top-rate skipper."

And how did Liverpool respond? With 20 wins, three draws and two defeats from the next 25 league games! A new generation of stars were coming to the fore such as Ian Rush, Ronnie Whelan, Sammy Lee and Craig Johnston, in place of David Johnson, Ray Kennedy, Jimmy Case and Terry McDermott.

Nottingham Forest and Liverpool were both looking for Craig Johnston's signature in April 1981. Johnston, who played for Middlesbrough, wasn't sure which side to pick: Liverpool, who were European champions in 1977 and 1978, or Forest, who had won the European Cup in 1979 and 1980. He phoned his dad in Australia and his advice proved decisive. "Liverpool is an institution and Brian Clough is just a man. If I were you, I'd go for the institution."

On May 1, 1982 at Anfield, Johnston played his first game for Liverpool against Clough's side after turning him down the previous year. Craig scored Liverpool's goals in a 2-0 victory and secured a club record of 11 straight league victories. Brian Clough, Forest's manager, was clearly a man holding a grudge.

"I was playing on the wing and Cloughie ran up and down the sideline calling me a cheat," Johnston recalled. "And it caused a bit of a problem because Ronnie Moran started shouting at Cloughie and calling him a cheat. So I'm running up and down the line with Cloughie running after me and now Ronnie Moran is running after Cloughie, having an argument about whether I was a cheat or not."

Ronnie was extremely protective of his players and would never allow any criticism to be directed at them from the opposition bench.

Forest and Liverpool clashed again the following season when Johnston featured in a 1-0 defeat at the City Ground on May 2, 1983. Once the game had finished, the teams used to have a drink or two in the players' bar.

"I had a bit of an injury and I was getting strapped up so I was a bit late," Johnston said. "And when I tried to get in, they wouldn't let me in and I said: 'Why?' They said: 'Because Brian Clough said that you're not allowed in.' Ronnie Moran heard about it and he went in, got all the players and said: 'Well, if he can't go in, no-one's staying in.' Then we left," Johnston said.

Paul Moran remembers his dad telling him that Clough was a tricky character to deal with. "My dad said that Clough would hardly go in the Bootroom for a traditional post-match drink because he was a contrary character, so if everyone else was doing it, then he wouldn't, just to be different." Clough's assistant at Forest, Peter Taylor, also had a problem entering the Bootroom and he was one of the few people in football who Ronnie disliked.

Ronnie used to get on Johnston's back as he wasn't that mobile in training sometimes, but Craig never forgot how Moran stood up for him. Ronnie had fond memories of 'Skippy' too.

"Craig was certainly different," Ronnie said. "Despite being a bubbly character he never seemed at ease at games. He couldn't sit still and he would rub his hands and constantly push back his mop of hair. Players are made differently and that was his way of easing tensions.

"He had strength and pace and could whip crosses in for Ian Rush and Kenny Dalglish and also score goals himself. Defenders found him difficult to knock off the ball and he was difficult to check when he ran at them. He was erratic on occasions but he responded well to team briefings."

Ronnie not only noticed how players behaved in training and matches but how they carried themselves in general. "I was struck with Craig's popularity with the supporters and the time he spent talking to them after training. He got on well with everybody and he had the ability to mix with people from all walks of life."

Ronnie wasn't the only Moran working at Anfield in the 1981/82 season. Paul was employed by the LFC Development Association, that over 40 years raised money to help fund the development of Anfield, and in later years the Academy as well. The scheme came to a close in 2010. "I sold the golden goal tickets for a club lottery outside the Main Stand on a few occasions on match days," explained Paul. "It was run by Ken Addison and was a fundraiser for the club, based in an office behind the Kop. It was all cash in hand and I used to enjoy it and all the money went to the development of the club."

The most memorable incident for Paul from this particular campaign occurred as Liverpool were about to face Barnsley in a fifth round League Cup replay on January 19, 1982.

"When we arrived at the ground I had to go to the players' entrance at Oakwell to pick up my tickets that my dad had left for me at the ticket office," Paul recalls. "When I asked for the tickets left for Paul Moran by Ronnie Moran, the fella in charge said someone had already collected them, I started to argue but the fella was blanking me and another steward was trying to make me move along as there were no tickets for me.

"I was getting angrier and the first fella said that he would go and check if there had been a mix up. As he moved away from the door a laughing Sammy Lee appeared with my tickets and said he'd been watching me get more and more annoyed, but thought he should give me them before there was a fight.

"Sammy had seen me walking towards the door and had asked the fella for our envelope as a joke that the stewards played along with. We won the game 3-1 but I remember telling my dad later that Sammy should be dropped for the next game for taking the piss!"

Liverpool held on to the League Cup in 1982 by beating Ray Clemence's Tottenham Hotspur in the final in dramatic fashion. Whelan equalised in the 87th minute after Spurs had led the game for 76 minutes. Whelan added another in extra-time with Rush getting on the scoresheet as well. This was a joyous day for Paul Moran, but also a bit stressful.

"I went on a coach from Anfield early on the Saturday morning which was going back to Anfield after the game," Paul remembers. "My dad wanted me to take his car home from Anfield because the team was staying in London. Along with the car keys, my dad gave me the keys to the main gates at Anfield so I could get in to get his car. As it turned out we never got back until 11 o'clock so I spent the whole day panicking about what would happen if I lost the Anfield keys, but luckily that didn't happen and we won the cup."

Liverpool retrieved the league title from Aston Villa in the penultimate game of the season with another win over Spurs. The night prior to the last game of the campaign at Middlesbrough, captain Souness took the players out to sample the local drink. They finally returned to the hotel at 2am and caught a few hours of sleep before being woken up by their taskmaster.

"Ronnie must have smelled beer in every room he entered but to the best of my knowledge never said anything to Bob or Joe," Ian Rush recollects. Ronnie suspected most of the players had been up to no good but knew for sure that Craig Johnston had been out drinking. Johnston stumbled back to the team hotel, trying to find the room which he shared with Bruce Grobbelaar.

"I had started thumping on the door to wake Bruce up," said Johnston. "Instead of Bruce, a very bleary-eyed senior coach, Ronnie Moran, answered the door to be confronted by an extremely drunk midfielder who had broken curfew by eight hours. My punishment was playing the next day nursing a force 10 hangover!"

The game ended goalless in an uneventful affair as most of the Liverpool players were worse for wear and making a run for the bathroom as soon as the whistle sounded for half-time.

Ronnie's job on the team trips was to look after the players and make sure they weren't degrading Liverpool's good name, although Ronnie and the coaching staff were known to turn a blind eye to their antics as long as they were performing to their standards.

Joey Jones said that sometimes he could have got drunk on Terry McDermott's breath at Melwood, but he excelled on the field, which was the most important thing.

Roommates Jimmy Case and Ray Kennedy were usually quite a handful for Ronnie and never more so than in Wales on March 2, 1980. The day before, Liverpool had beaten Everton 2-1 at Goodison Park. Everton great, 73-year-old Dixie Dean, died while attending this game. Before facing Tottenham a week later in London, Liverpool's hierarchy decided to arrange a few days' break for the players, staying at the Bryn Howell hotel, near Llangollen in North Wales.

Case and Kennedy stayed up late the first evening, drinking with the hotel proprietor, Albert Lloyd, who Case knew well, and his son, John. Ray had already had an altercation with Terry McDermott, for failing to let him know when the players left the hotel for the pub earlier in the evening. At the same moment the phone rang and the landlord's son asked Ray whether his name was Alan, thinking he was Alan Kennedy. Ray was very sensitive about being confused with his namesake and promptly punched John with his right fist. Ray and Jimmy left the room, but returned a few minutes later, launching into John Lloyd again as well as his father, Albert, throwing bar chairs at them. The police arrived at the scene and arrested the players.

Joe Fagan and Ronnie Moran followed the pair to the station. Ronnie stayed with Ray, who was sitting quietly in his prison cell. Meanwhile, Jimmy was hammering on the cell walls, shouting "Let me out!" Moran berated them for their stupidity. Ray retaliated by claiming that Moran's stressful training sessions at Melwood were responsible. Joe Fagan, who was locked in with Jimmy, was desperately trying to calm him down. After about an hour, Moran and Fagan returned to the hotel.

Both players were fined £150 and Case remained on the fringes of the team the following season before leaving in August 1981. Ray followed suit six months later.

"Fines, court appearances, jail... we were bad for each other," Ray said. "At hotels, when we asked for the room key, the receptionist would dive under the desk and say: 'Not you two!'"

Even though they contributed to the loss of his hair, Ronnie didn't hold grudges with the pair, judging by his decidedly tongue-in-cheek remark when asked about the duo's friendship many years later.

"Theirs was always the tidiest room by far. There was never anything out of place. They had come from good, tidy homes," Moran said.

Ronnie Whelan made his breakthrough in the 1981/82 campaign, having survived the school of hard knocks at Melwood. He became well aware of Ronnie Moran in his first day of training. The two Ronnies were on opposite sides in the five-a-side when Moran tried to tackle Whelan. The up and coming Irishman went past Moran easily...or so he thought.

"Next thing, this leg came round the back of me, dragged

the ball back, and the bloke pushed me over," Whelan says. "And he had a right go at me: 'Don't run past me with the ball, young fella.'"

Whelan had no idea who this bald, old fella was before this incident but soon learned he wasn't to be messed with. Whelan saw Moran do this to a number of young players throughout the ensuing years. Moran wasn't just showing his displeasure because his disciples went past him, but was teaching them the lesson of not running with the ball when they could have passed it. This was lesson number one.

Striker David Hodgson was signed from Middlesbrough for the sizeable fee of £450,000 at the start of the 1982/83 season, but he struggled to make an impression. Ronnie welcomed him in his own unique style and kept on going at him as Hodgson wasn't learning enough to fit in, as Ian Rush remembers. "In the end Hodgy turned to Ronnie and said: 'For Christ's sake, just leave me alone.' Ronnie Moran said: 'That's him finished.' It's the pressure of being a Liverpool player. You had to do it in training. You had to do it on the pitch. I'll never forget that. Three or four months later Hodgson left."

Around this time, Paul Moran came upon a cheap solution for travelling to away games to follow the Reds.

"I was a steward on the special trains from 1982-84. The lad who ran the buffet on the special was called Jimmy Jones. He knew my dad and it was him who suggested that I could get to the away games as a steward," Paul says.

There was no pay involved, but at least it was a free ride to see Liverpool play.

"You were supposed to patrol the train and make sure no-one was damaging anything or hanging out of the windows, but there were about 10 stewards so it wasn't crucial for me to join in," Paul continues. "I always had four complimentary tickets with me so the other lads would say: 'No it's alright, Paul, you sit there and we'll go and walk up and down,' in a desperate attempt to earn a ticket.

"A lot of lads would ask me for training gear and I would say to them, 'if your dad was a solicitor would you ask him for a load of pens and pencils?'

"When the train arrived I would just wander off with the fans and go to the ground in the escort. It was always a bit of a pain having a comp because the Liverpool fans would be on the terraces behind the goal and the comps would be in a stand so after the game we'd have to make our way round to the away end to try to join the Liverpool fans without being too obvious.

"I remember one game at Swansea's Vetch Field when we were winning 3-0 and we asked a policeman to walk us down the touchline to the Liverpool fans who were in a pen behind the far goal. After a bit of persuasion, he took the four of us down the touchline past the dugouts. My dad was in there so I said: 'Alright, dad' and the look on his face was classic. I remember Alan Harper had gone to the game in the squad and he was laughing when he saw me.

"When I saw my dad the next day he said they were all saying in the dugout I had been arrested and was being ejected from the ground. He said if that was the case I was hardly likely to have said 'Hello' and waved to everyone as I went past."

At away games, Ronnie was, on many occasions, called a 'baldy bastard'. That didn't bother him in the slightest, but it wasn't the only thing he was called.

"I went to away games with a lad called Ashy who would

always shout 'Dad' as loud as he could when my dad was walking in front of the Liverpool fans after treating an injured player," said Paul. "I told my dad loads of times not to look up because it wouldn't be me shouting, but occasionally he did and the lads around us would take the piss out of me because he thought I was trying to get his attention.

"Generally, my dad never commented on trouble at matches other than to warn me to keep out of the way and that if I did get caught up in anything, he would take my tickets away.

"I remember an incident at Coventry when a scuffle broke out and a Liverpool youth player got arrested. The lad wasn't involved at all, so I told my dad what I saw. We ended up going to Anfield to tell Bob Paisley what I'd seen. They were thinking of sacking the player, but luckily Bob realised I was telling the truth and the club eventually sorted the matter out.

"My dad used to wind me up about tickets all the time, especially the away ones, saying he couldn't get them until the day of the match, because I used to go and get them off him at Friday dinner time before the team left. He did the same joke nearly every week but then sometimes he couldn't get them and I wouldn't believe him! I used to get four tickets for each away game and I'd always ask for another one just to annoy him."

Liverpool won the league in the 1982/83 campaign at a canter despite failing to win their last seven league games. This sort of indifference angered the coaching staff, but as stern-faced Paisley attempted to address the situation at a team meeting he pulled the curtains down with a sharp tug which caused them to fall down on top of him.

Liverpool retained the League Cup after beating Manchester United in Paisley's last game at Wembley as manager due to his retirement at the end of the season. Captain Graeme Souness insisted that Paisley went up to collect the cup.

Paul Moran says that Paisley and his dad were first and foremost workmates rather than friends off the pitch. "Obviously Bob's time as manager at the club resulted in the most successful period for Liverpool Football Club in terms of trophies, therefore he had respect for him as a manager," said Paul. "However, he saw Bob as a work colleague, who he got on extremely well with on a daily basis. I can never remember my dad having a bad word to say about him. In my dad's own words, he was a 'great bloke', which is the highest praise he gives anyone."

Moran and his fellow coaches had trained Liverpool under Paisley's management to six league titles, four European trophies and three League Cups in nine seasons. The domestic success was remarkable on its own but to couple it with unparalleled success in Europe was almost beyond belief.

"It's been said before that there was no special formula at the club; no amazing training ground techniques or no secret plans. I always used to joke with my dad that we never scored from corners or free-kicks in matches and he'd say to me: 'We do practise them at Melwood, son, but in matches the opposition players wouldn't stand where we wanted them to!'"

– *Paul Moran*

Chapter 7

1983-1991

BOB Paisley revealed in May 1983 that he wished his successor to be one of his closest associates at the club, either Joe Fagan, Ronnie Moran or Roy Evans. It was no real surprise that assistant manager Fagan was announced as the chosen one on July 1, 1983 as he had effectively been next in line. Moran later said that he would have been ready to take over, but there were no complaints from the Bootroom boys at the time.

Captain, Graeme Souness, said: "Ronnie Moran and Roy Evans were constantly mentioned as likely candidates but they were hardly practicable suggestions as they both looked on Joe as a father figure and to have leapfrogged over him would have been embarrassing for them as it would have been for him."

Moran felt that it was a natural progression for Fagan to go into management.

"To me, Joe was a manager long before he was made manager because I had been brought up through the ranks of the Bootroom with him and knew all about the work he'd been doing," Ronnie said.

"A lot of the players had also worked with Joe for a long time and everyone at the club was well aware of his managerial potential."

Sixty-two-year-old Fagan wasn't pining for the job; quite the contrary.

"When Bob decided to retire, it frightened me that they might ask me to take over," Fagan said. "I said years ago that I'd never take on a manager's job, that coaching was my game. My first reaction at the time was that I wouldn't take it. But I thought about it carefully and realised that someone else might come in and upset the whole rhythm. I finally decided to take it and keep the continuity going for a little longer."

Just like Bob Paisley, Fagan put his neck on the line to ensure the status quo remained at Anfield.

There were no real changes in the way things were run at Anfield and Fagan kept the same staff when he took over as manager. Ronnie was now going into his 10th season as first-team coach and his 35th at the club.

The 1983/84 campaign was notable in the Moran household as this was the time when Ronnie decided to premiere his moustache that he wisely shaved off after the season finished.

Paul and Janet used to call the tash 'Harry' and asked their dad what he fed it.

One of Ronnie's most successful products of his former reserve team from the early Seventies was Phil Thompson, who went on to play 477 games for Liverpool, 147 of them as captain over 14 seasons. He won the league seven times, the FA Cup in 1974 and two European Cups; in 1978 and then in 1981 where he lifted the trophy as captain.

Although Thompson regards Bill Shankly as his hero, Ronnie Moran was his mentor.

"When Joe Fagan got promoted to the first-team in 1971, Ronnie was given the reserves and brought me through with him. I had always been a midfield player but I became more defensively-minded when Ronnie Moran started playing me at centre-half for his reserves side," Thompson recalls.

Larry Lloyd's injury led to Thompson playing centre-half for the first-team. Shankly obviously saw that Ronnie was on to something and that led to a whole new playing style for the Reds.

"People always say it was the Dutch who invented Total Football. I say it was Liverpool," Thompson concludes. "Emlyn and myself were not centre-halves like Big Yeatsy and Larry Lloyd, just as a stopper. It was now a totally new ball game. It was Ray Clemence rolling the ball out to me or Emlyn and we pass it and we go across one side, we go across the other side. People couldn't get the ball off us for minutes on end."

Thompson was both shaped as a player and as a coach by Ronnie's training methods that were tough but necessary to keep Liverpool's success going. "Ronnie was a hard task master, but it was always to ground the players. During the small-sided games in training he would be constantly shouting instructions at us: 'Close down together, move forward together, give it easy, give it early.' He wouldn't stop. We had won 5-0 on a Saturday and we'd come in on a Monday morning and Ronnie Moran would say: 'We've got a game next week; you've got nothing for what you have just done on Saturday.' He would be hammering you and the players coming back to that were thinking: 'What is up with this guy?' 'We have just won 5-0!'

"Over time I realised how right he was and this was his way of keeping the hunger for success alive. If you couldn't accept that, you simply weren't good enough, because on a Saturday you would be playing in front of a 50,000 crowd at Anfield, so you needed to be tough. If you couldn't take it, they would find someone who could."

Ronnie could spot players' weaknesses and strengths in an instant and was very perceptive about the mentality of the players as he observed them very closely.

"Once a week we used to have a 'staff versus apprentices' game on one of the pitches at Melwood, which we used to call 'Little Wembley'," Thompson recollects. "I used to get chosen to play on the staff side all the time. At first I thought they just picked me because they were lacking pace, therefore I would do a bit of running for them.

"I asked Ronnie a few years later: 'What did you ever see in me?' And he replied: 'Ability… and we picked you to play with us as we wanted to give you our experience. But it wasn't just that, son, we were always watching you; how you sorted out the kit, polished the boots and washed the baths at Anfield. You never cut corners. You always gave 100 per cent and showed the right attitude.'"

Ronnie had his own special ways to toughen up the players and had a feeling who would need tougher love than others. Thompson explains: "In the depths of winter you could choose between long-sleeved shirts and short-sleeved shirts and Ronnie would ask: 'Who wants long-sleeved, lads?' and I'd say: 'Yeah, I'll have one.' Ronnie, however, would go: 'Nah, you're not getting one.' I asked: 'Ronnie, why can't I have a long-sleeved shirt?' and he replied: 'You will go to sleep and it makes you too comfortable. You've got to be wide awake and keep everybody else on their toes.' I was freezing with my little arms. But that's the way he was and he knew these little things were important."

Ronnie was never in doubt of the Kirkby lad's ability though.

"I still remember Tommo's first morning with us when he arrived with a batch of the other kids," Ronnie said. "Sometimes you can instantly spot players who are going to make it all the way to the top. You could see it in him straight away. His attitude was right, he was positive and he wanted to win. He was the Liverpool prototype, who did the right things without being prodded along all the time. You don't make them, they make themselves.

"When things went against him, his heart took over. That's what makes Tommo tick; guts and character plus the fact that he could play."

Ronnie did reveal Thompson's one weakness though. "We always joke that if Tommo hadn't been a professional footballer he could have been a male nurse. Between you and me, he just about passes out at the sight of blood, even when it's not his own!"

Liverpool participated in testimonials at least twice a year, most often for former players. These were light-hearted affairs and the staff had their way of passing the time while sitting on the bench, as Kenny Dalglish recalls.

"Joe Fagan and Ronnie Moran kept a half-bottle of whisky in the dugout," said Dalglish. "'We'll have a nip if we score,' Joe always said. 'Okay, we'll have a wee nip if we get a shot on goal.' When the game meandered on with Liverpool still not threatening, 'Bugsy' said. 'Joe, why won't we just do it for a free-kick?' Still no joy. 'Let's just settle for a throw-in!'"

Although Fagan was now the manager, Paisley assisted him with the general organisation of the team and any transfer dealings that took place as the 1983/84 season approached. Striker Michael Robinson flew to Holland where the team was taking part in a mini tournament in Rotterdam to complete his move from Brighton & Hove Albion.

Michael settled in well at his boyhood club, but struggled to adapt to Ronnie's training sessions at first, especially the one-touch football in the practice matches that was all about getting the ball, giving it and moving into space to support the man with the ball.

"I remember the exact phrase Ronnie used to bellow at the players: 'Give it! Get it! Go!'" Robinson says.

When Joe approached Robinson in training to ask if every-thing was okay, the striker complained that Ronnie's constant shouting got on his nerves.

"Ronnie's voice haunts me at night," Robinson complained. Then Fagan handed Robinson the Liverpool philosophy in a nutshell.

"Joe asked: 'Do you know why we play like that, Michael, and shout: 'Give it. Get it. Go?' Well, imagine you're a hunter and the ball is a hare. If the hare was two yards in front of you and it was still, do you think you would hit it with your rifle?' I said: 'Probably yes.' He then said: 'Right, but what if the hare was moving all over the place, would you still be able to hit it with your rifle?' I answered: 'Probably not, no.' 'Well, Michael, so there is your answer, that's why we play like that, the opposition is the hunter and the hare is the ball. We give it, we get it and we go. That's the way Ronnie and myself want you and every player to play. The Liverpool Way, Michael: 'Pass and move'.''

John Wark, who joined from Ipswich during the same season as Robinson, also had to familiarise himself with new training methods if he wasn't to become a spare part in a well-oiled machine.

Wark recalls his first training session at Melwood. "The ball came to me and I sprayed a 30-yard pass down the touchline," he said. "I was standing there admiring what a great pass it was, then Ronnie Moran marched over and gave me a right bollocking.

"He was screaming at me, waving his hands everywhere, going: 'We pass and move, it's nice and short here, don't ever stand there admiring what you've just done.' He was a very angry man and then he gave a free-kick against me!"

Bruce Grobbelaar says that these rollickings weren't usually dished out in front of the other players. Instead they were invited for the dreaded walk.

"Ronnie Moran came after you if you did something completely wrong," said Grobbelaar. "But he took you to one side, and if he did do it in front of the players it was because you had deserved it. If he did it behind your back then that was even worse than doing it in front of the players. About three or four times he did it to me.

"He would say: 'If I could get rid of you, I would do it tomorrow, but I'm not the boss!'

"I saw many other players with Ronnie going for a quiet walk together. He used to say: 'Come and walk with me, son,' even in the rain and when they came back he would just say: 'Now, get back to it.' Everyone then knew that you'd been in the shit."

Liverpool were top of the league with a four-point lead when they played at Highfield Road on December 10. The Reds were out of sorts and 3-0 down at half-time.

"I said to one of my mates as a joke, 'if this gets much worse we will have to start singing 'Fagan out',"' Paul Moran says. "Terry Gibson scored late on in the second half to complete his hat-trick and made it 4-0 to Coventry, which my mate took as the cue to start singing. A few others joined in but only to cheer themselves up.

"As we were sitting in the comps, someone reported back to whoever they had got their tickets off, who knew my dad. A few days later he asked me why we had been singing. I told him it was only a joke and obviously done with irony. It was very rare that we saw Liverpool get beat in them days, never mind by such a large scoreline. My dad understood and wasn't fazed by hearing the chant at all. He said: 'I was more annoyed with the person who was trying to grass you up, rather than the fact you were doing it.'"

After winning the League Cup for the fourth time in a row, Liverpool became league champions for the third time in succession and the seventh time in nine seasons. A historic treble was now on the cards as they faced Roma in their own back yard in the European Cup final on May 30, 1984. Alan Kennedy recalls: "We weren't favourites for that game against Roma;

however, we weren't afraid of going there and getting the job done. Regardless of our opponents, Ronnie never let us change our policy or our approach to the game.

"Roma were never in control of play and they never pushed us back. The game could have gone either way, and fortunately for me, my penalty went in. I glanced over to the touchline and I could see Ronnie doing a little jump of joy when I scored."

Ronnie, being a former full-back himself, must have been particularly pleased with Kennedy and Neal's contributions that night. Right-back Neal scored Liverpool's only goal from open play and left-back Alan scored the winner in the penalty shoot-out. Grobbelaar's spaghetti legs did the trick, but Ronnie didn't really approve of such antics.

"If Bruce had told us beforehand that he was going to start larking about during a penalty shoot-out of a European Cup final, he would have been hit in the head," Ronnie claimed.

Kennedy remembers the night: "Ronnie always celebrated winning trophies in his own way and the right way. He would take it all in and it didn't have to be through alcohol."

One of Liverpool's most glorious nights was in the bag, but Ronnie was already looking ahead to pre-season. After parading the cup in Liverpool, the players disembarked the bus at Anfield. As they walked away, Ronnie said: "I'll see you on the fourth of July; don't be late!"

The versatile Scot, Steve Nicol, made his breakthrough in the 1983/84 campaign, after arriving from Ayr United two years previously. He started 32 out of 67 games in this treble campaign and came second in the PFA's vote for the 'Most Promising Player of the Year' behind Luton's Paul Walsh. Nicol was soon made aware of what was demanded from a Liverpool player.

"It was really hot at training one day and one of the players said he could do with a drink to combat the heat," Nicol says. "The request was met with a classic Ronnie Moran statement: 'You don't stop during the game for a drink of water, do you?' 'No,' replied the player. 'Well, why would you do it in training?' It was hard to argue with that reasoning. Back then it was, 'do as you're told' and we did.

"If we won a cup final and any of the lads who played ever failed to help put the kit hampers back on the bus then Ronnie would accuse them of being 'Big time Charlies' and that such menial tasks were clearly above them now. It wasn't done to spoil your enjoyment; it was simply done to bring you back down to earth. Don't forget where you came from. That was always the message."

Paul Moran went to every game in 83/84, having missed a handful in the previous three seasons. A couple of games in that memorable campaign stood out for Paul. One was the away leg in the second round of the European Cup. Liverpool and Athletic Bilbao drew 0-0 at Anfield before Ronnie took Paul with him for the return leg at San Mames on November 2, 1983.

"We went to Spain on the Monday and spent Tuesday and Wednesday with the players in their hotel," said Paul. "I knew all the players then and it was a brilliant experience. I still have my massive Bilbao flag to this day."

The drums of the Basque fans and their intimidating chanting would have caused most opponents to cave in, but not the Reds. Ian Rush, who had scored five goals against Luton the previous Saturday, headed in the winner in the 66th minute after a pass from Alan Kennedy. The *Liverpool Echo* named Graeme Souness the man of the match as 'he ran the show for the Reds with skill, energy and total commitment, giving a real captain's performance.'

Paul will also never forget his trip to watch Liverpool play QPR at Loftus Road on October 22.

"Four of us set off early Saturday morning in my mate's car from Liverpool down to London," Paul says. "Everything was going to plan until we approached Northampton where the car engine decided to pack in. We ended up having to flag down a lift into the town centre after just abandoning the car to increase our chances of actually getting to the game. Finally, we managed to get to Northampton train station and caught a train down to Euston. Luckily, as we arrived in London, we met up with the Footy Special Service, which had just arrived. We jumped on the Special with all the lads which took us directly to the underground station near the stadium."

The match was pretty awful on QPR's plastic pitch, but substitute Steve Nicol came to the rescue in the 83rd minute by drilling an unstoppable left-foot shot past Peter Hucker. Three points were in the bag, but Paul and his friends were now faced with the task of getting home.

"Two of the lads decided to try and get back on the Special with a secondary plan of bunking home on the ordinary service," Paul remembers. "I was left with young Steve Purcell and came up with the idea of trying to get back home on the team coach.

"We were hanging around the players' entrance for a while when eventually an employee asked us who we were waiting for. I told him I was Ronnie Moran's lad and asked if he could get him for me. He looked a bit suspicious but finally wandered off. Five minutes later my dad appeared. We told him what had happened and asked him to give us a lift back up to Liverpool. He said: 'I'll check with Joe [Fagan] but it should be okay.' He came back and told us that Joe said it's no problem and to wait for us here. So we just hovered around by the dressing room door until all the lads were ready.

"The fella who got my dad for me asked us if we wanted a kick-about on the pitch while we were waiting; he even gave us a ball! To our amazement, after such a stressful start to the day, myself and Steve found ourselves on the pitch at Loftus Road reliving the game. Our fun was short-lived though as an extremely loud shout from the touchline alerted us to the fact that the bus was going and we should stop messing about on the pitch. It was my dad. The coach was parked by the players' entrance and as we were getting on we were abused by various QPR fans, so we had a little word back and then finally got on.

"Just as I sat down the driver came over: 'Hello, Paul, can you do me a favour and go to the chippy up the road and get the order for Liverpool FC? It's already paid for.' He was about to give me a free ride home so I couldn't really say no. I got back off the bus and walked through another corridor of abuse to the chippy. The players were all on the bus when I got back with 25 portions of fish and chips and I started to hand them all out to the team, being randomly abused by them for not having enough or there was too much salt and vinegar on them.

"I eventually sat down at the front and someone behind me

passed me a bottle of Carlsberg. As I was about to take a well-deserved drink my dad appeared and said: 'You're not having a drink, lad, you're driving us home when we get back to Anfield.' We got back to the ground about half past ten, after what can only be described as a tiring but truly brilliant day. The other bonus about being able to get to the QPR game was I managed to achieve my goal of attending all of the 42 league games that season," Paul says proudly.

The 1984/85 season was the first time since 1974/75 that Liverpool ended a campaign without any silverware. During this ten-year period as well as winning the League Cup four times, every season they would finish with either a European trophy or the league championship, or on three occasions with both in their trophy cabinet. Moreover, Liverpool started the season in contention to win seven trophies.

The loss of captain Graeme Souness to Sampdoria proved to be the biggest setback for the club as he wasn't readily replaced. Midfielder Jan Mølby honed his trade at Ajax in Amsterdam for two-and-a-half years prior to joining the European champions in August 1984 but he was in for a shock when he moved to Merseyside.

"When we arrived at Carrow Road for my first game, we filed into the away dressing room," Mølby recollects. "I asked Ronnie Moran, 'What do we do now?' 'Just get changed,' growled Ronnie. 'Get yourself ready for the game, son.' 'What time do we go out to warm up?' I asked. 'You don't have time to warm up, save your energy.' I couldn't believe what I was hearing. At Ajax, we spent about 25 minutes warming up."

When Mølby got changed his teammates decided to have a little fun with the newcomer and encouraged him to ask Ronnie for a massage prior to kick-off as that was the standard for every player. Mølby somewhat timidly approached Ronnie: "'Er… Ronnie, can I have a massage?' 'Fuck off!' shouted Ronnie. 'You earn the right to have a massage. Go out and play some games and then I might consider it.' Then I saw all the lads pissing themselves. That was my introduction to Ronnie and the Liverpool dressing room humour," Mølby remembers.

The season began on August 18 when Liverpool travelled down to the capital to face arch rivals Everton in the Charity Shield. The Toffees enjoyed a rare win over their neighbours at Wembley. The only goal of the game came after Grobbelaar had done well to block Graeme Sharp's close-range shot in the 55th minute. The loose ball pinged from one player to another before Grobbelaar sadly misfired the pinball into the net as he tried to recover.

The next disappointment Liverpool suffered was a 1-0 League Cup fourth-round exit at the hands of Tottenham Hotspur at White Hart Lane in October. This was only Liverpool's second defeat in their last 42 games in the competition, putting an end to their hopes of winning the League Cup for the fifth year running.

At the end of October, the European champions were 20th in the league, only two places from rock bottom. In December, Fagan's men travelled to Tokyo to face Independiente in the Intercontinental Cup. Liverpool were defeated by a single goal and left furious with the referee, who they thought should have awarded them two penalties.

This was only the second time Liverpool were involved in this competition as they refused to play Boca Juniors in 1977 and 1978.

"We never played Boca in 1977 because of a history of trouble in previous years in the competition and the following year in 1978 both teams simply refused to play each other," Paul Moran recalls. "I also think the problem of arranging a trip to Buenos Aires during the season led to the management swerving the game and blaming previous problems as the primary motive for not taking part. In 1981 and 1984 Liverpool were more or less forced to play by UEFA so the main consideration was for no-one to get injured as winning the cup was not a major priority.

"I honestly believe the games were approached and played by us like friendlies. I can recall my dad saying, tongue in cheek: 'Flamengo had cheated in 1981 by passing the ball to each other without letting it hit the floor,' but, joking aside, the South Americans placed much more importance on these games than Liverpool did."

On January 16, 1985 Liverpool travelled to Turin to face Juventus in the European Super Cup. At the time, the Super Cup was generally a two-legged tie, but due to fixture congestion only the first leg was ultimately played. Liverpool lost 2-0 to goals from Zbigniew Boniek. One more cup had slipped out of Liverpool's hands.

During the 1984/85 season, Liverpool travelled further than in previous seasons and Ronnie made sure everything went without a hitch.

"My dad always used to treat foreign trips the same, no matter where the destination was," Paul remembers. "It was never anything other than a game of football that we had to prepare properly for and ultimately try to win.

"There would never be any comments like: 'It's nice there' or

'I've never been there before.' He used to enjoy the organisa-tional side of the trips, making sure the training kit and such was right, as he felt any problems or mistakes were his respon-sibility. I can honestly not recall any problems. Sometimes I would go to Anfield to help pack the skips for away trips, which I always enjoyed."

Liverpool were knocked out of the FA Cup in a semi-final replay at Maine Road against Manchester United in April while Everton were running away with the league championship. All that was left was the European Cup final against Juventus at the Heysel Stadium on May 29, 1985. It was a game remembered for all the wrong reasons as 39 people died.

"The events of that day took away all the importance of the game," Ronnie says. "I was devastated by the deaths of innocent people which overtook any feelings of upset about the football side. I was also very worried about my son, Paul, and his girlfriend at the time, now wife Julie, if they were okay, as we never spoke to each other until teatime the next day when we all got home."

Due to Fagan's imminent retirement, Ronnie wasn't sure at the time if he would still have a job the following season. New manager Kenny Dalglish soon put his mind at ease on the flight back to Liverpool from Brussels, when he informed Ronnie and Roy Evans that he wanted them to carry on with their jobs. It wasn't a difficult decision to make for Kenny as he had been under their tutelage for eight years.

"I trusted Roy and Ronnie implicitly," Kenny said. "They

were totally honest, loyal men who'd never be stool-pigeons in the dressing room. Ronnie and Roy watched us like hawks, scrutinising every move and word. I know modern day clubs use technology to chart performances in training, but I'd back the eyes of Ronnie and Roy ahead of anyone's computer."

Ronnie had to make the adjustment of stopping shouting at Kenny in training to calling him 'boss'. He was happy that he was asked to stay on and not at all upset that he wasn't offered the manager's job. "I don't think my dad really wanted to be in the limelight position of team manager, as he was happy to carry on doing his coaching duties in the background," Paul claims.

Kenny Dalglish became the first player-manager in the English game. That was a daunting task in itself, but he also had to deal with Liverpool's ban in Europe. Ronnie had enough to take care of at the club to be too worried about what was going on outside.

"My dad never really reacted or cared about what other people thought about the club," Paul says. "He was only ever concerned about what was happening on a day to day basis at Anfield or Melwood. He adapted to the idea that once we were banned, he couldn't change it. He had to get on with the situation as it stood."

Moran seemed to have had a premonition about Kenny's new role as Dalglish explained years later.

"Just before the end of the 84/85 season at training I had a pass that, as usual, never went where it should have gone and Ronnie said: 'Play it easy.' I said: 'It was easy. I just made it difficult.' He went: 'You're clever but you're not manager yet, you know.' There had never been a mention about me being a manager or anything. I never knew I was going to be manager then either."

Ronnie was very impressed, though, by Dalglish's work ethic as manager.

"Kenny did his homework on opposing players; he knew an awful lot about their strengths and weaknesses," Moran said. "He was also a person who studied football videos at length. I remember one away trip when we moved into Roy Evans' room on the Friday evening and watched two games at the same time."

Dalglish was certainly happy with Ronnie's work.

"The contribution and help Ronnie gave me was enormous and I am eternally grateful for him, both as a player and as a manager," Kenny said. "I don't think anybody that worked with him during his spell at Liverpool will have anything but total admiration, respect and gratitude for what he did for them.

"I don't think it's a coincidence that in the most successful spell in the club's history, Ronnie Moran was of great importance. He was there at the outset when Bill Shankly came in and revamped everything. Bill changed the philosophy, the principles, the beliefs. The football club as it stands today is there because of what Bill Shankly set in place, and Ronnie was a big part of that."

Liverpool scored an incredible 138 goals in all competitions during the 1985/86 season, which to this day is a club record. The coaching staff at Liverpool had plenty of goals to savour but on one occasion they had to keep their celebrations to a minimum.

Liverpool had won five games in a row before they played at Birmingham on November 23, 1985. The Liverpool bench had been asked by the police not to come out of the dugout if they scored because away team staff had had objects thrown at them in previous games.

In the 10th minute Craig Johnston burst into the box on the right side and crossed hard and low for Ian Rush, who hardly put a foot wrong that campaign, to make it 1-0; cue the celebrations! Ronnie couldn't get up and celebrate so he joyfully punched Roy Evans on the thigh and gave him a dead leg instead. Sixteen minutes later Jan Mølby's free-kick on the left found its way to Paul Walsh who headed in from close range. A big scuffle seemed to break out on the bench as staff tried to hit each other on the legs.

Liverpool scored three or more goals on 23 occasions during this season, as happened on April 26, 1986 as Birmingham visited Anfield.

"A couple of weeks before the Birmingham game, Paul Walsh had an opportunity to get a hat-trick by taking a penalty," defender Gary Gillespie recalls. "Walshy missed and when we got back into the dressing room Ronnie Moran went absolutely berserk at him, as at the time it was thought the league could be decided on goal difference. He really went mad with him. If Ronnie had any hair left he would have been pulling it all out.

"Rush won a penalty against Birmingham when the score was 4-0. I could hear the Kop shouting my name," Gillespie says. "I glanced over at Ronnie Moran who was stood on the touchline shaking his head at me. Dalglish, who was on the pitch as player-manager, told me to come forward. I took the ball off Kenny and with Ronnie Moran still shaking his head at me, I was feeling rather nervous. Fortunately, for Liverpool and myself, it went in and I completed my hat-trick."

Liverpool clinched their 16th league title on the last day of the season, beating Chelsea 1-0 at Stamford Bridge. Seven days later Liverpool travelled to Wembley to face Everton in the hope of adding the FA Cup to their collection. For the best part of a century football had waited for an all-Merseyside FA Cup final. Ronnie believed all games should be approached in the same way. In those days there weren't 25 players to pick from, so the first-team played every game and there was "none of this resting players rubbish," as Ronnie would say.

Liverpool beat the Blues 3-1 and clinched their first-ever league and FA Cup double. Craig Johnston scored for the Reds, and Ronnie said: "Rushie's two goals against Everton in the 1986 cup final are up there as being my favourites. I might sound 'fuddy duddy' but every goal that goes in for us is a good one and any we concede is a bad one."

Ronnie Moran was consistently quite willing to join in with the dressing room banter and despite the hard work, the staff wanted the players to enjoy training. There was a lot of messing about at Melwood but it had to be done at the right time and curtailed to a point. The better the mood was around Melwood and Anfield, the better the results were.

The aura that has been built up around Ronnie Moran makes it seem like he stomped around bellowing at players and swearing all the time. He certainly wasn't someone who suffered fools gladly, but at the same time he wasn't averse to having a laugh and having the mickey taken out of him too.

The majority of the players would never call him 'Ronald', 'Ronnie' nor 'Ron'. To them he was always 'Bugsy', named after a 1920s American gangster called George 'Bugs' Moran. Bill Shankly started the 'Bugsy' name off and that is why Ronnie was always okay with it. Everyone called him 'Bugsy' apart from Tommy Smith who insisted on calling him 'Moransco'.

At home, Ronnie's children used to refer to him as 'Archie', but he soon made them stop when he found out it was short for 'Archibald', the emphasis being on the 'bald' part of the name.

Moran would always refer to the players by the names they called each other in the dressing room, which was usually a shortened version of their name. He would also call the first-team players 'Big heads' to keep their feet on the ground. At training he would say, "Right, you big heads over there, let's have you," and everyone would know what he meant.

Kenny Dalglish's second season as player-manager, and Moran's 13th on the first-team staff, started on August 16, 1986 with another trip to Wembley to take on Everton for the second time in three seasons in the Charity Shield. The game finished 1-1 after Rush cancelled out Adrian Heath's second-half goal for the Toffees.

Five weeks later the Reds hit double figures, beating Fulham 10-0 at Anfield in the League Cup second round. This was Liverpool's biggest win in domestic football, a record that still exists. Nonetheless, as far as Ronnie was concerned, a win was a win, whether it was by 10 goals or one. However, sometimes he would come up with a jokey remark in the dressing room after the game, such as: "Any danger of getting the killer goal a bit earlier next time, lads, so we can relax on the bench?"

In September, Liverpool secured a 7-2 aggregate victory over Everton in the final of the Screen Sport Super Cup, a competition founded to compensate the teams that would have otherwise qualified for European competition. This minor trophy turned out to be the only one the club won during this season.

Liverpool came second in the league to Everton and were runners-up as well in the League Cup, having lost the final 2-1 to Arsenal.

In the summer Liverpool parted ways with what many considered their greatest asset, Ian Rush, who wanted to try pastures new. The club received a healthy sum of £3.2million from Juventus.

Rush's replacement as centre-forward came in the form of Liverpool-born John Aldridge, who signed from Oxford United for £750,000 in January 1987 during Rush's farewell season. 'Aldo' had big shoes to fill and despite claims that Ronnie always behaved the same way to players at the club, whether they were super stars or up and coming youngsters, Rushie was a notable exception.

"Ronnie loved Rushie to bits and when I came in, I felt he was gutted that Rushie was leaving," Aldridge reveals. "I wasn't Rushie, but a different type of player. In shooting practice, we would line up and Ronnie would lay the ball off to us. I'd be first up and I'd put the ball wide and Ronnie would shout: 'Hit the target, you bastard!' Next up would be Ray Houghton and he would hit it wide and he would shout the same thing to Ray. Finally, Rushie would run up and hit the ball over the crossbar and Ronnie would shout: 'It doesn't matter, it happens in a game, son!'"

Rushie recognises this was the moment when he knew that Moran had a soft spot for him. "I would get away with murder in training," Rushie said. "He loved Ronnie Whelan as well. We got into the side together. He used to call us the Goat and the Racehorse. 'You do all the hard work. Let Rushie do the finishing.'"

Former Liverpool captain, Mark Wright, was also well aware of Moran's special fondness for Rushie. "If we ever went out for a Christmas party and we were in training the next day, and Ian Rush said he was feeling a bit dodgy, Ronnie would say to him: 'Go on, son, go and get yourself a nice massage.' If it was me he would say: 'If you can't handle it, don't do it.'"

Ronnie said of Rush: "He had this trait about him that you can't teach. What he can do is simple and you can't teach those. Some people in the game think they can make players like Ian Rush and they've got no chance. They can encourage them on certain aspects of the game, but he's got to have his own individual traits about him, which he has, and this is why he has been in the game so long and scored all these goals."

Ronnie not only valued Rushie's goalscoring instincts, but also his incredible workrate and how well he took instructions on board. Rushie frightened the opposition with his attacking skills, but also defended vigorously, helping the team's cause.

"I have to admit I found it very hard to adapt to Ronnie's tough nature but I wanted to do him proud as I saw so many similarities in him to my own father," Rushie says. "He would either make you or break you but ultimately he was laying the foundations for you to possess the necessary mental strength which would later shape my career as a player. His enthusiasm for the game resonated throughout each and every player. I will always admire him for guiding me in the right way."

Ronnie couldn't afford to dwell on Rushie's departure to Italy, but to focus on how he could get Aldridge to perform to the best of his ability.

"I've got tinnitus in my right ear. I think the reason why I got it was because Ronnie was always in it for the entire time

I was at Liverpool," Aldridge quips. "During training he kept on going on and on at me. I thought he had it in for me, but I later found out he was just trying to make me a better player. If I didn't move when I passed the ball he would call me a 'lazy bugger' and hammer me for it. That's what he wanted me to do and when I started to do it, he soon laid off me. It was all about making sure the new players like myself adjusted quickly to the Liverpool Way."

Whenever a new player arrived at the club during the summer the first thing he had to endure, besides Ronnie's undivided attention, was the fitness training that took place in pre-season.

"Get yourself to bed early tonight, lads. Big picture tomorrow," was the message from Ronnie as the players regrouped after the summer holidays. The veterans at Liverpool explained to the newcomers that it meant they would run laps around Melwood throughout the following morning.

John Aldridge soon felt the benefits of Ronnie's training and discovered that there was a method to the perceived madness.

"The training was excellent and the small-sided games were phenomenal," Aldridge says. "Ronnie used to join in and get involved, as it would be more effective to get the message over. You had to be quick, pass and move and be able to deal with the ball.

"Ronnie always had the utmost respect of everyone right throughout the entire club. I agree that managers usually get all the credit and the coaches do tend to be less appreciated. This does come with the territory of being a coach but it wasn't the case at Liverpool, as far as the players were concerned anyway. Nobody ever got anything out of Ronnie apart from football and he never got involved in any of the personal stuff either!"

Prior to the 1987/88 season, Dalglish brought in John Barnes from Watford and Peter Beardsley from Newcastle United to bolster his attacking options. The pair complemented Aldridge perfectly and Liverpool went unbeaten for 29 games from the start of the season and equalled Leeds United's record from the 1973/74 campaign.

"My dad said to me during the 1987/88 season that when Beardsley and Barnes were unstoppable, occasionally during games the staff on the bench could actually relax and were able to enjoy the game," Paul Moran recalls. "However, that luxury didn't happen that often as I used to ask my dad after games what he thought of one of our goals and he'd say: 'I'll have to watch it on the telly tonight as I was shouting at the back four when we scored.'

"If I told him an opposition player had played well he'd say: 'I never noticed, I was watching our players.' It goes to show that what the fans are watching – usually the ball – isn't necessarily what the staff are watching."

John Barnes was excited to partake in the training that had made Liverpool invincible throughout the years, but his initial impression was that the routines were too repetitive, no tactical work was done and that the players and staff were just fooling around in the small-sided games. He soon realised that all the strategy was forged in the eight-a-side games and the intensity that was on display was unlike anything he'd experienced at other clubs.

"The philosophy centred on passing, making angles and one-touch football. Liverpool's doctrine would help any ball-player," Barnes reveals. "If there was any secret to Liverpool's success it lay in the fact that the fixation with five-a-sides gave us an extra edge on match days. Bigger pitches and goals made us feel we had more room."

Kenny, Roy and Ronnie could have their pick of the first-team players to strengthen their team during the highly competitive training games with one exception, as Peter Beardsley points out. "They would also try and pinch Barnesy but that was always under protest."

John Barnes wasn't too keen at first to play with the staff. He said: "They gave me a bib and said: 'That's your team.' Ronnie is on my side. You thought: 'How are we going to win with Ronnie, Roy Evans and Kenny Dalglish on our team?' But we did, more often than not, because Ronnie was enthusiastic in his playing. He loved to play."

Moran not only relished playing against the seniors, but the youth team as well.

"They had the Friday afternoon games against the kids," Barnes says. "They would play until they won. They would be cheating and kicking. Ronnie would be kicking the kids. His will to win was incredible, whether he was playing against the people he was coaching, the under-16s or the young kids. He lived and breathed, ate and slept Liverpool Football Club."

Peter Beardsley was left in no doubt about who ran the show at Melwood.

"Ronnie was the main man as far as the coaching and training were concerned. He used to do the lot," Beardsley says. "You were just not allowed to be a prima donna with blokes like Ronnie Moran around. Ronnie was the hard man, he would be the one doing the shouting and he didn't mince words. If he thought you were a pillock, he said so in the kind of colourful language you became used to. But you respected him for that."

Moran tried to lighten up the mood with his usual joke. During the small-sided games, when Ronnie wanted a player to make a late run into the box to join the two strikers, instead of shouting 'third man', he would shout 'Harry Lime', referring to Orson Welles' character in the movie The Third Man. It soon became a well-known phrase to any newcomer among the players.

A typical day of training in the monumental 1987/88 season started with a jog for 6-7 minutes with Ronnie and Roy leading from the front around the perimeter of the pitch. Then the players formed a circle to do some stretches and practise passing before an eight-a-side was played across the training pitch, typically 65 yards long and 40 yards wide but the playing surface did vary in size as the staff saw fit.

Ronnie kept everyone on their toes by constantly changing the rules during the game, allowing players only to take one or two touches or keeping the ball below a certain height. The game would usually last about 15 minutes and then the players did some sprinting and practised crossing or shooting with the goalkeepers. The training finished with another eight-a-side and sprints.

"It's been said before that there was no special formula at the club, no amazing training ground techniques or no secret plans," Paul Moran says. "I always used to joke with my dad that we never scored from corners or free-kicks in matches and he'd say to me: 'We do practise them at Melwood, son, but in matches the opposition players wouldn't stand where we wanted them to!'"

Kenny Dalglish was likely to emulate the success of two seasons ago by achieving the league and cup double. After winning the league by nine points, Liverpool faced Wimbledon in the FA Cup final at Wembley. Wimbledon's ground, Plough Lane, was the one that Ronnie liked the least.

"Wimbledon kept the ground and facilities as basic as possible to put the glamour teams off," Ronnie says.

Wimbledon were outsiders at 33-1 before the third round took place in January, to win the cup in May. They had played in the Fourth Division only five years previously, but triumphed over Liverpool in one of the biggest shocks in the history of the oldest association football competition in the world.

Ronnie had plenty of other reasons to rejoice during the 1987/88 campaign. Paul and his wife, Julie, celebrated the birth of a daughter, Alix, on December 2, 1987. They had a son, David, a couple of years later, on June 19, 1989. Alix has always treasured the company of her grandad.

"At least once a year, during the school summer holidays, we'd go to Lytham St Annes where there was a mini golf course," Alix remembers. "David and I and Grandad played while my nan would find a bench to sit on to watch. While we were playing we let Grandad keep track of the score and he would always win. As we got older we realised that he cheated! He was the worst!

"When Grandad and Nan would visit us on Sunday afternoons, we'd guess the scores of whatever game we were watching. We'd all throw 20p in. No matter what we had written down for Grandad he would always at the end say he hadn't said the score that we had written for him and he'd got it bang on. Biggest cheat ever!

"Grandad always has his flat cap on, which to this day is his pride and joy. He doesn't leave the house without it and it is panic stations if we don't have eyes on it.

"People always come up to him when we are out and want to tell him how great he is, especially the die-hard Liverpool fans who grew up with Grandad as one of their favourites. I just stood there thinking: 'What's all the fuss about?' Even after all these years I still don't get the fuss as he is just my grandad. Even at my 18th, 21st and even engagement party the fuss people would make: 'Alix, can I have my photo taken with your grandad, would he mind?' My response would be: 'Oh, get a grip and just ask him; he's a normal person!' They could never understand why or how I couldn't see it! When I told my husband, Ryan, who my grandad was, he didn't believe me. I always remember saying to him: 'Why would I make it up?' 'Do I really look like I'd know who Ronnie Moran was if he wasn't my grandad?' I know deep down he has achieved more in his lifetime than anyone I have ever met but to me he is, and always will be, just my grandad," Alix concludes.

At the end of the 1988/89 season, Ronnie completed 40 years of service at Liverpool Football Club since starting out as a 15-year-old featuring for the youth teams during the 1949/50 season. Moran's landmark campaign at Liverpool was, however, the darkest in the club's history, the season when Liverpool travelled to Hillsborough to take on Nottingham Forest in an FA Cup semi-final on April 15, 1989.

Paul Moran had travelled to the game with three of his mates.

"I went to the game and was in the stand opposite the players' tunnel with three mates in the complimentary seats," he said.

A horrific crush was in progress in the Leppings Lane stand

behind Grobbelaar's goal that ultimately caused the death of 96 Liverpool supporters. The match was stopped after only six minutes and while the horror unfolded the players were in the dressing room not realising what was happening outside. They were still expecting that the game would continue. "Keep warm, lads, we will be going out in a minute," was the mantra repeated by Ronnie to the players until the match was called off.

"Once the game was abandoned one of the lads said to me: 'Why don't you go over the pitch and tell your dad you are okay,'" Paul recalls. "I said: 'No, there's enough going on and he knows I'm over here in this stand and not behind the goal.' Unbeknown to me, at the same time, someone had asked my dad if he'd seen me and if I was okay. My dad said: 'Yes, he's over there somewhere in that stand,' at which point the person said to him: 'He is, if he hasn't swapped his ticket and gone behind the goal.'

"I did have a habit of doing this. My dad would provide me with tickets for the games, but the complimentary seats wouldn't usually be for the stands at the ends of stadiums. Therefore, I would often swap my tickets before a game in order to stand behind the goal with the rest of the Liverpool fans."

Ronnie was extremely worried about his son's safety and whereabouts and at the same time trying to fully fathom the horror of the situation.

"As I was coming back from Hillsborough, we stopped in Stalybridge to ring home," Paul says. "There was no answer at my house or my sister's so I rang my auntie's and spoke to my Uncle Bill. He passed the message on to Julie and the rest of the family in Liverpool."

Six of the best: Bill Shankly, Bob Paisley, Joe Fagan, Ronnie, Reuben Bennett and Tom Saunders in 1971 after Shanks had just been given a new contract

Learning his trade: Ronnie casts his eye over an A team coaching session by Tony Waiters in 1969

Holiday retreat: The Morans loved a break at the Devon Coast Country Club

Crossing the divide: A rare picture of Ronnie in an Everton shirt – for a charity match in 1980

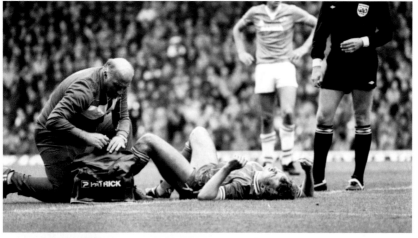

Magic sponge: For a while Ronnie acted as the club physio

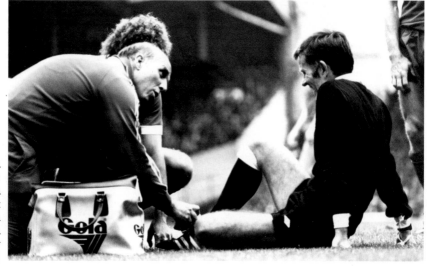

Are you okay, ref?: He even had to treat an injured referee in September 1981

Bootroom boys: Ronnie, Bob Paisley, Joe Fagan, Roy Evans, Tom Saunders and John Bennison share a joke in the hallowed store room

Trophies galore: Ronnie and the boys got their hands on the European Cup in 1984, and (below) showed off the league championship trophy, European Cup and Charity Shield in 1977

Brains trust: Bob and Joe were friends as well as colleagues

In charge: Ronnie took the role of caretaker manager for the first time at Luton after the resignation of Kenny Dalglish in 1991

Follow the leader: At the front of the queue at Wembley, leading the players out for the 1990 Charity Shield match against Manchester United

Close to the action: There was no need to use his piercing whistle when the players were within shouting distance

Terrific trio: With Kenny and Roy after the title win in 1990

That stare: The players knew not to mess with 'Bugsy' and this picture shows why!

Watch him!: Ronnie looks concerned as the recuperating Graeme Souness gets involved in the 1992 FA Cup final

Bringing it home: The family had a visit from a well-known silver pot after the Sunderland final!

Proud moment: One of the greatest honours of Ronnie's career was leading the team out for the FA Cup final against Sunderland

Roy's team: Sammy Lee, Roy Evans, Doug Livermore and Ronnie in 1994

Main Stand salute: Ronnie picks out a familiar face in the crowd

The yellers: There's as much action on the bench as on the pitch in 1997

Big thanks: Chairman David Moores presents Ronnie with a crystal bowl in recognition of his service to the club after retirement in 1998

Tribute night: Celtic were the visitors for Ronnie's testimonial in 2000

The Moran clan: A recent family photo with four generations of Morans

That flat cap: Ronnie wore his trademark cap when he met Jamie Carragher at Bootle, and when he caught a match at Anfield a few years ago

On the sidelines: Ronnie's appetite for football remained strong and when he wasn't at Anfield, he used to watch local matches with his son, Paul (right)

Ronnie's worries about his son were put to rest, without Paul realising how concerned he was at the time.

"I eventually met my dad and mum when they got back to their house about 10pm that night," Paul says. "I can honestly say the hug I got from them was something that I'll never forget. My dad then said to me: 'If you had been killed today, son, I would have permanently walked away from football.'

"My dad attended a few funerals with Kenny Dalglish and Roy Evans and we attended together the one of an old school friend of mine from Crosby, Paul Hewitson. He was a lad who I also played Sunday League football with, so my dad knew of him as well."

During the aftermath of Hillsborough all the players and staff were swept along with the outpouring of grief from the day.

"It's bewildering to think that all the players and staff dealt with many of the bereaved families with no training or counselling themselves," Paul says. "Kenny was at the forefront because he was the manager, but everyone at the club stepped up onto the same level. I think it wouldn't be right to say that more was done by others during this difficult period," Paul concludes.

Liverpool beat Forest in the semi-final replay and conquered Everton 3-2 in the final at Wembley. A familiar face was once again the bane of Everton.

"Rushie was happy to be back here and we were happy having him back, especially when the goals started going in again," Moran said about Liverpool's prodigal son, Ian Rush, who had returned from Juventus in the summer.

Rushie repeated his feat of three years earlier by scoring twice in a Wembley final against Everton.

Although most people on the red half of Merseyside always

savour a win against their neighbours more than victories against other teams, Ronnie didn't. He always treated teams the same and a win against one club wouldn't mean more to him than any other. It was always about the 90 minutes and whether a win could be secured. Ronnie also wasn't fond of the hype in the build-up to the supposed big games. All games were big games for Moran, regardless of the opponent and the occasion.

With the FA Cup now in the bag, the double was on the cards again. The destiny of the title was to be decided in the last fixture of the season against Arsenal at Anfield.

Alan Smith put the Gunners in the lead in the 52nd minute and one more goal would mean Arsenal would be champions. Barnes received the ball in the final moments of the game on the right flank and instead of holding on to the ball he tried to go past Kevin Richardson, who took the ball off him. With 91 minutes and 22 seconds of the game played, Michael Thomas scored in the most dramatic fashion possible. Some 40 seconds later the game was finished. Ronnie was furious with Barnes' decision.

"In the dressing room Ronnie Moran said to me: 'What were you doing? You should have taken the ball down to the corner flag.' But no-one else criticised me. Everyone was too shell-shocked," Barnes says.

"Ronnie would know the characters that he could do that to. There are certain players you can't criticise and certain players you can criticise. To get a reaction from you, to get the best out of you, he says these little things to you. It wasn't an issue with me. I didn't get carried away when we won and I didn't get carried away when we lost."

Liverpool strengthened their defence in the summer of 1989, bringing in the captain of Sweden, Glenn Hysen. Liverpool stole him right from under the nose of Alex Ferguson at Manchester United, who thought they had his transfer signed, sealed...but forgot the delivered bit.

"When I first joined Liverpool from Fiorentina, I was starstruck," Hysen says. "I remember sitting in the dressing room at Melwood for the first time alongside Bruce Grobbelaar, Steve Nicol, Alan Hansen, Ian Rush and John Barnes, thinking to myself how privileged I was to be with some of the best players in Europe. Then, in came Ronnie Moran and started shouting at us!

"At first, I was quite frightened of Ronnie. At Fiorentina I played under a softly-spoken Sven Göran Eriksson for two seasons, therefore Ronnie's approach was a real eye-opener to me. Right from the start I found his enthusiasm for the game magical. During the small-sided games, he would be really tough with us, constantly wanting us to give more. He used to join in too and although he didn't move much, he could still play a bit!"

Hysen admired the enthusiasm and drive that Ronnie displayed at training but discovered another side to him when they were not at Melwood.

"Away from the training field, Ronnie was a kind and polite man who to this day I have the utmost respect for," Hysen says. "Kenny Dalglish was the manager when I joined, but before a game he would only really read out the team while Ronnie Moran and Roy Evans spoke to the players individually before we went out onto the field. Ronnie would just say to me: 'Do what you do best, son! Head the thing, tackle and don't try to do anything else!' He would always keep me on my toes and strive to get the best out of me."

Liverpool launched another title assault after the disappointing end to the previous campaign and reached their goal on April 28, 1990 with two games still to be played. The Reds beat QPR 2-1 at home after going behind, while at the same time their main rivals for the title, Aston Villa, drew 3-3 with Norwich. At the final whistle Ronnie can be seen anxiously asking for confirmation of the Villa score, before celebrating jubilantly with Dalglish on the touchline.

Liverpool had won the First Division championship for the 18th time in their history and it was Ronnie's 10th in 16 seasons on the first-team staff. The trophy was presented three days later to captain Alan Hansen as Liverpool faced Derby County, a historic game as Dalglish made his final appearance as a player.

On August 18, 1990, Liverpool faced Manchester United in the Charity Shield at Wembley. Dalglish stepped aside to allow Moran to lead out the Liverpool team as a token of gratitude for his service over the years. It was a great gesture by Dalglish and one Moran had no time to prepare for.

"All the players knew what was going on, everyone but me," Ronnie revealed to the *Daily Express*. "The first I knew about it was when the bell rang in the Wembley dressing room and Kenny Dalglish turned to me and said: 'You're taking them out.' That's why I was still in my tracksuit. I hadn't time to change."

This annual showpiece was important in Ronnie's mind as it meant that Liverpool had either won the league or the FA Cup to be allowed to participate. His first message to the players each pre-season would invariably be: "Our ambition this year is to get into the Charity Shield."

Liverpool started their title defence with eight straight wins but when they faced their title rivals, Arsenal, at the start of December, their six-point lead was cut in half following a 3-0 defeat at Highbury. Dalglish had been unusually cautious in his approach to the game and his omission of Beardsley and Houghton from the First Division's most potent attacking team was deemed as incomprehensible. Rushie was left alone up front to fight Arsenal's towering defenders.

After a 1-1 draw against Wimbledon on January 19, *The Times* wondered: 'Even without a growing catalogue of injuries, it is increasingly clear that all is not well with Liverpool. But it is a brave man who suggests that the die is cast, for no club is better equipped for survival. The empire may yet strike back.'

There had already been doubts about the ages of the players. Bruce Grobbelaar (33), Glenn Hysen (31) and David Speedie (31) were all on the wrong side of 30; Gary Gillespie and Peter Beardsley were 30, and four key players – Ronnie Whelan, Steve McMahon, Ian Rush and Steve Nicol – were 29. Liverpool had always strengthened their team no matter how successful they were, but newcomers Jimmy Carter and David Speedie were hardly considered threats to any of the starting eleven.

It turned out that all was not well, despite the fact Liverpool looked in decent shape to make a run for the title.

By February 9, 1991, following a 3-1 win over Everton in the league, Liverpool had a three-point lead on Arsenal at the top of the table and had scored 46 goals in 24 games, 1.91 goals on average.

Liverpool met the Blues again, in the fifth round of the FA

Cup. A goalless draw at Anfield forced a replay at Goodison Park. Liverpool took the lead four times, but were pegged back each time.

At 4-3, with 103 minutes gone, Kenny wanted to strengthen Liverpool's defence, as he recollects. "'Let's shut up shop, Bugsy,' I said to Ronnie. 'Let's stick Jan back to sweeper.' 'Hold on,' said Ronnie. 'Just leave it,' I shrugged."

This moment of indecision was the last straw for Kenny as far as he was concerned. He no longer had the belief in himself to make big decisions. Tony Cottee equalised 10 minutes later and Kenny was left to rue this hesitancy. A second replay was on the horizon.

Dalglish was unusually quiet in the dressing room after the pulsating 4-4 draw while Ronnie tore the defenders to shreds for making such schoolboy errors and had a huge argument with Grobbelaar.

Glenn Hysen had worn the captain's armband in the absence of Ronnie Whelan in that game and didn't escape Ronnie's wrath.

"Deep into extra-time when we were 4-3 up, Jan Mølby played the ball back to me and I stepped over it," said Hysen. "I thought the ball was going to run through to Bruce, but Tony Cottee latched on to it to score the equaliser. When we got back into the dressing room, Ronnie hammered me for what I had done: 'What did you do that for?' he shouted. 'Sorry, I thought Bruce had it,' I replied. Ronnie was right. All I had to do was clear the ball and we would have seen out the remainder of the game and won the tie. Let's just say me and Ronnie weren't best friends for a few days after that."

This turned out to be Dalglish's last game as Liverpool

manager – at least for the next 20 years. The following morning, he attended a meeting that was held each month with chairman Noel White and chief executive Peter Robinson. Dalglish stunned them into silence by saying: "I want to resign. I just feel as if my head is exploding. I want to go now. Today."

"I was incredibly proud that my
dad was the manager of Liverpool
Football Club and that could never
be taken away from the record books.
I remember him saying that he
wouldn't take the job on a permanent
basis as he wanted to carry on being
a coach."

– Paul Moran

Chapter 8

EVERY ROLE IMAGINABLE

1991-1992

ON the morning of February 21, 1991, Ronnie Moran was in the Bootroom sorting out the kit and taking care of any minor injuries sustained by players the previous evening at Goodison Park, totally oblivious to anything else that was occurring at Anfield regarding the future of the club.

The players had a day off and after completing all his usual duties following a match day, Ronnie drove home to have lunch with his wife. He received a call around 3pm as he was on his way out to spend the afternoon in Southport with Joyce.

"'I've packed in,' Kenny said. 'I've had enough.' I thought he was joking, as he was a great practical joker and I told him to stop messing around," Ronnie recalled. "He must have filled up because he put the phone down and the line went dead."

Kenny Dalglish's resignation as manager of Liverpool was reluctantly accepted at an emergency board meeting at 4pm. The next call Ronnie received was from chairman Noel White in the evening to ask him if he would take over for the next few games while a decision was made on Kenny's successor. He accepted without hesitation.

Bill Shankly's resignation in the summer of 1974 had also caused a shock to the people of Liverpool. It had been Bob Paisley's calling to follow the great Shankly then and now Ronnie was being asked to step into the shoes of another Liverpool legend. The inexorable path to the top that had begun with apprenticeship in 1949 had finally delivered Ronnie Moran to the pinnacle of club football as manager of the league champions.

The following morning, before the news was delivered to the disbelieving press, the squad met up at Anfield prior to a little work-out at Melwood. The team anticipated leaving early for London to be able to train that afternoon on Luton's plastic pitch prior to their game the next day. The players were sitting in the players' lounge when Ronnie took everyone by surprise by telling them to gather in the home dressing room. Kenny walked in and with tears in his eyes told the players that he was leaving.

As Liverpool's finest sat there stunned, trying to come to terms with what just happened, Ronnie broke the ominous silence by declaring: "Okay, let's go training now." Life at Anfield had to move on without Kenny and the team had to prepare for the next challenge.

The press gathered for an 11am press conference in the Bob Paisley Suite at Anfield where Dalglish explained his reasons for leaving the club: "I've been in the front line and this decision is a result of those years at a very high and successful level. The pressure is in the build-up to matches and the aftermath of them, although I still enjoyed coming to the club and working with the players. It's a decision that many people will find difficult to understand, a decision that only I could have made. And it would have been wrong to mislead people that everything was fine with me."

White was respectful during the conference, but afterwards said that Kenny's decision "has thrown the club into turmoil and the timing is lousy, but we aren't going to lie down and die."

It was now Ronnie's job to make sure everything would move on as normal so the players weren't thinking too much about Dalglish's departure. Ronnie had too much respect for Kenny to comment on why he left and only told the press that "obviously this has shocked everyone here, but we will get by."

Throughout the decades Ronnie's working life had centred on doing his best for Liverpool. The weeks that followed were a great testimony to Moran's dedication to his one and only club.

The 56-year-old was the obvious candidate to come to the rescue in a crisis until a permanent successor to Dalglish could be named. He knew the club inside out. He inherited a team that was top of the table.

As the whole club was in shock after Dalglish's departure, Moran's first task was to lift the gloom around the team and prepare it for a trip to London that afternoon.

The only duties that were new to Ronnie were picking the side and then dealing with the press after the game.

He did this for the first time at Luton where Ronnie was forced to make two changes from Dalglish's last match in charge. Mike Hooper came in for Bruce Grobbelaar, who had a stomach virus, and Ray Houghton returned to the side in midfield so Barry Venison was moved to replace the suspended David Burrows at left-back.

Liverpool suffered a 3-1 defeat at Kenilworth Road, having led 1-0 at half-time, and Ronnie was left to explain Liverpool's performance to the press for the first time as manager: "I don't know if I'll be doing this again. The chairman asked me to pick the team and told me we'll talk again on Monday."

Ronnie seemed unsure about his future, but relaxed enough to display his sense of humour when asked if he felt any pressure: "Oh no, I can't lose any more hair, can I?"

He then gave his honest opinion on his team's display: "We didn't perform in the second half and Luton deserved the win. But I gave no rollickings to anybody after what's happened in the last 48 hours; it's my job to try to lift them up for the game on Wednesday."

Liverpool were described as 'sloppy and lethargic' in Moran's first game, but he could hardly be blamed for the disillusion among the players at the time, who were still coming to terms with Dalglish's resignation. At this point bookmakers William Hill rated Ronnie as the even money favourite to replace Dalglish permanently with Hansen (7-2), Souness and Toshack (6-1), Phil Thompson (8-1) and Phil Neal (12-1), also in the equation.

The following Monday, in a meeting between Ronnie and

Noel White, the chairman informed him that he would carry on with the job until they found a replacement. At this time Moran made it clear to him he didn't want to be the manager on a permanent basis.

"I spoke to the chairman and told him that I couldn't do the job long term," Moran said. "I would only have been cheating them and I told them I wanted to go back to doing what I had been doing in the background."

Moran's decision was supported by two people close to him.

"I was really proud my dad was the manager of Liverpool Football Club and that could never be taken away from the record books," his son, Paul, says. "I remember him saying at first he wouldn't take the job on a permanent basis as he wanted to carry on being a coach."

Phil Thompson, who was in charge of the reserves at this time, was prepared to help Ronnie during this transition: "I stepped up and helped Ronnie and Roy; it was the three of us. Ronnie straight away said: 'I don't want this. I can't handle the press. I can do all the things on the training field, but not dealing with the media, signings and everything.'"

Kenny Dalglish later spoke about Ronnie's decision of originally not wanting to be his long-lasting successor: "If you're happy with what you're doing, stay with what you're doing. If you want to have a go, then have a go. If he did have a go, Ronnie could always come back to what he was doing. Irrespective of whether he was manager or not, his contribution was massive."

On February 27, Moran took his team across Stanley Park to face Everton again in the FA Cup fifth round second replay. Moran was to turn 57 the following day and his only wish was to take Liverpool into the next round of the cup. However, it wasn't to be as Dave Watson, who represented Liverpool's youth team in the late Seventies, scored the only goal of the game after 12 minutes. Despite creating numerous chances to get back into the game, Liverpool's strike force was denied time and time again by Everton goalkeeper Neville Southall.

"One man saved Everton in the second half and that's what his job is all about," Ronnie told the press.

"Ronnie wasn't any different when he took over from Kenny, but I remember his half-time team talk in the second replay against Everton was different to his usual calm simple words of advice that he usually delivered," Glenn Hysen remembers. "Ray Houghton had a shocking first half and Ronnie didn't half let him know about it. This was the only occasion during my time at Liverpool that he really dished out a rollicking in front of the other players in the dressing room. Little Ray just sat there and said: 'Sorry, sorry boss.'"

The elder statesman of the squad, Alan Hansen, was named as a possibility if Liverpool followed tradition and hired a manager from within. Alan didn't have any interest in the job, but couldn't resist pulling everyone's leg as he was a practical joker at heart.

The morning after the cup exit Hansen announced to Roy Evans, Tom Saunders and Ronnie Moran in the coaches' changing room at Anfield that he had been hired as the manager of the club. He then walked out, listening in on their conversation, before re-entering a couple of minutes later to tell them that it was total fabrication. He then convinced Evans and Moran to call a meeting the following day with the players in the dressing room at Anfield before training at Melwood.

John Barnes described events: "Alan stood behind an old, creaky treatment table in the middle of the dressing room when he declared: 'The board have offered me the manager's job and I've taken it. Things are going to change. I know where you live and which pubs and clubs you go to. Your drinking has got out of hand and it's going to have to stop. Steve Nicol, you are not allowed to go out to the pub ever again.'"

Barnes continues describing the confusing scene: "Alan declared that there would be training every day and that Nicol would be his new captain. Hansen then left the stunned dressing room, where only Ronnie and Roy were in on the joke. Two minutes later Hansen came back in again and said: 'Only kidding, I'm just retiring.'"

Despite the team having suffered defeats in both of Ronnie's matches as manager, Barry Venison backed him for a permanent appointment as boss.

"Ronnie won't change his style, but it's different seeing him standing up and talking when Kenny Dalglish used to say things," Venison told the *Echo*'s Ric George. "Ronnie has got a lot on his hands, but he has got the respect of all the boys, and his approach will never change. The only thing that is different at the moment is one man's point of view. If he got the job, I think the players would be absolutely delighted. I think he'd be their choice. We know we can talk to Ronnie, whereas if an outsider was appointed it would take time to build relationships. A new man would change things because he'd have different ideas."

Only goal difference separated Moran's side and league leaders Arsenal, who had displaced Liverpool in the top spot the previous weekend. Their encounter at Anfield on March 3 was already dubbed the title decider. Paul Merson's 43rd-minute strike sealed Liverpool's first home defeat of the campaign and only their second since Arsenal grabbed the title from them in dramatic circumstances in the spring of 1989.

The club seemed in full-blown crisis after three defeats in a row and had already contacted former skipper, Graeme Souness, but wasn't ready to move ahead with a deal.

Liverpool had also enquired about the availability of former striker, John Toshack, who had just returned to Real Sociedad as manager. He had once left Sociedad mid-contract to guide Real Madrid to the La Liga title in the 1989/90 season and the Basque club made it abundantly clear that was not about to happen again and had put a £1.5million compensation clause into Toshack's contract that any interested club would have to fork out for his release.

"I found it very flattering Liverpool should be interested in me, but when I signed with Real Sociedad a few months ago I was happy to commit myself to them for five years and that has not changed," Toshack told the press.

Ronnie's mind was put to rest, at least for the time being, before a trip to eighth-placed Manchester City. Noel White announced to the players and press that caretaker Moran had been appointed manager until the end of the season and as far as a long-term appointment was concerned they were keeping their options open. The decision on Moran's continued stay as boss had been the last item on the agenda at the two-and-a-half-hour board meeting: "He (Moran) was highly delighted.

He's looking forward to getting stuck in and getting the results for us now," White declared.

Whether the vote of confidence in Ronnie inspired Liverpool is open to conjecture, but two penalties by Jan Mølby put Liverpool 2-0 up against City before John Barnes secured Moran's first win. A less than convincing 2-1 win over Sunderland was followed by a stunning 7-1 triumph at the Baseball Ground against soon-to-be-relegated Derby County on a day when the Reds went back to the top of the table. Liverpool had also cut the Gunners' superior goal difference down from 10 to four. The 7-1 landslide was the club's first away win by a margin of six goals in 33 years.

"I wouldn't say we had arguments in the dressing room, but we pointed out one or two things we'll have to work on," said the never-satisfied Moran to the media after the match. It wasn't in Ronnie's nature to boast or gloat about results. In fact, after the game he just told his son how badly Derby had played.

Next up was a visit from 17th-placed QPR. Liverpool crashed to a 3-1 defeat in front of a home crowd who witnessed their team play without commitment.

"I'm smiling, but I'm choked inside," Ronnie told the press. "I've never been able to understand why players can run around in the second half but not in the first half."

When he was asked if injuries were a contributing factor to his team's defeat, Ronnie answered: "Injuries? I hope some players have injuries in their hearts. I know I have."

Liverpool's hopes of winning their 19th league title took a blow as Arsenal overtook them in the league. A further defeat away to Southampton at the Dell two days later put the Gunners firmly in charge of the championship's destiny.

On April 9, Ronnie could only drive his side to an uninspiring 1-1 home draw against Coventry City and an astonishing game was to follow against Leeds United at Elland Road, which along with Goodison Park and Highbury, was Ronnie's favourite away ground. Liverpool won 5-4 after leading 4-0 with less than half an hour played.

The Sunday Times gave their assessment: 'Liverpool now resembled nothing so much as a dozing lion. In terms of sheer quality, what team in the land can match the electric skills of Rush, Beardsley and Barnes when they are truly on song, as they so emphatically were yesterday? All of which leads you to wonder how much the Liverpool crisis has essentially been one of morale, caused perhaps by the sheer trauma of Kenny Dalglish's going.'

Ronnie told his son, jokingly, after the game: "We were working on attacking plays all week and never had time to sort the defence out."

Barnes and Beardsley had been a handful for Leeds' defence, coming in from the wings. "It was a little system we'd been working on, something I remembered from our days in Europe," Ronnie told the press.

Around this time, Paul Moran says, his dad visited Liverpool's hierarchy with a dramatic change of heart. Ronnie told Noel White that he had realised that, in fact, he would like to try to do the job on a full-time basis. Phil Thompson recalls: "After a few good weeks Ronnie decided that he could handle the job. He went to see Peter Robinson and Noel White and said: 'I can do this. If you want to offer me the job again, I'll take it.' They went: 'Ronnie, I wish you had come last week because we've got a new manager. It's Graeme Souness.' Ronnie's chance of being the manager of Liverpool Football Club ended then and there."

Ronnie reacted to the news in typical style. "If Graeme wants me to work with him I will be more than happy to do so," Ronnie told Ken Rogers of the *Liverpool Echo* before the unveiling of Souness. "Graeme is exactly the right type of character for a big job like this. We all know that Graeme doesn't like losing. He is one of our kind. I was working with the first-team when he first arrived at Anfield. At first he was a bit of a gentle giant, expecting us to tell him what to do on the pitch, but he soon came into his own. He is a good organiser and always got the very best out of the people around him. He has got an easy going nature, but he is also tough. I would say he is a Liverpool type of bloke. I am sure he will come here and prove he is a winner."

Moran's managerial career had been cut short, but he had been a willing deputy with a record of four victories, one draw and five defeats. He was extremely proud of serving as the acting manager of Liverpool Football Club.

"I have enjoyed these last few weeks. We've not had the kind of results I might have wanted, but it has been an experience," Ronnie told the *Echo*.

Moran and Souness had been expected to reign at their respective clubs until the end of the campaign, but once the secret got out, Souness' position at Rangers had become untenable.

Souness had been present at Liverpool's game against Coventry seven days before he was officially appointed, but no-one had suspected what was going on, as Tommy Smith told the *Echo* after the news broke. "I was a little bit surprised. When I saw him at Anfield last week all we talked about was

Ray Kennedy's testimonial match coming up at Highbury. But that's typical of Liverpool. Do things first and then talk about it later."

Tommy added: "Ronnie Moran, Roy Evans and Phil Thompson all know Graeme and good luck to him. I've always thought Ronnie would get the job, but I'm sure Ronnie will be there after the appointment."

On April 16, Liverpool's former captain was unveiled at Anfield.

"How many people are asked to manage Liverpool Football Club?" Souness asked the press, before declaring that, at present, Liverpool "play the best football of any club side in Britain, maybe Europe and maybe the world."

One of Moran's former pupils from his reserve team side in the late Sixties, Phil Boersma, also swapped Ibrox for Anfield, but Souness swiftly informed Ronnie that he wanted him to continue as chief coach. He was obviously happy with Souness' decision as he still had a job at the club he loved.

Despite Souness' optimism, Liverpool failed to ignite and cut down the five-point lead Arsenal had when he took charge at Anfield. The second-place finish came with qualification for European football in the form of the UEFA Cup, which was the first time in six years Liverpool were eligible to qualify for Europe due to the Heysel ban.

The extra travelling that came with playing in Europe again was something that didn't bother Ronnie one way or the other. Sight-seeing in foreign countries wasn't something that particularly interested him. It was all about football.

When Ronnie came back from trips to places like Vienna and Athens, his son would ask him: "What was the place like?" and

Ronnie would simply reply: "I only left the hotel to go to the game."

"It had nothing to do with my dad becoming forgetful," Paul adds, "but if a big match was on the telly at Anderlecht's ground, for example, I'd say to him: 'You've been there' and he genuinely wouldn't know he had."

Souness introduced some changes to training as his first pre-season started that didn't go down too well with the Bootroom boys.

"Ronnie and Roy were looking to do it the old Liverpool Way; tried and trusted over the years. A load of 440m and 880m runs, done at intervals, rest periods in between," Ronnie Whelan said.

Whelan and his teammates discovered that Boersma and Souness had other ideas and ordered two pre-season sessions nearly every day.

"We'd face 20 minutes of envelope running as ordered by Boey and Souey," said Whelan. "Across the back of goal, reach the corner flag, then a long diagonal run to the flag in the bottom corner, up the side of the pitch, reach the corner flag, then a long diagonal down to the other corner: half-pace, three-quarter pace, jog across the back of goal and repeat the process for 20 minutes."

Strains, hamstring and groin injuries became commonplace and Ian Rush, Barry Venison and Jimmy Carter all fell victim to Achilles tendon injuries that could be linked directly to a change in training methods.

"I'd just come from holiday and my limbs and muscles weren't up to such strenuous work at such an early stage," Ian Rush noted. "Long runs were of little benefit to me. My game was all about speed off the mark and I needed short, sharp sprints, not seven-mile runs."

Since the days of Shankly the players were used to meeting up at Anfield prior to training, then go on a coach to Melwood and return to Anfield after training.

"When we were developing Melwood I decided against having a place there where the players could eat," Shankly explained. "I felt it was most important that, after training, the boys should have a cooling-off period before they took a bath and had a meal, and the 45 minutes between the end of training and arriving back at Anfield was just right. If you have a hot bath when you're perspiring, you perspire all day. Our system prevented the players from catching colds and it also made sure they were not strangers to their home ground."

Souness scrapped this system and made the players meet up at Melwood, arguing that it would be easier to have the headquarters at one place, keeping the players away from the ever-increasing hustle and bustle at the stadium. Even the hallowed Bootroom made way as Liverpool needed bigger space to accommodate the media.

Peter Robinson, who was the club's chief executive at the time, said that Liverpool simply had to move on from the Shankly era and those important decisions were ultimately taken by the hierarchy of the club.

"Initially a lot of players didn't have cars and we felt that it would be better for the players to report directly to Melwood each day and to train and be fed there rather than to ride up and down in an old coach as they used to," Robinson said. "Football was moving on. We also needed to have an after-match press room and the Bootroom was the ideal area for it."

The diet also changed as Souness brought with him what he'd learned while playing for Sampdoria in Italy. Boiled fish, chicken, pasta and salads made their way to the Melwood canteen. Ian Rush's quip that Liverpool won the double on fish and chips only produced a wry smile from Souness.

Rob Jones was the signing of the 1991/92 season for the Reds, a throwback to the days when the club found gems in the lower divisions, like Ray Clemence and Kevin Keegan at Scunthorpe, Phil Neal at Northampton and Ian Rush at Chester.

"When I first joined the club my grandad, Bill, would come and watch me play and also a couple of times popped down to Melwood during training," Jones says. "What was always nice to see was my grandad and Ronnie reminiscing about the old days with huge smiles across their faces. It was obvious to anyone that they had a lot of respect for one another.

"Ronnie started playing when my grandad was coming to the end of his career, but they did go on the tour of America together in 1953.

"What I liked about Ronnie was he always treated the players in exactly the same way, whether it was Rob Jones coming from Crewe or an already proven star coming from a bigger club. Ronnie's attitude was always the same towards them: 'Come on lad, get your kit on, put your boots on and get out there and train.' That's the way he was brought up and was taught by Shanks."

Jones says it was evident that Souness' new training methods were not to Moran's liking.

"I remember when the sports scientists were brought in by Graeme Souness," Rob says. "Ronnie, being old school, was obviously against this. He would always want to keep things basic, playing the five-a-side games and being in favour of correcting mistakes within these mini-games. Ronnie never wanted things to be complicated."

Glenn Hysen agrees that the experienced coaching staff weren't keen on the changes Souness was implementing.

"I can never understand why Souness did this," Hysen says. "He would be in almost everyone's all-time Liverpool XI. He knew how things were done at Liverpool and won endless titles doing it the Bootroom way. He knew first hand it worked. Therefore, changing it didn't make sense.

"He dropped me for his first game and I went from being captain to playing for the reserves. All he said to me was: 'You're out, big man!' Ronnie was very supportive to me during this time and would always say to me: 'Keep working, keep going and you'll get another chance.' Ronnie's advice was very helpful and I came back into the team for the last game of the season versus Tottenham."

Souness picked Hysen only five times from the start in the 1991/92 season with two further substitute appearances. He left for his native Sweden in February 1992.

Graeme Souness had been far from a well man since he had been appointed boss at Liverpool. "I took the Liverpool job without realising I'd need heart surgery," he said in 2000. "It must have affected my day-to-day relationships because I lived with permanent, terrible headaches. I used to take Solpadeine when I woke up in the morning, Solpadeine at lunch-time, Solpadeine at tea-time and Solpadeine before I went to bed.

I didn't know what was wrong with me. Taking Solpadeine was the only way to get through the day. It wasn't the stress of being Liverpool manager that was causing it – it was high blood pressure. I would think it made me a very difficult person to be around."

On April 6, 1992, Moran took over the reins as manager for the second time in two seasons as Souness had to undergo triple by-pass heart surgery at the Alexandra Hospital in Cheadle. At this stage of the season, Liverpool's hopes of European glory were gone and their inconsistent league form meant they were sitting fourth in the league. Liverpool's only chance of silverware was the FA Cup and a semi-final replay against Portsmouth was on the horizon.

Ronnie was more than happy to deputise as manager again but knew for sure this time around it was only ever going to be temporary. Souness was effectively still in charge and Ronnie was in constant telephone contact with Graeme, who was still making all the important decisions from his hospital bed.

Ronnie's first task of his second managerial stint was to entertain Wimbledon at Anfield on Wednesday, April 8, 1992. As it was only a day since Souness' operation, Liverpool's team selection was Moran's responsibility.

With the semi-final replay only five days away, Moran was in no mood to take risks, fielding just five members of the side that began the game against Portsmouth the previous Sunday in the original semi-final. John Fashanu's penalty sealed a 3-2 victory for the Dons.

After the game Ronnie told the press: "We started off a bit shaky, I don't know whether it was because the manager was in hospital but the players were warned about this yesterday and today." Ronnie then commented on his team's injury problems that had clearly influenced poor results: "I don't like making excuses, but we were down to the bare bones again. We have had so many injuries we can't get any rhythm going."

Three days later Ronnie's side visited Aston Villa and crashed to a 1-0 defeat. The only goal of the game came from Tony Daley, who robbed left-back Mike Marsh and ran 60 yards with the ball. Daley's shot lacked power but a diving Bruce Grobbelaar could only help the ball in.

"You always blame the last man," Ronnie told the press, "but you have to remember where the ball was lost."

He couldn't resist a little humorous remark when asked about Souness' condition: "Graeme is doing fine but he might be back in bed again after hearing this result."

Two days later, Liverpool revisited Villa Park, this time to face Portsmouth in the FA Cup semi-final replay that turned out to be a dramatic affair. Liverpool had salvaged a draw three minutes from the end of extra-time in their previous encounter. If Portsmouth could reach England's biggest showpiece they would face Sunderland in the first-ever FA Cup final between two Second Division sides. The tie was decided on the cruel lottery of penalties.

Whenever a game had the possibility of going to a shoot-out, Liverpool practised penalties the day before in training. However, the coaching staff never sorted out the penalty takers beforehand as it affected the players' mindset during the game. They would be constantly thinking about the possibility of having to take a penalty later on. It was always a case of asking the players who fancied one the most and then sorting out the order from their reactions. Ronnie could barely watch the proceedings, but Dean Saunders' successful penalty and John Beresford's miss guaranteed Liverpool their fourth FA Cup final in six years, against Sunderland at Wembley on May 9.

The following weekend Liverpool played host to league leaders Leeds United. Although the game finished 0-0, Ronnie was more than happy with his side's performance: "We looked like the team that was going for the championship. Their goalkeeper kept them in it."

However, Ronnie's satisfaction wasn't long-lived as two days later Liverpool suffered their heaviest league defeat for nine years when they visited Highbury. This 4-0 defeat was also the club's worst against the Gunners in 39 years.

Liverpool had strength in depth but their resources were spread a bit thin with the absence of Grobbelaar, Thomas, McManaman, Burrows, Whelan and Wright, but Ronnie couldn't accept such a defeat no matter what the circumstances.

"I'm sick inside, but you can't show that; life must go on," he admitted. "It was embarrassing the way we lost the goals. That was Sunday league defending, but it is not only the men at the back who were at fault."

Ronnie seemed relaxed enough with the press, taking the same approach as Joe Fagan had done during his couple of years at the helm. Never make any excuses and if you played badly, just tell the reporters you played badly. Don't blame anyone and everything was our fault. That way the press can't argue with you and it will be over quicker.

The Arsenal defeat had been Liverpool's fourth game in nine days and the Reds only got two days' rest before a 1-1 draw at Nottingham Forest. The *Guardian* speculated after the game about Moran's future: 'The grapevine on Merseyside has it that

Souness is determined not only to prune the playing staff this summer but to dismantle the Bootroom. Apparently he wants a new No. 2. Steve Coppell's name has been mentioned which would effectively mean no place for Moran, who has support among the board.'

Paul Moran believes Souness had a certain agenda that he wanted to get through.

"Souness did try to change things and we had obviously heard the rumour that he wanted to get rid of my dad," Paul said. "I think Souness didn't want people saying the Bootroom had helped him if he achieved success at Liverpool. He wanted it to be thought of as being a Souness legacy, not a Bootroom one."

Liverpool's final two games before their trip to Wembley were a 2-0 home victory against Manchester United that extinguished their arch enemy's title hopes and a goalless draw at Sheffield Wednesday. Liverpool ended up sixth, with just 64 points, 18 behind eventual winners Leeds United. It was their worst finish in 27 years. This was something Ronnie simply wasn't used to.

Since he joined the first-team staff in 1974, Liverpool Football Club only finished outside the top two on one occasion and in that year, 1981, they won the European Cup and the League Cup.

"If my dad was concerned about our league position he never let it show while away from the ground, but by the same token he never used to strut around claiming all the glory when we were winning things," Paul explains.

Ronnie's task was now to prepare the team for Liverpool's

10th FA Cup final. He had witnessed all the club's previous eight Wembley finals, his first 42 years earlier.

Souness was now out of hospital and recuperating well. Under close supervision of a doctor he was able to attend the final. Despite his presence at the game, Souness was unable to carry out all of his match day duties as manager. He later admitted that he had been in no condition to be there and should have stayed away.

Ronnie would have the honour of leading the team out at Wembley for the second time in his career. However, this time it was different. It wasn't the Charity Shield; it was the FA Cup final!

"I'll have a humdinger of a tie with my jacket. My daughter will think her old dad has gone hip," Ronnie told the *Daily Post*.

Though Ronnie was pleased with the club suit that he'd been given to wear, he was always more comfortable in his daily outfit: "There is a little room near the touchline where I can change into my tracksuit. I can't sit on the bench in my suit. I'll take my tracksuit out there in a bag." Ronnie stayed true to his word.

Ronnie led out the players onto the Wembley turf alongside Sunderland manager, Malcolm Crosby, in front of almost 80,000 spectators.

"It was a very proud moment for me," Ronnie said years later. "I've still got the video at home and it will be something for my grandchildren to watch in years to come. It was a great occasion for us and I introduced the side to the Duchess of Kent."

Prior to the game Ronnie had told his family to take nothing for granted in case Souness had a change of mind and thought he was up for bringing the team out.

"I wasn't certain my dad was leading the team out until he actually emerged out of the tunnel at the front of the team," Paul Moran recalls. "He had obviously told me there was a chance he would be doing it, but it was never a definite thing. Therefore, I got into the ground slightly earlier than usual. It was a great honour for him and gave the whole family a massive buzz seeing him do it. I think it was the high point of his 49 years there."

Liverpool's right-back that day, Rob Jones, vividly remembers Ronnie's big moment. "I can just see him now in his suit and how proud he was in his face. After all those years, seeing the team win all sorts, for him to lead us out gave me and all the players such a lift. Although Graeme was there, he had no intention of leading the team out. We all knew that Ronnie was going to do it and what a good job he did. He led us to victory!"

Liverpool beat Sunderland 2-0 to clinch their fifth FA Cup. Michael Thomas and Ian Rush were the goalscorers. Steve McManaman came into the side after Barnes failed a late fitness test. This was McManaman's first game in a month after injuring his cartilage in the first semi-final against Portsmouth. He had undergone knee surgery to remove a piece of bone. Ronnie paid a glowing tribute to the 20-year-old who was named man of the match.

"We don't usually individualise at Liverpool," he told the press, "but Steve's switch from left to right in the second half changed the game for us. Steve has always been a lad of tremendous potential and today he proved how good he is. He's come through to make the best of the situation with all the injuries we have had this season and now he has got a great chance to go on from here."

As well as dishing out rare praise, Ronnie admitted that "our passing wasn't sharp enough in the first half and give credit to Sunderland, they had a couple of chances to score. Once we got the break in the second half we were on our game. But we never eased up because you need a third goal before you can get the cigars out."

Captain Mark Wright lifted the trophy, but the presentation of the medals left the Football Association's officials sporting faces as red as the Liverpool shirts. Dejected Sunderland players stared in disbelief at the medals they received from the Duke of Kent that were labelled: 'FA Cup winner 1992', but the mishap was quickly corrected.

"The Sunderland lads came over to our players at the end and told them about the problem," Ronnie said. "Most of them swapped on the pitch and there were just one or two missing, but that's all sorted out now."

More joy was to come for the Morans when they got back to Liverpool.

"My dad phoned me and my sister the following morning and told us to meet him with the kids at the police grounds in Aigburth as he was going to take the grandkids on the bus to parade the trophy around the city," Paul says. "Unfortunately, my sister Janet and her husband Chris got stuck in traffic and we just arrived as the bus was leaving. Everyone was already on the bus and my dad said: 'You're here now, just get on!' so we all piled on the bus, another great memory for us all."

Kirkdale-born Steve McManaman joined Liverpool as a schoolboy in 1987 and quickly got to know the inner workings of the club and the man who made sure everyone was on their toes.

"I started working at Anfield as an apprentice," McManaman said. "I was forever pumping the balls, washing the kit, hanging the kit up, doing all the menial work that the YTS lads did and it was Ronnie Moran who was checking my work."

"As a YTS we travelled to Melwood with the first-team for training, so we were in contact with the first-team staff on a daily basis. The young lads used to train separately to the first-team, but if they had any injuries or any problems you would get the shout over from Ronnie or Roy."

McManaman was eager to impress his mentors. "As a young lad I was extremely privileged to be in the presence of people who had been involved in winning European Cups. Ronnie was very well respected and any sort of knowledge and advice that he gave me was like gold dust really."

By the age of 17, Steve trained regularly as part of the first-team and was always moving closer to his big break. "Before my debut against Sheffield United in 1990 I was with the first-team for about a year, but due to the small number of substitutes allowed, I was always 15th or 16th man from a squad of 16. Ronnie was watching the reserves all the time, so I was in constant contact with him," Steve says.

McManaman scored 14 goals in 26 matches in the Central League in the 1990/91 season, but the highlight of the campaign was when he came on for Peter Beardsley in a 2-0 win against Sheffield United on December 15, 1990.

He got another short run-out in January but had 20 minutes to impress in the last game of the season, a 2-0 victory against Tottenham. Liverpool had lost out on the title and the Spurs players had their sights on Wembley, where they eventually beat Nottingham Forest.

Dalglish had been replaced by Souness as Liverpool boss but Moran was still the man who guided Steve throughout his introduction to top-flight football.

"Anything he said was never too complicated and he made it sound as simple as possible," McManaman said. "As far as I'm concerned they are the best instructions you can ever get as a player.

"As a youngster, if I felt I wasn't getting a kick of the ball for a long time, I would go hunting for it. Ronnie would always shout: 'Steve, be patient.' 'Get your boots on the touchline, Steve!' 'You've got the beating of him, so go and take him on.' Ronnie knew that if I made the pitch as wide as possible, then I would only have to take on one player to create a goalscoring opportunity, rather than going inside and having to beat three or four."

The word 'simple' played a big part in Moran's football philosophy that had been inherited from Shankly.

"Everything we do here is for a purpose," Shankly once said. "It has been tried and tested and it is so simple that anybody can understand it. But if you think it is so simple that it is not worth doing, then you are wrong. The simple things are the ones that count."

Ian Rush remembers Ronnie Moran's simple philosophy of condensing what might be a 15-minute message into something that could be said in 30 seconds, but the striker did sometimes grow tired of Ronnie's constant striving for perfection.

"In training, it wasn't the nine good things that Ronnie focused on, but the one bad thing you had done. He kept going at you."

Liverpool's hold on the league championship had been loosened when Steve McManaman came to prominence but the club still had the personnel who had seen the glory days of the club and carried that winning mentality.

"Nobody had big egos at Liverpool and that's why I think the place flourished really," McManaman says. "It was all about: 'How can we go forward?' It was all very low key. The place was so special; steeped with history, steeped with wonderful players and steeped with people like Ronnie who just passed on information and advice to try and make you a better player. Simplicity was the key for 'Bugsy'. He would always tell us to 'pass the ball to each other as soon as possible, so the team can move through the field,' which is what Barcelona are doing today; exactly the same thing Ronnie Moran was telling Liverpool teams to do 40 years ago."

The wisdom that McManaman picked up from Moran not only benefited him as a player but also in his current advisory role at Liverpool's academy.

"Everything Ronnie told me when I was a player, I now pass on to the academy lads when I work with them," McManaman said. "I'm forever telling youngsters to get wide and make the pitch as big as possible in order for them to be able to beat the full-backs one-on-one with their technique and ability."

The day after having been bestowed with the ultimate honour of leading the Liverpool team out at Wembley, it was evident that Moran was worried that this would be his last hurrah at the club, as Phil Thompson remembers. "I recall a conversation between Tom Saunders, Ronnie, Roy and myself. Ronnie said: 'I am not feeling safe.' I said: 'I have a distinct feeling that something is happening behind my back. I could be looking for a new job in the summer.'"

It turned out that Ronnie was safe but Phil Thompson's

instincts had been spot on. Thompson had earlier that season been reassured by Souness that he had a future at the club by telling him: "I see you as my young Ronnie Moran. I want you with me."

Once the campaign was over Thompson sought reassurance from Souness who, in turn, told him he was going to be sacked and the reason he gave him was that he had been rollicking the young lads in the reserves too much. Thompson had based his modus operandi on Ronnie and believed that while he dished out the verbals he still had a great relationship with the youngsters. They needed to take the negatives and turn them into positives because if the reserves took the next step to the first-team they would be introduced to Ronnie, where they would learn what a real tongue-lashing was.

Ronnie was disappointed to lose one of his best disciples but Thompson's replacement, Sammy Lee, was no stranger to him. The Bootroom spirit at the club was still hanging on.

"When me and my dad were having conversations about the decline he would say: 'Some of the players we have signed aren't Liverpool players and don't fit in to how we have played for a long time or don't want to fit in.' However, my dad would rarely mention any particular players or talk negatively about them behind their backs."

– Paul Moran

Chapter 9

CHANGING OF THE GUARD

1992-1998

THE 1992/93 season didn't get off to the best of starts; in fact it was the worst for 39 years.

An Eric Cantona hat-trick denied Liverpool the Charity Shield in a 4-3 defeat to Leeds at Wembley and by Christmas the Reds were out of Europe and 10th in the Premier League.

Manager, Graeme Souness, was given the dreaded vote of confidence by chairman David Moores.

"The board supports the manager and is fully behind him," Moores said in October. "How can you judge him when seven top players are out injured? I am certain Graeme Souness is just as concerned as the board and really the time to judge is when we have a full-strength squad."

Souness was desperate to improve his defence and brought in Stig Inge Bjørnebye from Rosenborg.

"I made my Liverpool debut in a 5-1 defeat against Coventry City at Highfield Road," Stig Inge says. "Ronnie told me after the game that the result was a huge disappointment for the club, never mind my debut! I soon learned that Ronnie was very critical of everyone who played in the left-back position. The boys told me to get used to it, as it was 'his position'."

Bjørnebye learned that instant positive feedback was not always forthcoming from Ronnie, but once in a while the gods smiled down on him.

"When I scored, he used to say: 'I told you I wanted you to shoot more, son!'" Bjørnebye remembers. "He was also very positive towards my crossing and he used to keep me behind for extra training sessions, solely for crossing and mainly to Rushie. Ronnie was very tough on me and didn't always make me feel good enough or ready for the next game. Later I realised that insecurity kept you on your toes and I thank him for that now."

Liverpool's league position didn't improve and by February they were 15th and chairman Moores was now in a less forgiving mood. "Let me be perfectly frank. Being halfway down the Premier League and out of three major cup competitions is totally unacceptable to Liverpool Football Club."

Liverpool dragged themselves up the table by winning seven of their last 12 league games and ended sixth in the newly-formed Premier League. It was widely expected that Souness would leave before the start of the following season, but the board decided to stick by him, although it rather poignantly appointed Roy Evans as assistant manager.

During the summer of 1993, Souness strengthened his side by spending close to £5million on Nigel Clough and Neil Ruddock. Ruddock's first experience of Ronnie Moran was a positive one. "Liverpool visited the Dell in October 1989. We beat them 4-1 and I was given man of the match. When I was given the award I walked up the stairs and Ronnie Moran was waiting at the top to congratulate me. He just shook my hand and said: 'Well played, son!'"

When he moved to Anfield, though, he discovered that Ronnie wasn't to be messed with.

"'Bugsy' gave an absolute roasting to Don Hutchison for messing around, attaching Budweiser bottle stickers to his dick," Ruddock remembers. "Ronnie used to give me some right bollockings after games. I would have been at fault for a goal by giving away a silly free-kick or the man, who I was supposed to be marking, scored from a corner. The following Monday it would all have been forgotten and he would take me aside and go over what had happened during the game. 'That's football, son' he would say and sometimes he would even apologise, but never in front of the other players as that would show weakness."

Ronnie had to keep an eye on 'Razor' and some of his teammates, and the defender recalls a man the squad were anxious not to upset.

"We would always have respect for 'Bugsy', but we would always be wary of him," Ruddock says. "When we were staying at hotels around England and Europe a few of the lads would get together to play cards of a night. In them days, we had to be in our rooms by 21:30-21:45 and when that time had passed, someone would suddenly shout, 'Shit, Bugsy's coming!' There would be lads in the wardrobes, under the beds and in the bathrooms, so that we could carry on and play the last hand!"

Again, Souness was unable to get his team off to a successful start as his side won just four of their opening 10 games in the 1993/94 season. The League Cup came as a welcome distraction, not only because they beat Fulham 8-1 over two legs, but also because the Kop had a new hero in 18-year-old Robbie Fowler, who scored on his debut in the first leg.

The Toxteth-born striker started two Premier league matches without getting on the scoresheet before the second leg of the Fulham tie took place at Anfield. Fowler wrote himself in the club's history books by becoming only the fifth player to score five goals in one game for the club. Fowler learned that even the most incredible feats failed to impress Ronnie.

"After playing against Fulham and scoring five goals I was feeling well pleased with myself when Ronnie came in the dressing room and said: 'I don't know what you're looking so smug about. You should have scored seven.' Those words will live with me forever and I think they sum up the greatness of the man," Fowler recalls.

Ronnie had followed Robbie's progress long before his breakthrough into the first-team as his finishing skills had been admired in the club's youth teams. Fowler's talent was there for all to see and he was the toast of the town after scoring 18 goals in 34 matches in his debut season.

"It is an incredible thing to become an overnight sensation in the pop era of professional football," Fowler said. "It was a force of nature that I had absolutely no control over. One minute, I was a kid cleaning the baths and throwing the bundles, going home to me mum's little terrace where my nan and grandad also lived. The next I was all over the papers and across the telly, the Toxteth Terror."

Moran's main concern was to help Fowler remain focused and handle his stardom.

"When Ronnie spoke, you listened," Fowler said. "He had your respect before he even opened his mouth. He has a deep, gruff voice, Ronnie, and he doesn't speak loudly, so he was almost whispering when he talked to me.

"He said that a good player would build on the start, would take it into the next game and show he could do it again. The trick was to be doing that in six months, and then six years. Ronnie Moran was a big influence on my career, because he helped me understand what I had to do to be a success, and more importantly to stay there. Ronnie always said getting there was the easy part compared to what came next."

Robbie scored 129 goals in 216 matches for the first-team as his career blossomed until he tore his cruciate knee ligament against Everton in the 1997/98 season. Ronnie knew how important Fowler was to the team's cause and would give him a piece of his mind if he felt it was needed.

"I'm not saying we always saw eye to eye, because he could be a hard man and he often chewed you out," Fowler said. "He didn't bother about reputations. If you did something wrong, he told you and you listened, because you knew he had been there before with the great players of the past."

On January 19, 1994, a 1-1 draw away to Bristol City in the third round of the FA Cup caused concern that later changed to panic when Liverpool lost the replay at Anfield 1-0. This was totally unacceptable and Souness knew it, handing in his resignation the following week.

After a manager's departure, Moran would expect to go through the usual rigmarole of wondering if he still had a job but as it was widely tipped his good friend, Roy Evans, would be Souness' successor, he had less to worry about.

As expected, Evans had enormous faith in Moran and felt more confident in taking on this huge responsibility with his friend in charge of his troops at Melwood. He still felt, though, the need for a right-hand man that came in the form of former player, Doug Livermore, who was appointed assistant manager.

Evans wanted the coaching staff to revert to the tried and trusted methods of the past, but some of the players simply weren't good enough to do what was required of them.

"During my later years at the club, we started to get players in who questioned the way we did things," Ronnie recalled. "They wanted us to change the training depending on whatever system the next opposition would be using. Then after games we had lost these players would say things like: 'If we'd done this and if we'd done that.' I used to say to them, 'well, if you realised that, why didn't you change it out on the pitch?'"

Jamie Carragher emerged as a first-team player in the late 1990s and he remembers the atmosphere in training at the time.

"Ronnie always told the players they were too much of a soft touch," Carragher said. "No-one paid attention, brushing off the comments as the ramblings of an old man. The generation gap couldn't be bridged, even by such a legend as Ronnie."

Paul Moran says his dad complained to him about the lack of quality in the Liverpool squad.

"When me and my dad were having conversations about

the decline he would say: 'Some of the players we have signed aren't Liverpool players and don't fit in to how we have played for a long time or don't want to fit in,'" he said. "One player that springs to mind was Souness' last signing, Julian Dicks. However, my dad would rarely mention any particular players and talk negatively about them behind their backs."

During Roy Evans' time as manager, Moran turned 60 on February 28, 1994. For his 60th birthday Ronnie enjoyed a joint party at his son's house along with daughter-in law, Julie, who turned 30 on the 26th. Apart from friends and family, the party was attended by Sammy Lee, Tom Saunders and Roy Evans.

Evans' task as manager wasn't going to be a straightforward one. The remainder of the 1993/94 season was dreadful. The Reds only managed five wins from their final 16 league games and ended the season eighth, the club's worst finish since 1963.

Liverpool's defence needed bolstering and in September 1994 Evans spent £7.1million on centre-backs Phil Babb and John Scales to provide competition for Neil Ruddock, Mark Wright and 21-year-old Dominic Matteo. The latter was brought to Liverpool at only 11 after catching Kenny Dalglish's eye when he was watching his son, Paul, play for Birkdale United.

"When I first joined the club as a young boy, I remember seeing Ronnie watching us train on a Tuesday and Thursday night," Matteo recalls. "When I left school and became a YTS lad, that's when I worked with Ronnie every day and soon realised that there was something special about him. He just had this unique way of talking to you and helping you out.

"I had plenty of bollockings from Ronnie when I was a YTS. Ronnie and Phil Thompson would check all our jobs and if they weren't done properly we would soon know about it. Ronnie would say: 'Go and clean that again!' I think sometimes with Ronnie he would be testing the water to see how you would react. Ronnie and Phil had been through it all themselves. We all kind of moaned about it, but deep down we enjoyed it as it was part of being a footballer. I just kept my head down, worked hard and did what I was told.

"I found whatever Ronnie said to me throughout my career was always very simple: 'Do things quicker, be better on the ball,' basically just reinforcing all the basics of the game that a footballer needs. He would be constantly reminding us of the little things like your positional play on the pitch or your movement off the ball. When I needed a little push or a little kick, Ronnie would be the one who would give me one and I needed one every now and again! Most of this would be done during the small-sided games in training."

Matteo knew that Moran had the best interests of the players at heart.

"People would say: 'Don't mess with 'Bugsy',' but as far as I am concerned that was all a myth," Matteo says. "When Ronnie told us to do something we just did it. This all came down to the respect he had throughout the football club for everything he had done. Before my debut what made me relaxed was seeing Ronnie relaxed. All the shouting was done on the training field and 'Bugsy' was the complete opposite before a game. He would just give me a few reminders and then tell me to go out there and enjoy myself and win the game.

"Don't get me wrong, if we had a bad result or you didn't play well he would tell you how you should put it right and for me that's what we're missing in the game today. Players will lose too easily now, but in my day Ronnie would make sure that players hated losing."

Just like many players who had experienced working under Ronnie, Matteo had received the best education available, one that he cherished after he had left Liverpool.

"Ronnie was always my reference to where I should be on a football pitch, not only when I was at Liverpool but throughout my entire career," Matteo says. "When I was playing for Leeds, during the games I would be constantly reminding myself of all the little things he had told me. I would later tell the young lads at the club I was with all his tips and advice; the basics of football. Once a player has learned the basics, he will never forget them."

In common with the previous three managers, Fagan, Dalglish and Souness, Roy Evans won silverware in his first full season as manager as his team won the League Cup.

On Sunday, April 2, 1995, Sir Stanley Matthews presented Ian Rush with the trophy as Steve McManaman again grabbed the headlines in a cup final, scoring both of Liverpool's goals as they beat Bolton Wanderers 2-1. This was the club's fifth League Cup and Moran claimed his 23rd trophy as first-team coach. Liverpool improved their final league position from eighth to fourth. The old Bootroom boys had made the players enjoy their football again.

Ronnie's good friend, Kenny Dalglish, was crowned a Premier League champion at Anfield that season, despite the fact Blackburn lost 2-1 to Liverpool in their final league match. Prior to kick-off, Kenny came out of the tunnel and reached across to greet Ronnie, who tried to pull his old boss into the Liverpool dugout. Five years earlier Moran and Dalglish had celebrated a title victory together at Anfield, but despite being on opposite sides this time around, Ronnie was still delighted on Kenny's behalf.

In the summer of 1995, Evans entered the transfer market in search of a future replacement for the great Ian Rush, who was now approaching 34 years of age. Liverpool broke the British record transfer fee by paying Nottingham Forest £8.5million for Stan Collymore's services.

Ronnie started calling Stan 'Fog in the Tunnel' because he was late for training on numerous occasions or just didn't turn up at all. Collymore lived in Cannock, a one-and-a-half-hour drive down the M6.

The relationship between Moran and Collymore came to a head after Liverpool reserves lost 2-0 to Bolton in November 1995, as Jamie Carragher recalls.

"'You'll never get back into the first-team playing like that,' Ronnie told Collymore, before turning his attentions to Mark Walters, who had also been on reserve duty. 'And I could have played against you tonight,' said Ronnie, to which the winger responded, 'Why don't you get your kit on then?'"

Carragher then overheard Collymore in the shower laughing, saying: "I can't get the image of Ronnie trying to run around in his shorts out of my head."

Paul Moran remembers his dad's impressions at the time.

"Of all the players in my dad's time at the club, Collymore is the only one I can remember him saying he never liked," Paul says. "Dad thought Stan was a disruptive influence who felt he was better than everyone else. My dad's career was 49 years at Anfield, winning numerous trophies, whereas Collymore played for many different teams."

One player who was re-emerging was Mark Wright, who had been bought from Derby at the start of the 1991/92 season. He had been criticised for his poor form and attitude in general by Roy Evans, but after a year's absence from the first-team he returned in March 1995 and had two fantastic seasons in 1995/96 and 1996/97. He credits Ronnie as having a lot to do with his rise in fortunes.

"I like the fact that Ronnie was forever kicking my backside and making me think about whether I should be a better player," Wright said. "Roy Evans brought in Scales, Babb and Ruddock. There were offers for me to go. I refused to go. Not only did I want to stay to do a job for Liverpool and say to the fans of Liverpool: 'Listen, I'm still here and I'm not giving in until I make my mark,' it was for Ronnie Moran, who was chipping away: 'You've got to prove yourself.' That, for me as a person, worked."

John Barnes also revealed how Moran tried to make the players simplify their game in order to get them to play to their proper standards. "I remember what he said to Mark Wright once after Wrighty did something. 'Wrighty, what were you thinking?' Wrighty knew it was a loaded question, so he thought, 'I better not answer.' So he put his head down. Ronnie persisted: 'Wrighty, what were you thinking?' Wrighty went: 'Ron, what I thought was…' And Ronnie went: 'See, son. You're thinking too much. Just get on with it.'"

Although Liverpool made a disappointing early exit in the UEFA Cup at the hands of Danish outfit Brøndby, their domestic from continued to improve under Evans during the

1995/96 season, finishing third in the league and reaching the FA Cup final against Manchester United. Liverpool turned up at Wembley in their infamous white Giorgio Armani suits except Ronnie and Roy, who both wore navy blue. "I'm not an ice-cream man!" Ronnie snarled when it was suggested that he should also wear this suit.

"There was no danger of my dad or Roy wearing the white suits, but again it was one of those things that the press focused on," Paul says. "My dad said at the time: 'The players could have even worn dresses if it had meant we'd have won the cup.' The fact that we got beat by United provoked all the criticism. If we'd have won, no-one would have mentioned the suits."

Despite the Liverpool team being dubbed the 'Spice Boys', Ronnie always thought things were blown out of proportion by the press as it wasn't the Liverpool Way for players to be out of line. Things that the press were reporting on had been happening for years. The only difference was that the press coverage had got more intrusive and players at the time weren't ready for it.

It was always Roy's job to sort out the press side of things as Ronnie would concentrate on the football side, but he would always tell the players not to talk to the press as they would twist things round to cause as much trouble as they could. Ronnie only trusted a couple of people in the press. One of them was veteran reporter for local and national papers, John Keith.

Keith followed the Reds as they rose to prominence under Bill Shankly and reigned supreme in England and Europe under the guidance of Shankly's disciple, Bob Paisley.

"I have known Ronnie since the 1960s when the Shankly revolution was in full swing at Anfield and it is a great tribute to him that despite the cascade of success he experienced at the club, he never changed," Keith says.

Ronnie was very appreciative of Keith as he was part of the inner circle at Liverpool as much as any non-football person could be. They told him things off the record because they knew he wouldn't report it. Keith also valued Ronnie greatly.

"Ronnie was one of Liverpool's marathon men and if you asked him something there was no prevarication. He answered directly and forthrightly. He has been a football man in the finest sense, a member of a rare breed and one, I fear, we will never see again. I'm just very glad I've known him and feel privileged to be a friend of his," Keith says.

Midfielder David Thompson, who had been on Liverpool's books since he was a kid, made his first appearances for the first-team in the 1996/97 campaign. Thompson always appreciated Moran's candour, though he could be brutal at times.

"Ronnie could cut you down with one comment," Thompson said. "He was black or white. That's what was good about him. You knew what was going to upset him and you knew what was going to make him happy. He was very passionate."

Thompson was the quintessential cheeky Scouser, who was starting to make his presence felt among the big heads. One day, just after signing a new contract, he was sitting with Jamie Carragher in the foyer at Melwood, looking pretty smug, haggling over how many tickets they were entitled to for first-team games.

"Ronnie just walks past and goes, 'What are you two dickheads doing here?'" Thompson remembers. "'I've just signed a new contract, Ronnie,' I told him proudly. 'What, they've given you a new contract? You've only been doing well for two minutes. You're nowhere near good enough yet.' Then he jumped on the bus and left me there. I felt like I had been buried in the ground."

Steven Gerrard was a YTS player at the time whose growth spurt had caused him back problems that had severely restricted his progress as a teenager. Just like any youth player on the books of the club with big dreams to fulfil, he had certain menial tasks to perform and that included pumping balls at Melwood, supervised by Ronnie.

"Ronnie Moran, that great old Liverpool coach, would fine us if we failed to inflate every single ball to perfection," Gerrard says. "So we pumped and pumped and pumped in the ball room, and yelped with laughter because, every time, we had to battle through one of Joe Corrigan's shites."

Former Manchester City great and then Liverpool's goal-keeping coach, Joe Corrigan, had been part of the setup at Melwood from 1994. "It was the time of the morning when Big Joe settled down on the toilet. His favourite cubicle was right next door to the ball room. While we pumped the footballs we had to listen to Joe's clockwork rituals in the khazi and, even more disturbingly, risk being suffocated by the powerful fumes he generated," Gerrard remembers.

The club's youth players would arrive at Melwood at 8.30am on a typical day during the 1996/97 season. One of their first tasks upon arrival was bringing the coaching staff's kit from the laundry room to the changing room, leaving it there nicely folded. An hour later, the YTS players, the reserves and the first-team were supposed to be fully kitted out, ready for that day's training session.

"We didn't need a bell or anything to let us know when it was time to get going because Ronnie Moran always made a point of banging on all the dressing room doors and bellowing out, 'Away the noo, lads!'" YTS apprentice, Mike Yates, recalls.

The whole group, ranging from hopeful youths like Yates and Gerrard to experienced first-team campaigners such as John Barnes and Jamie Redknapp were all assembled, awaiting instructions from the trainers; Ronnie, Sammy Lee, Steve Heighway and Hughie McAuley.

A gentle warm-up was followed by a couple of laps, the first a jog and the second at a quicker pace, around the perimeter of the training ground, taking care to stretch at any corner. The youth team, reserves and the first-team were then split up, having their own routines to follow. The first-team played small-sided matches and did passing/shooting drills, while the YTS lads focused on the technical aspects of the game that the seniors were already supposed to have mastered. Once the training was over the apprentices had to clean all the boots used by the squad.

"Ronnie Moran had a habit of popping his head into the boot room while I was in there to constantly remind me to put a ring of Dubbin (wax to waterproof leather) around the soles of the boots so they wouldn't crack," Yates recalls.

On November 27, 1996, Yates and a couple of other apprentices were asked to stay behind after training by Joe Corrigan to take shots at the three goalkeepers to prepare them for a League Cup game against Arsenal that evening. Ronnie was almost fanatical that all the balls were pumped up to the full

12psi air pressure as he wanted them to 'zing and ping at all times', otherwise he would hunt down the apprentices and really give them an earful.

After the shooting drill had wound down, Ronnie Moran, Roy Evans and Joe Corrigan were still out on the training pitch along with the apprentices. "I was banging a few balls into the net when I heard Jamie Carragher shout to me to knock one over to him," says Yates, who became a Liverpool academy coach.

"There was a shiny, new Mitre Delta right in front of me, so I just touched it out of my feet with the outside of my right foot and then absolutely pinged it. I really caught it sweet and it flew like a rocket towards Jamie. As I was admiring its trajectory, I suddenly realised that big Joe Corrigan was heading back to the dressing room and he'd walked straight into the line of the ball's flight path. Before I could shout any kind of warning it clocked him straight on the back of the head, sending him sprawling forward across the A team pitch.

"The gloves he was carrying flew out of his hands and into the air before landing next to his prostrate body. Everyone saw it happen and immediately burst out laughing," Yates recalls.

Corrigan suffered a concussion and by doctor's orders he was absent from the Arsenal match that Liverpool won 4-2. Yates was mortified about this incident – that Steven Gerrard later called the funniest thing he had ever seen at the training ground – but at least it must have given Ronnie some satisfaction that the balls had been pumped up to his required standard!

Jamie Carragher made his first-team debut during the 1996/97 pre-season, but had already caught Ronnie's eye a couple of years before making his breakthrough.

CHANGING OF THE GUARD

"In 1994, I left school and started playing in midfield for the reserves and Ronnie used to come and watch," Carragher recalls. "We got to the final of the Youth Cup in 1996 and the normal centre-back was suspended. The youth team coaches at the time – Hugh McAuley and Steve Heighway – didn't know what to do. Ronnie told them to play me there as it looked as if I was going to end up playing at centre-back. It was Ronnie's initial idea and it turned out well in the end, I think.

"I always remember something Ronnie Moran used to say when I first joined: 'If your two centre-backs play well, no matter how everyone else plays you've got a chance of winning the game,' and I think he's right. If your two centre-backs build a partnership, don't get too many injuries and can play week-in week-out you can build from that."

Ronnie was eager for Carragher to make his debut with the first-team.

"In the summer of 1996, the first pre-season game we played was away at Crewe," Carragher says. "During the second half I was hoping to get on to make my debut. I always remember sitting behind Ronnie and Roy Evans and Ronnie turned to Roy and said: 'Shall we give him a go?' I thought 'here's my chance' but Roy said: 'No, we'll leave it how it is.' When he said that, my heart sank. However, I did get my chance four days later and funnily enough I made my debut for Liverpool's first-team against Everton, the team I supported when I was a boy, at Goodison Park, which at that stage was the ground I had been to watch more games than anywhere else."

Carragher wasn't overawed when he took his first steps with the first-team as Ronnie didn't bombard him with instructions.

"He would say: 'The reason why you're here in the first-team, son, is because of everything you have done in the youth teams and the reserves,'" Carragher remembers. "People think when you reach the first-team you need a lot of advice from all different kinds of people but that isn't true; you're there on merit. This philosophy was one I used to pass on to the younger players who were just breaking through into the first-team. Nevertheless, Ronnie would always give me a few pointers before the game and at half-time, but nothing too complex and you would then go out there and play your own game."

Carragher made his full debut against Aston Villa at Anfield and got booked 20 seconds after kick-off.

"I wasn't sure if I was going to get a rollicking at half-time for getting booked so early and putting the team under a bit of pressure," said Carragher. "But Ronnie Moran said to me at half-time that this was the best thing that could have happened to me as it calmed me down and stopped me from going into stupid tackles. His words made me feel a lot better! Moran also really made me laugh as he had a great sense of humour."

Carragher recalls with fondness playing in the staff games on Mondays when it was the senior team's day off.

"I used to get picked for the staff team, and everyone knew they felt highly of you if they picked you to play with them," Carragher says. "Ronnie would put himself on the left wing and told us all where we should be moving and what we should be doing. So I would be getting coaching all the way through playing alongside the staff in these small-sided games."

Liverpool's first league match of the 1996/97 season was at Middlesbrough. Liverpool were leading 3-2 when Fabrizio Ravanelli, who the Reds had been chasing that summer, equalised in the 81st minute, completing his hat-trick. Carragher, who was sitting on the bench, had a hard time not to burst out laughing as Boro fans celebrated the equaliser. "As the third goal went in, Ronnie had been squirting the contents of a Lucozade bottle into his mouth," Carragher says. "A screaming woman in a Boro shirt raced, arms aloft, towards where we were sitting, as though she had just witnessed a cup final winner. Cool as you like, Ronnie aimed the bottle towards her and squirted her in the face."

Liverpool were aiming for the title and if they beat Manchester United at Anfield in mid-April, they would go top of the Premier League with just three games to go. Liverpool were without Robbie Fowler, who had been sent off in the previous game, along with Everton defender David Unsworth in the 156th Merseyside derby. Once the players had been shown the red cards, Robbie retaliated again and had to be escorted off the pitch by Ronnie and physio Mark Leather. Liverpool were without their star striker for the remainder of the campaign. A 3-1 defeat to United virtually gave Alex Ferguson's men their fourth Premiership title in five years. Although they ended up finishing fourth, Liverpool had been playing their best football since the late Eighties.

During the 1997/98 season Moran missed a game on the Liverpool bench for the first time since he was promoted to the first-team staff in 1974. His wife, Joyce, was taken ill on the morning of the match against Arsenal at Highbury on November 30, 1997. Liverpool beat Wenger's Gunners 1-0 and went on to win six out of the next eight league matches, moving up to third, five points behind leaders Manchester United.

Liverpool lost their way, but still managed to finish in third place, 13 points away from champions Arsenal. For the fourth season in a row Liverpool had finished in the top four. Although Evans would have been content with his team's progress, the board wasn't and radical changes were looming.

In the late 1990s only the top two clubs from the English league used to qualify for the Champions League. Since Liverpool's last participation in Europe's elite competition was in 1985, the club was desperate to find a way to get back. Principally, the role they were looking for was a director of football. They approached John Toshack at first, as not only did he understand Liverpool Football Club but he also had experience of the continental game in Spain where he had won La Liga with Real Madrid and the Spanish Cup with Real Sociedad. Toshack was considered the best man for the role, but he declined as he was only really interested in being the boss.

After the completion of the 1997/98 season, manager Roy Evans had been made aware of the club's new vision and had to carry out the most difficult task of his time as manager, if not his entire life. He was asked by chief executive Peter Robinson to inform Ronnie, Roy's friend of 35 years, that he wanted to see him and to let Ronnie know, as well, what this conversation with the hierarchy was going to entail.

Evans approached Ronnie at Anfield one morning in May 1998 and told him that Robinson wanted to see him. Moran was optimistic about his imminent meeting with PBR (as he was known) and speculated that maybe he was going to be given a new contract as his current one was up for renewal.

Roy revealed to Moran that 'the powers that be' had brought in a new club policy which set the compulsory retirement age of all full-time employees at 65 years old and that Robinson was not going to offer him a new contract.

CHANGING OF THE GUARD

In the meeting that Ronnie dreaded by now, Robinson explained to Moran that the club was exploring new options and there was no longer any room for him on the coaching staff.

Ronnie, who was turning 65 in February, did as he had done all his career at Liverpool and put the club first. He did not want to cause Liverpool Football Club any problems. Roy Evans was disappointed with the board's decision as he felt Ronnie was far from past his best, but he would have had to take on all the board to overturn this ruling.

"There is a common misconception about my dad's retirement," said Paul Moran. "He did not willingly retire as he had no plans of retiring whatsoever and wanted to carry on as normal. He left the stadium in tears and drove home to break the news to my mum and then obviously the rest of the family. I can remember the devastation in his eyes when he told me and all the family tried to rally round him."

In May 1998, Moran's 49 years at Liverpool Football Club came to an abrupt end. Ronnie Moran sat on the Liverpool bench for an incredible 1,365 out of a possible 1,366 official first-team games from 1974-1998. In 24 seasons he had coached Liverpool teams to achieve 23 of the club's 34 major honours that were won prior to 1998. Ronnie could rank himself as one of the best-ever coaches in Europe with 10 league titles and four European Cups to his name.

"My dad never had a bad word to say about the club after leaving as he loved his time there. Kenny kindly brought Celtic down for the [testimonial] game. There was a fantastic turnout by the former players. My dad had 49 wonderful years at Liverpool and you can see to this day what he means to Liverpool fans."

– Paul Moran

Chapter 10

LIFE AFTER LIVERPOOL

1998-2012

THE English game was going continental and supporters were now getting used to the arrival of foreign players and coaches.

In the summer of 1998, Peter Robinson, on behalf of the Liverpool board, contacted the technical director of the French Football Federation, Gérard Houllier, who had already been offered jobs as boss at Celtic and Sheffield Wednesday. Robinson and Houllier had become friends when the Frenchman spent a year in Liverpool from 1969-70 as an assistant schoolteacher at Alsop Comprehensive School.

"The board and Roy Evans agreed we needed to strengthen the management and coaching staff. We discussed names that might have been suitable, when I noticed in the papers that Gérard was considering offers from a couple of British clubs," Robinson told the *Liverpool Echo*. "I picked up the phone and said: 'I'm just ringing to congratulate you on wherever you go.' I was fishing, of course, and then told Gérard that whatever club he was going to, it was the wrong one. I told him he should be coming to Liverpool. He then told me he was not committed. I was on a plane to Paris the following morning."

After further discussions with Evans, Houllier was appointed joint-manager on July 16, 1998 and brought with him his former coach from Lens, Patrice Bergues, who took Ronnie's position on the coaching staff.

Houllier's appointment was a drastic move away from the old Bootroom philosophy that had reigned since Shankly's arrival in 1959. What made it highly unusual was that Liverpool opted for joint-managers, an idea that Peter Robinson claimed he had been hesitant in approaching at first.

Roy Evans had initially thought that Houllier was being approached to be Moran's successor as chief coach. If not, then a director of football, the position John Toshack had refused to contemplate taking on. It certainly looked like Evans, was, in fact, a dead man walking and only three months into this experiment another Bootroom boy was gone.

"Arsène Wenger had revolutionised Arsenal, and France had just won the World Cup. It seemed like a sensible idea to get Houllier in as joint-manager and work together," Evans said. "I let my heart rule my head. Deep down, I knew it wasn't right. I wasn't strong enough to insist that he would only be a director of football. I should have said that under no circumstances can two men do the same job. The board should have known that too. It had been tried at other clubs and it hadn't worked," Evans said.

The last of the Bootroom boys had gone, but Liverpool kept a local connection with the appointment of Phil Thompson as Houllier's assistant manager after a six-year absence from the club.

"The hardest thing for my dad is when he realised his day-to-day involvement at the club had finished. It devastated him," Paul Moran says. "He wasn't the same person for a good few months after that. He was okay with the family but he had to bite his lip when people wished him a happy retirement. As always he put the club first and if that's what Liverpool wanted, he would go along with it and not cause a fuss."

Moran certainly didn't let on anything was amiss when he was interviewed in the autumn of 1998.

"Of course it was a wrench to leave because this place has been my life, but I have adjusted quickly," he insisted. "I'm finding plenty of things to do to occupy my time and it's nice to wake up in the morning, look at the weather and decide what I'm going to do for the day. It's a new way of life for me and one I'm enjoying at the moment."

The most successful coach in Liverpool's history was typically understated when he summed up his time at the club.

"I have been lucky enough to work with so many great managers and so many great players," Ronnie said. "It has been an absolute privilege. I like to think that I have been a cog in a wheel and that I have helped in some way with all that the club has achieved.

"It was a great feeling for me to work on things on the training field during the week and then see what we have practised come off during a match. Liverpool Football Club is in my blood and I will forever wish them every success."

'Bugsy', who had seen players come and go in their hundreds during his time at Anfield, was asked to compile his all-time Liverpool XI. This was a team that any player would be proud to be a part of as Ronnie had seen the best in English football up close.

In a 4-3-3 formation he went for Ray Clemence in goal and full-backs were his old teammates Chris Lawler and Gerry Byrne, who had, as well as playing with Moran, been responsible for keeping him out of the team. Alan Hansen and Tommy Smith were in the heart of defence, a blend of silky skills and solid steel. Moran opted for a three-man midfield of Ray Kennedy, Graeme Souness and Ian Callaghan and up front were John Barnes, Kenny Dalglish and Ian Rush. Moran rated Dalglish the best player he had ever worked with and the goal-hungry Welshman was, of course, his favourite. Surprisingly, there was no place for Ronnie's idol, Billy Liddell.

Ronnie had a hard time staying away from the club he had called home for five decades. "I still go down to Melwood two or three mornings a week and do my own thing out of the way of the management team and the players," Ronnie said in 1998.

"It's nice to still be able to go to the training ground as it has been like a second home to me for almost 50 years," he said of the place he renamed his 'prison exercise yard'.

Realising that Ronnie still has something to offer, the club sent him on scouting missions.

"The club scout role was a bit of an honorary title," Paul

says. "I honestly think the club was desperately trying to keep my dad involved. He used to go to watch Chester a bit and I went with him to Port Vale and Burnley, but his heart was never really in it. It was just something for him to do. He was not on the payroll then and received no wage, but did get his expenses covered."

Ronnie's trips also made him miss a number of Liverpool matches throughout the 1998/99 season, although this time he would only have been a spectator at Anfield.

The club did reach out to Ronnie by inviting him and Joyce as guests of the club when Liverpool faced Valencia at the Mestalla in the second round of the UEFA Cup on November 3, 1998. The Reds conceded a goal in first-half stoppage time, but responded with goals from Steve McManaman and Patrik Berger in the last 10 minutes. Paul Ince and McManaman were then both sent off close to the final whistle along with Valencia's Amedeo Carboni. A thrilling match ended 2-2 and Liverpool went through on the away goals rule.

The following week Ronnie was guest of honour at Anfield at a special retirement dinner hosted by Liverpool FC's board, attended by Ronnie's old friends, Joe Fagan and Tom Saunders as well as joint-managers Houllier and Evans and the coaching staff. David Moores thanked Ronnie for his service by presenting him with a cut glass crystal bowl with the Liverpool crest engraved on it.

November proved to be a busy month for Ronnie. On the 16th he was again the focus of attention, this time at the Liverpool Moat House Hotel where John Keith hosted a special Variety Club of Great Britain tribute dinner in Ronnie's honour to support children's charities. Present were former

Liverpool players who wanted to pay tribute to Ronnie. Guests included Peter Thompson, Alan Kennedy, Jimmy Case, David Fairclough, Ian Callaghan, Tony Hateley, Geoff Strong, Dave Hickson, David Johnson, Gary Gillespie and other football luminaries like Mike Summerbee and Brian Labone.

Liverpool FC didn't feel the same to the Moran family after events in 1998.

"I had watched his team home and away for 24 years and suddenly he wasn't there," Paul says. "If my dad had been offered a job by another club, I would have gone and watched them. It's like with my son playing for Bootle, Runcorn Linnets and then Ashton Athletic. I watch him wherever he is and it would have been the same with my dad but he never went anywhere else. I went to roughly 5-10 games a season at Anfield after dad left, usually European games or if we played someone I'd not seen us play before."

Liverpool finished their first season without Moran seventh in the Premier League, their worst finish in five seasons.

"I think it's fair to say Roy knew before my dad left what an influence on the club he had been and that he could still have done a good job in that first season with Houllier," Paul concludes.

By this stage Liverpool had a new goalscoring hero in Michael Owen as the 19-year-old finished as the club's top scorer for the second season in a row. Michael certainly had an admirer in Ronnie.

"All the talk at the moment is of Michael Owen and rightly so because he has done very well," Ronnie said. "He is an excellent player and always has been right through the youth ranks. I've seen a lot of players who were good at 14 or 15 but then they reach that difficult age when other distractions come into their lives and they maybe lose their way a bit. Michael hasn't had that problem though and he is the best youngster I have seen since I have been at the club."

Three years later Owen was voted European Footballer of the Year, becoming the first Briton to win the Ballon d'Or since Kevin Keegan in 1979.

Gérard Houllier's first full season as sole manager didn't start well. After Everton beat Liverpool 1-0 at Anfield at the end of September 1999, the Reds were 12th with only 10 points to their name.

Liverpool's fortunes swiftly changed and they were only defeated twice in the league until the end of April. The team had climbed the table to second place, within reach of finally securing a spot in the lucrative Champions League.

The club had strengthened their defensive resolve with the triumvirate of Sami Hyypia, Stephane Henchoz and Didi Hamann, but weren't scoring enough goals.

Liverpool were nine points behind leaders Manchester United and five points ahead of third-placed Arsenal, who had a game in hand. But it all fell apart in the final weeks of the season during which Houllier's men didn't score a single goal in five matches. Liverpool finished fourth.

Ronnie still followed the fortunes of Liverpool Football Club, but at the start of the millennium his health was failing. On Thursday, January 13, 2000, Paul went to his parents' house to visit them just like any other normal day.

"I was off work at the time and had been to their house to see them," Paul says. "By the time I'd got home, my mum rang me and said my dad had suffered a problem. She sounded startled so I told her to phone an ambulance. As I got back to their house I saw my dad being wheeled into the ambulance and I was told by the paramedics it looked like he'd had a heart attack. I followed the ambulance to hospital but he had another heart attack on the way. He was in Fazakerley hospital for 10 days."

Four months later on May 16, 2000, Moran was back at Anfield as he was rewarded with a testimonial match against Celtic.

Ronnie's testimonial was organised by a man called Mike Berry, who still contacts the family from time to time.

"Mike was a brilliant organiser and my dad used to just turn up where he was told and meet and greet the fans," Paul says. "My dad never had a bad word to say about the club after leaving as he loved his time there. The way he left was unfortunate but he would never do anything to disrupt the club.

"We spent the afternoon and evening at Anfield in the Carlsberg Lounge. Kenny had kindly brought Celtic down for the game, which obviously guaranteed a great turnout.

"Three of the four grandchildren went onto the pitch with him before the game and it was a fantastic turnout by the former players.

"My dad had 49 wonderful years at Liverpool and you can see, even to this day, what my dad means to Liverpool fans. We've never won the league since he left!"

Kenny Dalglish, who was Celtic's director of football, also performed on the night, although in a Celtic jersey. He was more than happy to honour his good friend and former colleague, as he told the *Liverpool Echo* before the game.

"Tonight will be magnificent for Ronnie and although he deserves it after giving his working life to Liverpool, he would never have expected it," Kenny said. "Ronnie is very well respected, not only at Anfield but throughout the game and he is a very decent and down-to-earth bloke."

Kenny also put emphasis on Ronnie's rare gift to make the beautiful game so easy to understand. "When I was there he had very simple ideas and very simple tastes and perhaps that is what is most appealing about him. He was never afraid to bark when he needed to but his simplicity in coaching sessions, which many would find difficult to put across, came to him with ease. He served the club as well as anyone and can take credit during the successful years as well as any of the players."

A special match day programme was published in which Ronnie revealed who had been his favourite characters in his time at the club.

"Fifty years is a long time to look back on and remember the great managers and great players I have worked with," he said. "I could fill this programme with friends from the past who made Liverpool Football Club into what it is today. Some were quite special; Bill Shankly and Bob Paisley, Joe Fagan and my old mate Roy Evans. On the playing side were Billy Liddell, Ron Yeats, Kevin Keegan, Rushie, Dalglish and Robbie Fowler to name a few."

Ronnie also revealed some of his off-the-field favourites. When asked about his favourite film and favourite music he answered with 'Titanic' and 'Marching bands' respectively. Less surprising were his choices for favourite drink (whisky), TV programme (Only Fools and Horses), other sport (cricket) and holiday (cruises). He added that Joe Fagan and Bill Shankly had been the biggest influences on his career and although Gerry Byrne took his place in the Liverpool side as a player eventually, Ronnie regarded him as his favourite left-back of all time.

It was a pleasant surprise for the family to see Ronnie's old foe from Manchester United, Alex Ferguson, contribute to the testimonial programme.

"Ronnie is a true professional, a loyal servant to Liverpool FC and a nice guy," Ferguson said. "I know his links with Liverpool go back to the days of the late, great Bill Shankly and the other famous members of the Anfield Bootroom, but his place in history is down to much more than longevity.

"As long as I have known him he has always been 110 per cent Liverpool. Anything asked of him in forwarding the club's cause would be done without further enquiry.

"It is fair to say that Manchester United and Liverpool have had their moments over the years. The rivalry between our two clubs is well documented and I wouldn't have had it any other way while the game is on. But that is where it ends as far as coaches, managers and players are concerned. Ronnie Moran has always been one of the first to shake the hand of an opponent, whether that be following a win or defeat. I wish I'd had a pound for every argument I've had with Ronnie, but after the game he was always the first to offer you a drink. There is no question Ronnie Moran is one of Liverpool's all-time greats."

Ferguson was actually somebody who Ronnie liked, as Paul Moran reveals.

"My dad admired Fergie for what he achieved at United in the 1990s and don't forget that the hatred between the fans wasn't carried onto the staff," Paul says. "My dad would have a go at Fergie and the rest of the United bench during games but afterwards in the Bootroom the discussion would be about football and players.

"It's a cliché but Fergie is a 'football man' and my dad has always said that there needs to be more of them in the game, and that's why they got on so well."

Alex Ferguson always kept Ronnie in mind and in April 2003 the Scot sent him a couple of tickets to the second leg of the Champions League quarter-final between Manchester United and Real Madrid at Old Trafford. Paul went with his dad and saw the Brazilian Ronaldo score a superb hat-trick for Real. United won 4-3 on the night, but lost 6-5 on aggregate.

"I was obviously delighted United lost but my dad kept muttering to me: 'Stop smiling, you'll get us killed,'" Paul reveals.

Ronnie Moran was deeply touched by the tributes paid to him during a memorable testimonial night at Anfield. When he was introduced on to the pitch, the crowd chanted his name. Ronnie wasn't too fond of the fuss made over him, but this was his special night and he was going to savour it.

"Tonight will stay with me forever because the support has been brilliant from the Celtic supporters and the Liverpool supporters!" Ronnie said before his name was chanted once again. Gerry Marsden sang 'You'll Never Walk Alone' with Ronnie heartily joining in out on the pitch.

"I'm overwhelmed by the attendance and support," Ronnie told the *Echo* on the night. "I've been involved in the game a long time, but this has really opened my eyes to what football is all about. The support from the Liverpool and Celtic fans has been magnificent. When I was here we enjoyed a bit of success but throughout that time the support given to us made a big difference. With fans like this, hopefully both clubs can go that little step further and have the success they deserve next season."

Liverpool beat Celtic 4-1 in front of 33,300 fans with Erik Meijer netting two of the goals, and Titi Camara and David Thompson grabbing the others. Gérard Houllier was delighted that his side had produced a fine display on such a special occasion for Ronnie and noted that this had been an unusual game for Ronnie, especially in one respect. "Ronnie sat alongside me on the bench during the first half, but he was very quiet throughout the game."

Ronnie's heart problems were far from over and after complaining about chest pains he eventually needed a bypass operation at Broadgreen Hospital in October 2000.

Ronnie eventually returned to Anfield as Houllier's French revolution gathered pace. Liverpool secured Champions League qualification in the 2000/01 season for the first time since the European Cup was rebranded in 1992 – and the club celebrated an unprecedented triple success in cup competitions.

It took penalties to beat a stubborn Birmingham City side in the League Cup final and Liverpool certainly enjoyed some huge slices of luck in the FA Cup final against Arsenal, being outplayed for most of the match at the Millennium Stadium in Cardiff, before Michael Owen's two late strikes saw some sort of revenge for three previous final defeats to the Gunners, in 1950, 1971 and 1987.

Gary McAllister's delivery then ensured a golden own goal in the closing minutes of extra-time in the nine-goal thriller of a UEFA Cup final against Alavés in Dortmund. Moran attended the finals of the FA Cup and the UEFA Cup as a guest of the club.

Despite the sensational cup victories, Moran was proudest of Liverpool's return to Europe's strongest club competition.

As football had been Ronnie's life for the previous five decades, he hadn't had the opportunity to explore other pastimes. But now, with more spare time on his hands, he and Joyce took an interest in antiques and used to attend the antique fair at Charnock Richard in Chorley every week. Ronnie spent a lot of time refurbishing furniture they had picked up.

"It was a family joke that my mum always asked my dad to paint the furniture glossy white," Paul says. "We always used to ask her: 'Why don't you just buy white furniture in the first place?'"

Ronnie and Joyce also went to Lowther Park in Lytham St Annes every week to watch the crown green bowls.

"My dad seemed to enjoy it, and it was certainly a different environment to a packed Anfield," Paul says.

Since his retirement, Ronnie was able to spend more time with his grandchildren, but despite his busy schedule at Liverpool FC he always tried to be a big part of their lives. Ronnie and his two children all lived within two miles of each other.

"My dad has always been great with kids," Paul says. "He would just do grandad-type things with them, going to see them in school plays or watch the boys play in their school matches. Ronnie followed Janet and Chris' son, Ian, closely all the way through his career from St Luke's under 9s to Wigan.

"My grandad was a massive influence on my career from a young age," Ian says. "When my grandad was at Liverpool I always went to the match with my Uncle Paul, my nan and my mum. I used to love watching and listening to my grandad. I loved the way he treated everybody the same, apart from Rushie, his favourite. My own personal favourites were Robbie Fowler and Jamie Carragher so I used to tell him to lay off them. But I don't think he did.

"He would take me to Melwood with him every time I was off school and most days over the summer holidays. He was always giving me bits of advice, apart from Sundays if Liverpool had lost on the Saturday because he wouldn't be in a very good mood.

"His main advice from an early age was to go out and enjoy myself. But as I got older and got picked for the Sefton team he would start giving me tactical advice. I was a right-back when I was younger so he knew quite a bit about that position I suppose, being a full-back himself. He told me when and when not to join in attacks, where to be if the winger had the ball and so on."

After one year playing for Sefton, Ian joined Wigan Athletic's centre of excellence when he was 15 in 1998. Once Ronnie had retired he had more time to support Ian in his promising career. Ronnie drove Ian to training and watched his games for the reserves.

"We would play on Wednesday afternoons so he and my nan would take me up there," Ian says. "I always remember my nan wouldn't get out of the car if it was raining. My grandad would talk non-stop all the way home about the things I could have done better during a particular game. If I'd done well he wouldn't tell me directly, he would say the winger I was up against had an off day or that the other team weren't much good. But I knew that was praise.

"My dad always reckoned I played better when my grandad was watching from the sidelines. I suppose it was just a natural thing for me to do because of his standing in the game."

Although Ronnie wasn't vocal on the touchline, Ian still has nightmares about his grandad's whistling during games when he thought Ian was daydreaming or had drifted out of the game.

"If I was ever standing still on the pitch he would whistle," Ian says. "Even if the ball was out of play, I still had to be moving. He used to call me 'Seagulls' because every time the birds flew past I was looking up. Then the whistle would come out."

Whether they were part of his own family or First Division superstars, many shudder at the memory of Ronnie's whistling.

"There could be 100,000 at Wembley but you could hear that whistle. And everyone goes: 'Is it me or is it you? That's the power Ronnie had," Ian Rush said.

Ronnie's grandson, Ian, made two appearances for Wigan's first-team in the Football League Trophy in January 2001. The attacking midfielder subsequently played for Southport, Marine, Burscough, Bootle FC and Kendal Town.

During the 2008/09 season Ian suffered a cruciate ligament injury and, after making 14 appearances for the newly formed AFC Liverpool, he had to hang up his boots. Nevertheless, Ian didn't leave football altogether and has followed in his grandad's footsteps.

"I have taken up coaching at non-league side Clitheroe FC, who play in the Northern Premier League Division One North with my ex-Wigan teammate and former Welsh international Simon Howarth and player-assistant manager Gareth Roberts, who played for the Liverpool youth sides," Ian says. "Both are fully qualified coaches trying to make it in the game. I haven't done my coaching badges yet but will be looking to do them in the near future because I will need them if Clitheroe go higher up the leagues."

Ian knows it will be difficult for him to reach the same heights as his grandad, but his experiences will benefit him in his own career.

"I watched my grandad coach some of the best players in the world for years, first hand, so hopefully I've picked up a few ideas from him along the way that I will implement into my own coaching," Ian said. "I will also look at the diaries he made of the training sessions he did at Melwood. I will try not to shout as much, though. I don't think anyone could shout as loud as my grandad."

Ronnie and Ian have always been extremely close on and off the field. "I was always round at his home watching football with him," Ian says. "He shouted at the telly when players gave the ball away or dived."

The idea was for Ronnie to watch football in a small front bedroom that had a settee in it and an armchair with pictures on the walls of his grandsons in action for their teams and of Ronnie with his ex-colleagues. The Trophy Room, as Ronnie called it, was set up to give Joyce a break from football, but it didn't last long as Ronnie would always watch the football in the main room.

Ian hopes he can channel his grandad's energy in his own ventures in the game. "The amount of success he had during his coaching career can only help me and if I can keep his passion for the game, I'm sure he would love that. He's not a bad coach to have learned from, is he?"

Ian's mother, Janet, Ronnie and Joyce's only daughter, was diagnosed with breast cancer in early 2002. After receiving chemotherapy, she was given the all clear later that year.

Janet's husband and Ian's father, Chris, had a history of indigestion problems and had an operation in 2003 to remove part of his gullet in an attempt to resolve the problem. In June 2005, Chris had begun to lose weight rapidly and looked jaundiced. After a lot of persuasion from the family he went to hospital and was diagnosed with esophageal cancer. He died six weeks later. It became apparent that his earlier operation was to remove a cancerous growth but he had never told the family because they were all still worried about Janet's condition. "It was an incredible act of bravery," his brother-in-law Paul says.

On April 8, 2006, Ronnie and his family attended the Grand National at Aintree racecourse. Daughter Janet was not well on the day, having trouble with her eyes that were twitching as if she was extremely tired. She went to the opticians early the following week. He noticed spots on her eyes and referred her to hospital where she was later told her cancer had come back and spread to her brain. Janet died after a courageous battle on November 30, 2006, only five weeks after she had become a grandmother as her daughter, Christine, gave birth to Emmie.

"I remember when we all went to the hospital after Janet had passed away," her brother, Paul, recalls. "I stood in a waiting room with my son David, Janet's son, Ian, and Stuart, Janet's son-in-law. My dad walked in and told us we had to be brave and do everything possible to help my mum and Christine to get through this. In all the years I watched my dad at matches and saw what he achieved during his career, this was the time I felt the most respect towards him.

"My mum never wanted to talk about Jan's death and still doesn't, but when I went with my dad to watch Ian or David play, he used to talk about Jan and ask if I was okay.

"He couldn't talk to Mum about Jan, but I liked talking about her so we would recollect things we'd done as kids and after a few months, we could laugh about things again."

Ronnie started to attend games at Anfield more frequently to take his mind off his daughter's passing.

When Ronnie started to go again to Anfield, he would attend around 15 games per season. He parked by Stanley Park and walked over to the Main Stand to his seat in the directors' box. Despite having left the staff in 1998, he was still a part of the club's fabric.

When Liverpool faced AC Milan in the Champions League final in 2005, Ronnie was not in Istanbul, but in the Centenary Stand at Anfield. He was invited to attend a screening of the match with him answering questions before, during and after the game. With the Reds 3-0 down at half-time he hadn't given up hope and said the next goal would be crucial.

Even though Ronnie couldn't have predicted the dramatic fashion in which Liverpool eventually won this incredible match, he had witnessed a similar glut of goals in April 1976 in the UEFA Cup final, still played over two legs. It was home advantage first for Liverpool, but it was a rude awakening for the Reds when they found themselves 2-0 down inside the first 15 minutes of the tie. Paisley showed his tactical nous at the break and withdrew the ineffective Toshack for Jimmy Case, who was told in no uncertain terms what to do once he came on.

"You're supposed to prepare the player to go onto the pitch," Case remembers. "I thought I'm gonna get a big speech, 'Do this, do that.' All they said was: 'Go on and cause fucking havoc.' And those were the exact words from Joe Fagan and Ronnie Moran." It was a move which had an immediate effect. Ray Kennedy's thunderbolt reduced the arrears before the same player dragged a shot against a post and Case, following up, stabbed the ball home from close range. Then Heighway was chopped down in the area and Kevin Keegan calmly sent Jensen the wrong way from the spot. Three goals in five astonishing minutes had completely turned the game around.

Liverpool's club TV channel started utilising Ronnie's expertise in the 2004/05 season and did so until 2007. He was Steve Hunter's co-commentator during live games and offered pre- and post-match analysis.

Hunter says he was extremely fortunate to have worked alongside Ronnie, as well as the rest of Liverpool's last title-winning management team; Kenny Dalglish and Roy Evans.

"Ronnie was absolutely brilliant and what a genuine, lovely bloke," Hunter says. "Our commentary position was above the old Main Stand in an old white box which has now sadly been dismantled. It was a long way up, climbing a number of stairs, and I used to have great banter with Ronnie and his wife about taking him up there. Our position on the gantry was right near the Kop at the far end."

It was a humbling experience for Hunter to work with Ronnie.

"I used to have a season ticket right behind Kenny's dugout from 1987 to 1998 and Ronnie's head kept popping out of it with his famous tone bellowing out," said Hunter.

"It was an incredible insight into the game working with Ronnie. He would constantly shout: 'Beat him!' to Harry Kewell when he was one-on-one with a defender, very similar to when he was on the bench. I always found working with Ronnie an education as during the commentary he would give the listener a unique insight into the Liverpool Way."

A glimpse into the coaching mind of Ronnie Moran was given in his analysis of Liverpool's 2-2 draw with Tottenham on April 16, 2005. Rafa Benítez's team had previously lost six league games immediately after a Champions League game, but escaped this time with a point, having drawn 0-0 with Juventus in midweek at Stadio delle Alpi. Ronnie was asked why this kept happening.

"Certain players will take this to mind," Ronnie said. "They are a bit stale at the start for the first 10 minutes or quarter of an hour. Some have this in their minds: 'We've lost the last three games playing on a Saturday afternoon.' This is what you've got to look after. You don't dwell on it, the midweek game. That's gone." It was a simple message, yet would have been effective if Ronnie was the messenger.

Another example of what would have been in Ronnie's mind as a coach came after the same fixture the following season. Harry Kewell's 58th-minute strike, which Moran described as the "goal of the month", proved the only difference between the two sides.

At the time Liverpool were on an incredible run of eight consecutive home wins in the league with no goals conceded. It was a pleasing statistic, but one Ronnie wouldn't have necessarily embraced if still at the club.

"If you were involved with it, you would be frightened to death of the next home game. It might sound daft, but we had good runs at times. When the game was finished you would be looking to the next one. It doesn't necessarily follow when you have won eight and not lost a goal, you will play the next one and win that. You have got to work to win it," Ronnie preached. For the record, Liverpool drew their next home game against Birmingham.

In Moran's analysis on LFC TV, the players or the manager could never do any wrong. Ronnie was still clearly very protective of the club's employees, like he was during his coaching career. If anything was amiss at the club, it wasn't discussed. If anyone did something terrific, he didn't go overboard in his praise.

Ronnie never talked about Liverpool's recent managers to his son, Paul, but he knew that his dad was always grateful to Rafa Benítez for allowing him to carry on visiting Melwood.

After Liverpool had beaten Spurs in the aforementioned game in 2006, Ronnie did admit that he was impressed by Rafa. "It's only his second season but he (Benítez) has had a lot of success last season winning the European Cup, but this season has gone better, because now with him being here for a second year, he is sorting his players out and the players are responding to him and that's always a good sign."

Ronnie had witnessed the rapid changes that had taken place in English football, especially since the formation of the Premier League.

He was, at least initially, dismissive of continental methods that have invaded the shores of Britain in the last couple of decades. Ronnie's knowledge, common sense, and passion for the game, though, would have been useful at any time or place. Ronnie also felt that Bill Shankly would have thrived in modern-day football. "He would have been fine dealing with foreigners and all the big money because he would have just got on with it. He would have got through to them with his enthusiasm for the game. Can you imagine him dealing with the media? He would love being a manager today. They would have to drag him away from the TV cameras," Ronnie claimed.

Paul Moran has his own views on how his dad would have dealt with footballers today.

"My dad used to say the game was still as it always was, as at the end of the day any amount of correct nutrition or diagrams don't mean anything if the player is not up to it," Paul says. "He thinks the preparation side of the game is vastly overcomplicated now, particularly the 45-minute warm-up that seems compulsory even at non-league levels.

"I think the main problem my dad would encounter now would be one of communication with the foreign players, because trying to change a position or tactic during the game by shouting doesn't happen now. Can you imagine my dad shouting instructions at Coutinho or Firmino? No disrespect to the players but it would be a waste of time."

Wages for footballers have skyrocketed and Ronnie has his own perspective on whether the stars of today deserve so much money for playing football.

"My dad always used to say about the wages that if the players are offered the money then of course they would accept it,"

Paul says. "I always remember one lad who told my dad that players' wages were too high. Dad asked him what his job was. I think the lad was a painter and a decorator and my dad said, 'how would you feel if 40,000 people watched you doing your job while shouting 'Dickhead' at you, then you were criticised by old decorators on the telly?' The lad said: 'I'd want more money' and laughed."

Ronnie does have sympathy for young footballers of today, and what they have to contend with.

"I think all over the country now too much is being put in footballers' brains about what they must and must not do," he said. Moran also feels a certain nous for the game that players developed if given proper care and attention is being driven out of them. The hype manufactured by the media also held back the natural progression of talent.

"I do think that the media these days are too quick to build players up," Ronnie said a few years ago. "They go overboard on young players who have played just a handful of matches. The big test is whether a player can maintain his standards over a period of years, not just over a few games.

"I have seen plenty of players who have had a few good games and the papers have been calling them brilliant players. That can't be right. You have to work for a full season to get success at the end of it."

After he had just left the club in 1998, he felt optimistic about the future at Anfield, even though he was sad not to be part of it. "There are a lot of good young players at Liverpool. I think that is important. Some clubs buy foreigners, others invest in youth and I am pleased Liverpool do give youth a chance."

Ronnie turned 75 on February 28, 2009. He had been

retired for more than 10 years, but his birthday was recognised throughout the football world. Tributes flooded in from various clubs but the birthday message Paul appreciated the most was from boyhood Red, Steve Coppell.

"When I was nine or 10 I used to go to Melwood to watch the players train. When I was getting autographs off the players after training all the players just signed and left," Coppell said. "Your father was the only player who signed and had a chat. He was kind and courteous and I never forgot his down to earth approach. From then onwards we met on a number of occasions. I'm sure he never remembered our first meeting but he still had the same friendly nature. Mind you, most of the time Liverpool were beating my teams."

In the rapidly-changing football world, it wasn't just Melwood where life was different. From being a second home to Moran, access to Anfield was now more restricted.

"In 2009, my dad was going down the corridor towards the dressing room and was stopped because he didn't have a pass for that area," Paul says. "The steward who stopped him was upset because he obviously recognised my dad but someone had told the stewards that if they let anyone go by the dressing rooms without the right accreditation, they would be dismissed. Back in the day I often used to go down by the dressing rooms on match day and speak to my dad and other people I knew and it was never a problem."

This issue was soon resolved by Liverpool's assistant manager, Sammy Lee, who had returned to the club in 2008. He not only obtained a pass for Ronnie, but also offered him a new role.

"There was a room down the corridor from the dressing rooms which wasn't used for anything specific," Sammy explains.

"Ron was given that room to recreate a post-match Bootroom kind of atmosphere.

"When I approached Ron about this, I wanted everything to be done on his terms so that he was content and comfortable with everything. I wanted him to feel at home, which is more than he deserves. We put a television in there and a fridge, which was filled with wine and beer. A table and chairs were also brought in, but nothing too glamorous!

"I would see Ron at the ground before every home game played on a weekend. When I arrived with the team, he just said 'hello' to me and then went up to the directors' box to watch the game. After the match had finished Ronnie went down to his room and waited for the opposition coaching staff to arrive to greet them and offer them a drink while we were in the dressing room with the players. Myself and the rest of the coaching staff would soon join them in there, including Rafa if he wasn't needed anywhere else. The catering staff used to bring us some sandwiches and pies and we would all have a chat about the game and football in general before the opposition coaches left.

"Ron was extremely good at dealing with the opposition staff. He was brought up to respect them and did the same himself during the many years he was at the club as a coach. Therefore, it was a privilege for many of the younger managers and coaches to be greeted by Ronnie Moran. He would reminisce with the ones who had been in the game for a while and talk about the old days with them."

This was a great opportunity for outsiders to meet Liverpool royalty, but Rafa and his coaching staff would also benefit from Ronnie's presence.

"Ron's knowledge and experience was important as after games he would offer myself and the rest of the Liverpool coaching staff his take on games and give us a few pointers on what went wrong!" Sammy remembers.

Ronnie felt at home in the new Bootroom and told the *Liverpool Echo* about a visit from Manchester United's hierarchy.

After Liverpool had beaten United 2-0 on October 25, 2009, Ronnie met up with Alex Ferguson, who was knighted in 1999, and Bobby Charlton, who had been a 'Sir' since 1994. He invited them into the Bootroom. "As they approached the Bootroom I started joking about, bowing to them and saying: 'Good afternoon, Sirs.' They were having none of it. We had a cup of tea and a good catch-up, talking football and what not."

The likes of Ferguson and Charlton felt privileged to talk to Ronnie, who didn't need a 'Sir' prefix to his name to be respected throughout the football world.

During Sammy Lee's final spell at the club, from 2008 to 2011, Ronnie still stuck to his regime of exercising at Melwood a couple of times a week. In 2009, Fernando Torres pulled Sammy to one side at the training ground and asked him: "Who is that old guy who walks by the walls?"

"I'll show you who that is," Sammy told Torres and took him inside, past the changing rooms to a corridor where a print of Ronnie Moran in a white Liverpool shirt adorned a wall.

After that, when Moran crossed Torres' path, the Liverpool striker always shook his hand and stopped for a chat.

"Quite a few of the young lads will do that," Ronnie told the *Liverpool Echo*. "Glen Johnson is another one who went out of his way to speak to me when he arrived. I'm not sure how but he seemed to know all about me."

Sammy felt it was important for the players to get to know Ronnie. "I'd tell them about everything Ronnie had done for the club and tell them the reason they were enjoying such training facilities at Melwood was largely down to Ronnie Moran's contribution and dedication."

Ronnie visited Melwood faithfully until 2012 when his health deteriorated. "I can't run now. I couldn't run when I was playing," Ronnie explained to Steven Gerrard when the captain asked him if he had done a few laps.

Melwood had changed drastically since Ronnie's coaching days with the building of the Millennium Pavilion, a two-storey state-of-the-art facility that was completed in November 2001.

Ronnie had followed the careers of Carragher and Gerrard in particular, as they were the only links he had with the team from when he was there. Gerrard made his first-team breakthrough in the 1998/99 season but had been training as a youth player with the seniors for a couple of years before Moran's departure and didn't escape without a word or two from the intimidating taskmaster of the club. Gerrard was eager to prove himself but was seen as a little overzealous in his approach.

"I was told to calm down a million times by Liverpool coaches and Ronnie Moran pulled me aside once and said: 'Steven, the staff are telling me you're getting injured because you go into stupid tackles. You try to kill people in training. These are your mates, Steven. Relax. Save it for the games,'" Gerrard remembered.

One day during training in 1997, Roy and Ronnie had lined up the youth team to shadow the weekend's opposition as they usually did. Liverpool's captain, Paul Ince, played opposite Gerrard, who didn't care about anyone's reputation and virtually ploughed down the self-proclaimed 'Guv'nor' during the practice match. As Ince stood up angrily and complained about this young upstart, Gerrard told him to 'fucking shut up' and then all hell broke loose. Ronnie had to call a halt to the game.

"You don't have to put a whole career into a week, son," was the exact phrase used by Ronnie when he told an eager youngster by the name of Jamie Redknapp to calm down a few years earlier. That was equally apt in this case.

When Ronnie was analysing on TV a month before Liverpool's European Cup victory in Istanbul he gave his view on the club captain. Gerrard had missed a penalty at Anfield in a game Liverpool drew and in a post-match interview Gerrard blamed himself for the draw.

Ronnie said: "That's the type of lad he is; he's been the same since he was 15 and he is getting stronger and stronger. Probably in a couple of years when he has more experience he will start playing a lot easier.

"Don't get me wrong, I'm not saying he's not doing it now. If his brain takes more in, which it will do, as he is that sort of lad, he will go from strength to strength and he will be one of the world class players."

Paul Moran adds: "Carra and Gerrard would always come over and speak to my dad at Melwood, as did other players, but they were his favourites.

"Jari Litmanen ran over the first time he saw my dad as he was a Liverpool fan in his youth in Finland and was honoured to meet my dad."

Though Ronnie had left the club, his legacy ensured that he would never be forgotten.

"In 2016 I drove my dad to the Hillsborough Memorial Service at Anfield and went with him to help him along. He wasn't well that day but as it was the last one I knew my dad would have wanted to go. I remember walking across the Kop with the former players. We were at the back of the line and every time someone shouted to my dad he turned around to say 'hello' instead of walking on. It took us ages to get to our seats."

– Paul Moran

Chapter 11

AS MEMORIES FADE

2012-

RONNIE Moran agreed to a rare interview with Tony Barrett, then of *The Times*, in his retirement bungalow in Blundellsands in 2013. Ronnie welcomed Tony into his 'Trophy Room' where a legendary photo of the Bootroom boys, taken at Anfield in 1968, had a prominent place.

'Ronnie picked up the framed photograph and trailing his finger along the picture from right to left, he names his former comrades in arms one by one,' Tony reported.

"The first one is Reuben Bennett," he says. "Then there's Joe

Fagan, me, Bob Paisley and, last but not least, Shanks. They've all left us now. I'm the only one still here."

Ronnie seemed wistful for the old days, reciting the names of the men with whom he had spent the better part of his adult life.

The year 2012 had proved eventful for the Moran clan as Christine had given birth to Ronnie's second great-grandchild, Shea, in July. Ronnie had been getting increasingly forgetful, unable to recall what his family had just told him.

"As dementia has no physical symptoms, you might tend to delay dealing with it," Paul says. "At first I put my dad's memory loss down to old age, as even I forget things every now and again, like any other person. I thought as my dad was getting old he was more likely to be more forgetful.

"Dad wasn't a frequent visitor at Anfield any more, but he would always watch Liverpool's matches on TV.

"Most Sundays my mum and dad came round to our house for dinner and we watched whoever was playing. During the 2012/13 season I started noticing that my dad couldn't remember who was playing. He also started asking me strange questions like: 'How long does a game last?' At the time, although I found this rather odd, I didn't think too much of it. This wouldn't happen every game and then he would go another 10 more matches without asking anything unusual. He also stopped reacting to incidents in games like a foul or a goal and I'd say to him: 'Didn't you see that?' and he'd say: 'Yes, I did,' but there was no reaction at the time."

Ronnie, accompanied by Paul, had become a frequent visitor at non-league games to watch his grandsons, Ian and David, play. Paul's son, David, has played in goal for a number of local teams. Ronnie largely left David to it with only words of encouragement after a good save or good distribution as he used to say that it was up to David's managers and coaches to advise him.

"The first time I knew for sure it was more than just an issue with my dad's memory was when I took him to see David's team play," Paul says. "The goalkeeper in his team made a good save and my dad turned around to me and said: 'That was a good save from our Dave, wasn't it?' but David wasn't playing that game and was, in fact, standing next to us. Me and David looked at each other, thinking 'something is not right here.'"

Ronnie was diagnosed with vascular dementia, the second most common type of dementia after Alzheimer's disease, accounting for at least 20 per cent of dementia cases and estimated to affect around 150,000 people in the UK. In order for the brain to function properly its cells need constant blood flow through the network of vessels known as the vascular system. If the vessels leading to the brain leak or become damaged the brain cells will die. A person with vascular dementia will get easily confused, become agitated, see things that are not there, suffer memory loss, lack reasoning and control over emotions and experience a whole plethora of symptoms that will ultimately severely impair his or her daily life.

Paul continued to take his dad to non-league games, irrespective of whether a family member was taking part.

"Initially, we only watched the games Ian or David were playing in but it developed into watching any game every Saturday," Paul says. "It wasn't something that attracted me more than Anfield where we still have three season tickets, but attending games there had become too much for my dad.

"The atmosphere is quieter in the non-league but I had to

remind myself to be calm around my dad at the ground. I wouldn't be able to express my opinion as much because my dad would get agitated and join in."

Paul had to keep a watchful eye on his dad, as he had a tendency to wander off during games, up and down the touch-line. Paul particularly enjoyed taking him to the Delta Stadium, the home of Bootle FC, as Ronnie is well known around those parts. Fellow supporters would keep an eye out for Ronnie if Paul wanted to grab a cup of tea.

"In July 2014 we were watching Bootle FC play, when a friendly gentleman from Bootle approached my dad to ask for a photograph. It was Jamie Carragher. He stopped for a chat to ask how my dad was. He was really pleased to see Jamie," Paul says. "This happened during a pre-season game and one of the lads who had just joined Bootle spotted them and said with panic in his voice: 'There's Jamie Carragher and Ronnie Moran over there. They don't come to every game, do they?'"

Ronnie the coach was still alert and would always comment on games while watching them with his family.

"I would be watching the ball and I'd see my dad look the other way. I asked him what he was looking at and he said: 'Look at the right-back, he's out of position.' I would turn to where the right-back should be and I couldn't see him and my dad would say: 'I told you,'" Paul says.

"He would also watch on carefully during corner kicks to see how the teams were marking from corners. He would shout to the players to keep their eyes on the ball and don't turn their back. My dad was never a fan of zonal marking because you don't always know where the ball is.

"From a distance it was hard to see that there was anything

wrong with Dad. In fact, people were surprised that he had dementia when it was mentioned to them. Dementia used to be a disease that people never spoke about but now it receives a lot more publicity and there is no stigma attached to it."

Though his memories were fading, there were regular reminders of Ronnie's glorious past. On April 28, 2014, he received the Bill Shankly Memorial Award at the Liverpool Echo Merseyside Sports Personality of the Year Awards. Since 1996 the award has been handed to those who have served Liverpool FC with special distinction. Peter Robinson was the first recipient and the winners' list includes luminaries such as Roger Hunt, Tommy Smith, Ian Rush, Kenny Dalglish, Phil Thompson, Steven Gerrard and Jamie Carragher.

Two former recipients, Ian Callaghan and Ron Yeats, presented Ronnie with the award.

Ronnie was a hugely popular winner of the prize and former Reds skipper, Yeats, said: "Ronnie was tough as a coach. I remember he was always at the same place at the same time at the training ground day after day. He was very committed. Liverpool fans should be very grateful for everything he did."

The awards came thick and fast for Ronnie. The first-team was present at the Liverpool Football Club awards dinner, a glamorous event at the ACC Conference Centre on May 6, 2014. A Lifetime Achievement award was presented to Ronnie as someone who had dedicated his life to Liverpool FC while demonstrating the club's values.

In 2014 Ronnie had to have a pacemaker fitted because his heart rate was 'frighteningly slow'. At about 35 beats per minute it was affecting his dementia because of the slow blood supply to the brain.

Ronnie was moved to a day centre to help stimulate him and offset the advance of dementia, but this presented a whole new set of problems.

"Family members would receive phone calls saying my dad was trying to get out of the centre, and it became apparent shortly before Christmas 2015 that he needed more care," Paul says. "We had a family meeting and it was decided that I would leave work and look after him for as long as I could."

It became increasingly difficult to try to keep any sort of control over Ronnie.

"My mum, at 83 years of age, struggled to cope with my dad who tried to leave the sheltered accommodation they were in," Paul says. "He could never answer where he was going but repeatedly wanted the code number for the gates. He spent many hours looking out of the window into the car park and commenting on what he could see. It was very difficult to get him to sit down and relax, which I tried to do every morning when I got there.

"The problem with the dementia is that he is never settled at what he is doing at any one time; if we were out in the car he wanted to be home and if we were in he wanted to go out."

It was difficult for Paul's daughter, Alix, to watch her grandad's mind deteriorate.

"The man that you've seen at the ground and on telly and known as 'Bugsy' isn't there any more," says Alix. "He still goofs about and 'steals your nose' and puts the famous flat cap on backwards to look like Samuel L Jackson. These are the things that I'll remember most, not the big football man he once was."

As the dementia worsened, the less Ronnie could focus on a game and he talked less and less about Liverpool.

"I would tell him about everything that was going on at the club because I wanted him to know, and deep down he wanted to know too," Paul says. "My dad attended every Hillsborough memorial service at Anfield except the one in 2015 when he wasn't too well. In 2016, I drove him there and went with him to help him along. He wasn't well that day, but as it was the last one, I knew my dad would have wanted to go, so we made an effort to get there.

"I remember walking across the Kop with the rest of the former players. We were at the back of the line and every time someone shouted to my dad, he turned around to say 'hello' instead of walking on. It took us ages to get to our seats."

Ronnie's last trip to Anfield was on August 9, 2016, more than 70 years after his first visit there as a boy. Accompanied by Paul, Ronnie was also joined by his good friend Roy Evans and one of the authors of this book. The two remaining members of the Bootroom had a look at the rebuilt Main Stand.

Although there wasn't much dialogue from Ronnie, it was clear from his facial expressions that he was extremely pleased to see his old work colleague and happy to be in his company. Ronnie nodded in agreement with the points Roy was making that seemed to trigger some of his hidden memories.

Ronnie then stepped out onto the balcony of a box in the Centenary Stand. He took everything in and gazed over to the new Main Stand, trying to locate the home team bench.

It was now over 18 years since Ronnie had left Liverpool as an employee, but it was evident that he was still held in the highest regard. The staff at Anfield that day were very pleased to see him, stopping him to shake his hand, asking how he was and telling him he was an absolute legend.

One day in September 2016, Paul was driving around with his dad. Ronnie told Paul to stop because he thought he saw himself at a bus stop. Paul reminded his dad that he was in the car and couldn't be at the bus stop as well.

"I finally realised that if my dad had an illness such as cancer, then he would be in a hospital, therefore it shouldn't be any different with dementia and we made the heartbreaking decision that he needed to move out of his home to a place where he could be looked after by professionals," Paul says.

"The whole immediate family have been affected by my dad's illness but everyone has given every assistance possible to help out. It is something that a lot of people go through on a daily basis and I feel very sorry for anyone who has a loved one disappearing before their eyes and becoming someone who doesn't know them or have any idea what's happening."

Ronnie was moved to a full-time care home in Southport in November 2016. His family could not visit him for the first couple of weeks, but Paul phoned the staff there every day. Ronnie needed to be given time to settle, otherwise he would think it was time for him to go back home.

"The few first visits were hard for us as when it was time for us to leave, my dad would get up and try to come home with us," Paul says. "However, after he had been there a month, he just started to wave us off, as if he realised that this is where his home is now."

Paul and Joyce visit every week, usually with Alix, as does Christine who takes the great-grandkids to see him. Other close family members visit as often as they can. Ronnie is settled but finds it difficult to communicate.

"It is a care home for people with dementia and I'm happy

with the place we chose and with the people who are looking after my dad," Paul says. "The people who live there have communal areas and all do activities together. In one of the games that they play, they have to throw a ball to each other, but when it's my dad's turn, he puts it on the floor and kicks it to the next person!

"It's really difficult for them to form friendships, because, as sad as it is to say, every time they see each other, it is as if they're meeting for the first time."

A few days prior to the Capital One Cup final that took place on February 28, 2016, Ronnie visited Melwood, his beloved place of work for almost half a century.

"My dad had not been for quite a while and the lads on the gate were delighted to see him," Paul says. "We went into the reception and were taken upstairs to the viewing area above the pitches where we watched the players train.

"When they finished, we were moved to a lounge area, close to the players' dining area. The players walked past and those that spotted us said 'hello'. Eventually Jürgen Klopp came in and asked my dad how he was doing and we talked about the upcoming final against Manchester City that was on the following Sunday, which was also my dad's birthday.

"Jürgen said they would try to win the cup as a present for my dad, so I said to him: 'Weren't you going to try and win it until you found out it was his birthday?' He got the joke and then I asked if I could get a picture of him with my dad.

"As we were leaving Joe Allen came in from a fitness session and came over to speak to us as he knew all about my dad's time at Anfield."

Paul truly treasures this visit and the friendly and respectful manager of Liverpool, who immediately recognised his dad and called him a legend.

At a big gathering for Liverpool legends at the Hilton hotel in Liverpool a couple of months later, Ronnie made a rare appearance and met with several of his former disciples. As Jimmy Case saw Ronnie coming up the stairs in the hotel, by instinct he hid his glass of wine behind his chair so Ronnie wouldn't spot it. Old habits die hard!

Ian Callaghan made his way to Ronnie, who clearly recognised his good friend and was happy to see him.

Several fans wanted to greet Ronnie and an avid Red asked him about his eventful Melwood visit. Ronnie stared at him and asked him who Jürgen Klopp was and had trouble comprehending the term 'Melwood'.

In an instant it became apparent that Ronnie Moran had been robbed of his life's work.

The Moran Archives

Key documents from Ronnie's life

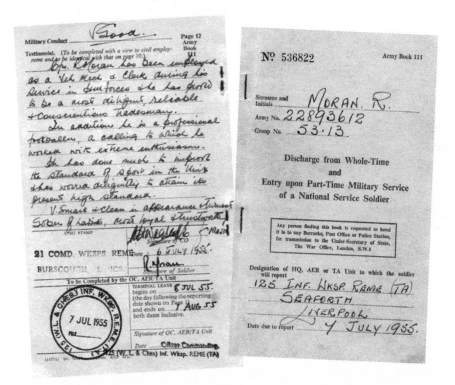

Military man: Ronnie's Army discharge notes call him 'diligent and reliable'

An Agreement made the ___Twenty fifth___

day of ___March___ 19 53 between ___T. C. Rouse___
of ___Anfield Road Liverpool 4___
___ in the COUNTY OF ___Lancaster___

the Secretary of and acting pursuant to Resolution and Authority for and on

behalf of the ___Liverpool___ FOOTBALL CLUB

of ___Liverpool___ (hereinafter referred to as the Club)

of the one part and ___Ronald Moran___

of ___85 Alexandra Road Gt. Crosby Liverpool 23___

in the COUNTY OF ___Lancaster___ Professional Football Player

(hereinafter referred to as the Player) of the other part **Whereby** it is agreed

as follows :—

    1. The Player hereby agrees to play in an efficient manner and to the best of his ability for the Club.

    2. The Player shall attend the Club's ground or any other place decided upon by the Club for the purposes of or in connection with his training as a Player pursuant to the instructions of the Secretary, Manager, or Trainer of the Club, or of such other person, or persons, as the Club may appoint. [This provision shall not apply if the Player is engaged by the Club at a weekly wage of less than One Pound, or at a wage per match.]

    3. The Player shall do everything necessary to get and keep himself in the best possible condition so as to render the most efficient service to the Club, and will carry out all the training and other instructions of the Club through its representative officials.

    4. The Player shall observe and be subject to all the Rules, Regulations and Bye-Laws of The Football Association, and any other Association, League, or Combination of which the Club shall be a member. And this Agreement shall be subject to any action which shall be taken by The Football Association under their Rules for the suspension or termination of the Football Season, and if any such suspension or termination shall be decided upon the payment of wages shall likewise be suspended or terminated, as the case may be.

    5. The Player shall not engage in any business or live in any place which the Directors (or Committee) of the Club may deem unsuitable.

Signed up: Two pages of the contract Ronnie signed at Anfield in 1953

9. In consideration of the observance by the said player of the terms, provisions and conditions of this Agreement, the said _J. C. Rouse_ on behalf of the Club hereby agrees that the said Club shall pay to the said Player the sum of £ _9 . 10 . 0_ per week from _25th March, 1953_ to _2nd May, 1953_ and £ _8 . 10 . 0_ per week from _4th May, 1953_ to _30th June, 1953._

10. This Agreement (subject to the Rules of The Football Association) shall cease and determine on _30th June, 1953_ unless the same shall have been previously determined in accordance with the provisions hereinbefore set forth.

Fill in any other provisions required

Amended Agreement.

As Witness the hands of the said parties the day and year first aforesaid

Signed by the said _J. C. Rouse._

and

Ronald Moran.

In the presence of

(Signature) _James L. McInnes_

(Occupation) _Clerk._

(Address) _Anfield Road_

Liverpool 4

Ronald Moran
(Player)

J. C. Rouse
(Secretary)

In the news: The *Evening Express* report on the day Ronnie had to take over in goal against Derby County in October 1957, and (right) his growing profile was used to advertise cars

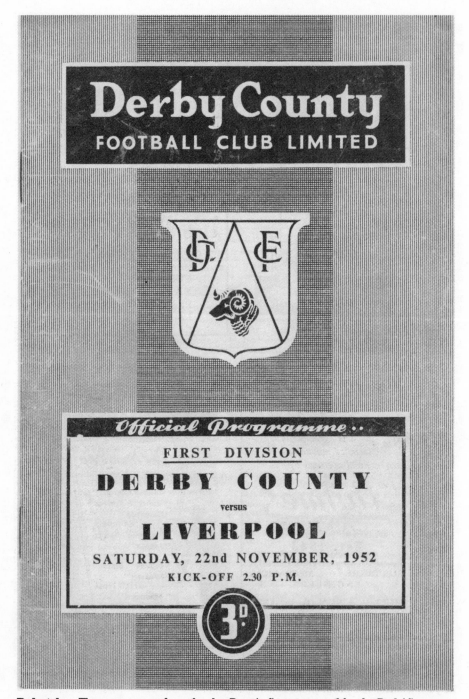

Debut day: The programme from the day Ronnie first appeared for the Reds' first-team

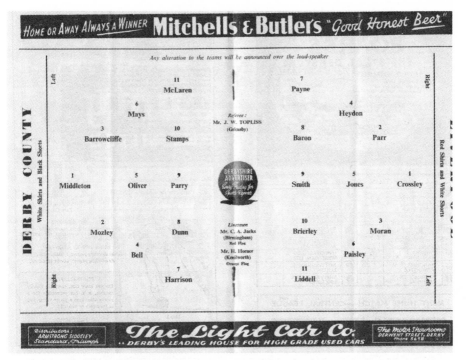

He's in: The Derby programme producers from 1952 knew Ronnie had made the team

Key moments: The programmes from the games where Ronnie scored his first Liverpool goal (left) and made his final Reds appearance (right)

Cup focus: Ronnie and the team were centre of attention before a big FA Cup quarter-final against Swansea Town in 1964. Unfortunately, the Reds lost 2-1

In print: A picture from the Daily Mirror in 1964 after the Reds had won the title and (far right) the Liverpool Echo mark Ronnie's 250th Liverpool appearance

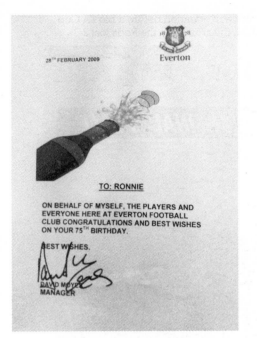

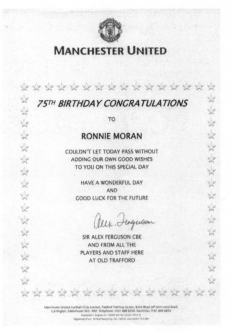

Congratulations: Everton and Manchester United sent their best wishes when Ronnie turned 75, showing how highly regarded he was, even by Liverpool's biggest rivals

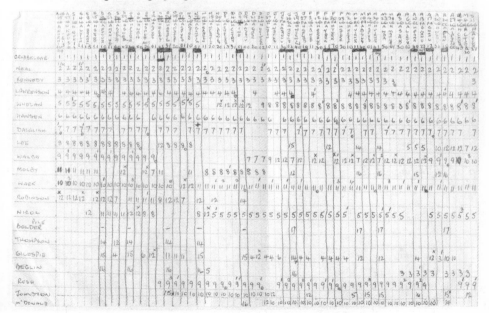

Stats man: How Ronnie kept a hand-written record of the 1984/85 season

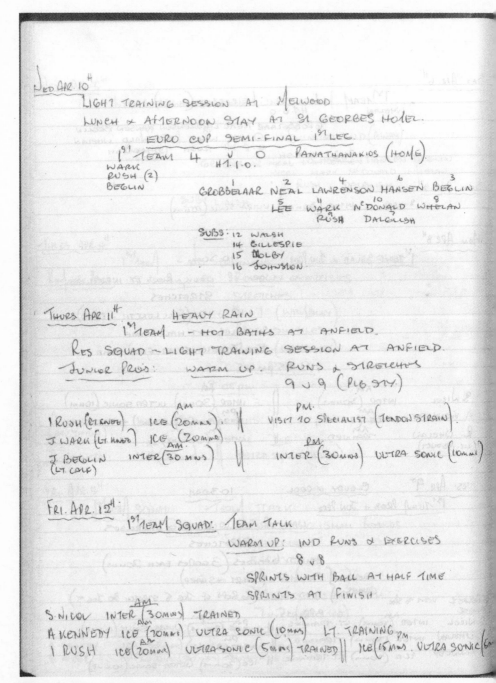

Wed Apr 10th

LIGHT TRAINING SESSION AT MELWOOD
LUNCH & AFTERNOON STAY AT ST GEORGES HOTEL.
EURO CUP SEMI-FINAL 1st LEG
1st TEAM   4   v   0   PANATHANAKIOS (HOME)
WARK   H 1 . 1 - 0.
RUSH (2)
BEGLIN

                        1   2   4   6   3
        GROBBELAAR   NEAL   LAWRENSON   HANSEN   BEGLIN
                        5   11   10   8
                    LEE   WARK   McDONALD   WHELAN
                            9   7
                        RUSH   DALGLISH

            SUBS: 12 WALSH
                   14 GILLESPIE
                   15 MOLBY
                   16 JOHNSTON

Thurs Apr 11th   HEAVY RAIN
            1st TEAM   - HOT BATHS AT ANFIELD.
    RES SQUAD - LIGHT TRAINING SESSION AT ANFIELD.
    JUNIOR PRO's: WARM UP. RUNS & STRETCHES
                                9 v 9 (PIG STY.)

                        AM   PM.
I RUSH (Ex KNEE)   ICE (20mns).   VISIT TO SPECIALIST (TENDON STRAIN).
J. WARK (LT KNEE)   ICE (20mns)
                        AM.   PM.
J. BEGLIN   INTER (30 MNS)   INTER (30mns) ULTRA SONIC (10mns)
(LT CALF)

Fri. Apr. 12th
            1st TEAM SQUAD: TEAM TALK
                            WARM UP: IND RUNS & EXERCISES
                                    8 v 8
                            SPRINTS WITH BALL AT HALF TIME
                            SPRINTS AT FINISH
                    AM
S. NICOL   INTER (30mns) TRAINED
                    AM
A KENNEDY ICE (20mns) ULTRA SONIC (10mns) LT. TRAINING PM
                    AM
I RUSH   ICE (20mns) ULTRASONIC (5mns) TRAINED || ICE (15mns). ULTRA SONIC (6mns

Melwood diary: An example of the records Ronnie and the staff kept during a season.
This one is from the 1984/85 season

SAT. APR. 13ᵗʰ   F.A. CUP   SEMI-FINAL

1ˢᵗ TEAM   2 v 2 MAN UTD (GOODISON) 1·1 F.T.
WHELAN   H.T. 0·0   A.E.X. TIME
WALSH

GROBBELAAR NEAL LAWRENSON HANSEN BEGLIN
              LEE WARK M°DONALD WHELAN
                 RUSH   DALGLISH
       SUB. WALSH CAME ON FOR WARK AFTER 60 MINS

SUN APR. 14ᵗʰ

S. NICOL   TRAINED

A. KENNEDY. ICE (20MINS)   TRAINED

P. NEAL.   INTER (30MINS) : ULTRA SONIC (10MINS)
(LT. THIGH)
K. DALGLISH   ICE (20MINS)   ULTRA SONIC (10MINS)
(LT. ANKLE)
K. M°DONALD   MICRO DIA (30MINS)
(LT. THIGH)

MON APR. 15ᵗʰ

1ˢᵗ TEAM — SAUNA & HOT BATHS AT MELWOOD.

RES. SQUAD — LIGHT TRAINING AT MELWOOD 10·30 AM

REM OF PROS & JUNIOR PROS: WARM UP: RUNS & EXERCISES
                                      STRETCHES
                             10 v 10 (B PITCH)

                            12·10 PM.
                          AM   PM
A. KENNEDY ICE (20 MINS) TRAINED || ICE (20 MINS) ULTRA SONIC (10 MINS)
I. RUSH   ICE & ULTRA SONIC (5 MINS)
                          AM   PM
P. NEAL.   INTER (30 MINS) || ULTRA SONIC (10 MINS)
K. DALGLISH   ULTRA SONIC (10 MINS)

            RES. 2 v 0 BARNSLEY (HOME)
          DEMANGE   H.T. 1·0
          MOLBY

          PILE TOALE SEAGRAVES GILLESPIE ABLETT
             NICOL JOHNSON MOLBY   WEST.
                 DE MANGE MOONEY
       SUB: CURRY CAME ON FOR ABLETT AFTER 70 MINS
                          (LT. THIGH)

Tributes to Mr Liverpool

George Scott (LFC 1960-1965):

"I loved Ronnie, we all did and it was obvious to me that he was destined for the coaching staff at Anfield. In his subsequent years at the club he was not only a great coach but an inspiration by his enthusiasm, fantastic determination and will to win, which Shanks admired so much. The word 'legend' is applied to so many individuals but in my view, and I know in the eyes of all true Liverpool supporters, Ronnie 'Bugsy' Moran will always be a true legend of the club who was right there at the start of the glory days with Bill, Bob, Joe, Reuben and the rest."

Gordon Wallace (LFC 1961-1967):

"I have had the pleasure of meeting up with Ronnie over the years since he has retired at Former Players' functions. He has not changed despite all he achieved throughout his career. Being in his company and reliving the past, he still had time to talk to people like myself who did not make greatness."

Kenny Dalglish (LFC 1977-1991 / 2011-2012):

"Titles are for people who believe in themselves. Ronnie had self-belief. You should never underestimate his contribution to this football club, although

it may be understated and he may be understated. He made a massive contribution."

Sammy Lee (LFC 1972-1986 / 1992-2004 / 2008-2011):
"Doing it Ronnie's way isn't everybody's way. But by the end of your term, however long your term was within the club, you knew exactly what was required of you. Certainly one of the reasons I am sat here today and I was able to play for Liverpool Football Club, to coach at Liverpool Football Club, a lot of that was down to Ronnie Moran. When you go through the Liverpool family as it was with Joe, Roy, Tom Saunders, John Bennison, Ronnie was, for me, the patriarch of that."

Alan Hansen (LFC 1977-1991):
"Regarding Liverpool's success over the years, Ronnie Moran hardly gets a mention, unless you were in there and you knew. I don't think anybody has contributed more to Liverpool's success than Ronnie Moran. He was there right through the lot of it. Thick and thin, ups and downs. He was always trying to lift players and deflate players whenever it was necessary. If contributions are underrated then he will be right up at the top of the tree."

Alan Kennedy (LFC 1978-1985):
"A lot of what Ronnie told me applied in life in general and I'm incredibly grateful for that. He was trying to get the best out of you every game. Sometimes I asked myself, 'What does he want? Blood, sweat and tears?' But from my point of view, and certainly the other players, we were prepared to give it. If I was at fault for a goal or made a mistake he would clatter me and tell me straight. Ron would never sit on the fence and told you what he thought at the time. There would be times when he would just flare up and say something he might have regretted, but we understood that Ron was so passionate about winning and that would rub off on me and the rest of the team. Ronnie was a winner and it was a good habit to have."

TRIBUTES

Bruce Grobbelaar (LFC 1981-1994):

"Ronnie Moran was the hard part of the three coaches when I first went there. Joe Fagan was the assistant to Bob Paisley and then you had the trainers; Roy Evans used to soften the blow but Ronnie Moran used to hammer you. Does Ronnie Moran know football? Like the back of his hand, and he was probably the most underrated coach in the entire league because you looked at him and you thought, 'he's just a trainer and he doesn't know anything'. Wrong; he knew everything, about the players, about their faults and their strengths. However, he would never talk to them about their strengths. He always wanted to combat their faults. There is nothing better for a player than to be coached by Ronnie Moran. For me, he was the ultimate coach, the constable. He was Liverpool's constant right the way from Shankly until the day he left. Ronnie isn't there now and I would say the reason that Liverpool have slipped up is that they haven't had a Ronnie Moran in the coaching staff. He kept everyone on their toes, and not just the players but the fans too. When they saw Ronnie they knew they had something stable and that they were going to be okay. Ronnie Moran is one of those men that if he was a general during the Rhodesia war, then Rhodesia would still be Rhodesia today, that's how I think of him. A character like Ronnie is what Anfield needs today."

Steve Nicol (LFC 1981-1995):

"Ronnie Moran was an integral part of Liverpool Football Club. He was woven into the club's fabric. Ronnie was a key figure in the development of my career, and not just me but also the hundreds of players who played at Anfield before and after me. No glitz or glamour, just a desire to do what was best for the club. Also, along with Roy Evans, he persuaded me to go and see Joe Fagan and tell him I should be playing in the first-team more often – a scary thing to do. Liverpool was about doing things the right way. The reason we were successful was because people like Ronnie ensured every

person at the club maximised what they had. And if you didn't maximise your ability then it was nobody else's fault but yours. Just like Kenny Dalglish, Ronnie was also always in my head when I became a coach at New England Revolution. I doubt I would have been the person I am today if it hadn't been for Ronnie Moran."

Steve McManaman (LFC 1987-1999):

"I've always said, as well as my father, who has been with me since I was born, Roy Evans and Ronnie Moran have been a huge part of my life and made me the player I was. Ronnie meant everything to me and whatever type of player I turned out to be was because of Ronnie Moran and the rest of the staff at Liverpool. The managers changed, but 'Bugsy' didn't!"

Jamie Carragher (LFC 1987-2013):

"Ronnie was the foundations of the success of Liverpool. He worked with Shankly, Paisley, Fagan, Dalglish and Evans; he was always there. I know the manager picked the team, but I know the players and people around the club knew of the massive impact Ronnie had. He was renowned for being a hard taskmaster and never made a big song and dance about anything. A part of his job was to keep people's feet on the floor and that contributes to how Liverpool got so successful, as the players never got carried away. There is no better title for Ronnie Moran than Mr Liverpool, for everything that he did as a player and achieved with the club as a coach, the most successful British side of all time, forever winning European Cups and league titles. All these players who won these trophies were coached by Ronnie Moran and I don't think that will ever be surpassed."

Rob Jones (LFC 1991-1999):

"Ronnie Moran is, in my eyes, Mr Liverpool and for me is right up there along with Shanks, Bob, Joe and Kenny. Liverpool wouldn't have been the same or achieved the same without him. Nobody had a bad word to say

about Ronnie. He was a gentleman. If you needed to sit down and have a chat he would always be there for you; however, if you weren't pulling your weight he would give you a kick up the backside!"

John Keith, author and broadcaster:

"Ronnie Moran has been a football man for all seasons and all situations; a member of a remarkable 'brains trust' who sat and talked in a smelly, windowless room off the Anfield corridor and plotted the conquest of Europe."

Terry Butcher, former England, Ipswich and Rangers player:

"Ronnie will be a real legend to those of us who grew up in his era of success. Liverpool FC were the benchmark of the old First Division and if you ever finished above them it was a remarkable achievement. I never heard a bad word spoken about Ronnie in all my time in the game and he will always be held in high regard for the way he coached and motivated that fabulous Liverpool side. Indeed, Graeme Souness always spoke extremely highly about Ronnie when I joined Rangers in 1986. One-club servants like Ronnie are now rare and exceptional. I still try to apply the same principles that made him one of the best coaches in Britain and the world."

Ronnie in Numbers

1949/50 - *C team player*

1950/51 - *B and A team player*

1951/52 - *Reserve-team player*

1952/53 - *12 games as first-team player*

1953/54 - *1 game as first-team player*

1954/55 - *21 games as first-team player*

1955/56 - *44 games as first-team player*

1956/57 - *43 games as first-team player*

1957/58 - *46 games as first-team player*

1958/59 - *41 games as first-team player*

1959/60 - *44 games as first-team player and club captain*

1960/61 - *12 games as first-team player and reserve-team player*

1961/62 - *19 games as first-team player and reserve-team player*

1962/63 - *39 games as first-team player*

1963/64 - *39 games as first-team player*

1964/65 - *18 games as first-team player*

1965/66 - *Reserve-team player*

1966/67 - *Reserve-team player / youth-team coach*

1967/68 - *Reserve-team player / youth-team coach*

1968/69 - *Youth-team coach*

1969/70 - *Youth-team coach*

1970/71 - *Youth-team coach*

1971/72 - *Reserve-team manager*

1972/73 - *Reserve-team manager*

1973/74 - *Reserve-team manager*

1974/75 - *53 games as first-team trainer*

1975/76 - *59 games as first-team trainer*

1976/77 - *62 games as first-team trainer*

1977/78 - *62 games as first-team trainer*

1978/79 - *54 games as first-team trainer*

1979/80 - *60 games as first-team chief coach*

1980/81 - *63 games as first-team chief coach*

1981/82 - *62 games as first-team chief coach*

1982/83 - *60 games as first-team chief coach*

1983/84 - *67 games as first-team chief coach*

1984/85 - *64 games as first-team chief coach*

1985/86 - *63 games as first-team chief coach*

1986/87 - *57 games as first-team chief coach*

1987/88 - *50 games as first-team chief coach*

1988/89 - *53 games as first-team chief coach*

1989/90 - *50 games as first-team chief coach*

1990/91 - *39 games as first-team chief coach and 10 games as acting manager*

RONNIE IN NUMBERS

1991/92 - *56 games as first-team chief coach and 8 games as caretaker manager*

1992/93 - *55 games as first-team chief coach*

1993/94 - *49 games as first-team chief coach*

1994/95 - *57 games as first-team chief coach*

1995/96 - *53 games as first-team chief coach*

1996/97 - *52 games as first-team chief coach*

1997/98 - *47 games as first-team chief coach*

- 13 seasons as a first-team player

- 379 games

- 17 goals

- 47 games as captain

- 24 seasons as a first-team coach

- 1,365 games as a first-team coach

- 1,744 games as first-team player and first-team coach.

- Only missed one game from 1974-1998, on 30 November 1997 at Highbury. Arsenal 0-1 Liverpool.

- Add to this number all the games between 1966 and 1974 when he was running the youth teams and the reserves and the friendlies he played and various minor competitions will bring this total to more than 2,000 Liverpool games.

Honours as a player:

First Division title: 1963/64

Second Division title: 1961/62

MR LIVERPOOL

Major honours as part of the first-team coaching staff:

First Division title: 1975/76, 1976/77, 1978/79, 1979/80, 1981/82, 1982/83, 1983/84, 1985/86, 1987/88, 1989/90.

FA Cup: 1986, 1989, 1992

League Cup: 1981, 1982, 1983, 1984, 1995.

European Cup: 1977, 1978, 1981, 1984.

UEFA Cup: 1976.

23 of Liverpool's 41 major honours won with Ronnie on the first-team coaching staff.

These numbers are worked out from official games registered at LFChistory.net and do not include friendlies.

Thanks

The following former Liverpool players have all contributed directly to this book for which the authors are very grateful.

John Molyneux (1955-1962)

Billy Howard (1955-1962)

Tommy Lawrence (1957-1971)

Ian Callaghan (1957-1978)

Chris Lawler (1959-1975 / 1982-1986)

George Scott (1960-1965)

Gordon Wallace (1961-1967)

Ian St John (1961-1971)

Peter Thompson (1963-1974)

Roy Evans (1963-1998)

Phil Thompson (1970-1985 / 1986-1992 / 1998-2004)

Sammy Lee (1972-1986 / 1992-2004 / 2008-2011)

Joey Jones (1975-1978)

Howard Gayle (1977-1983)

MR LIVERPOOL

Alan Hansen (1977-1991)

Kenny Dalglish (1977-1991 / 2011-2012)

Alan Kennedy (1978-1985)

Ian Rush (1980-1987 / 1988-1996)

Bruce Grobbelaar (1981-1994)

Steve Nicol (1981-1995)

Michael Robinson (1983-1984)

Gary Gillespie (1983-1991)

Dominic Matteo (1985-2000)

John Barnes (1987-1997)

John Aldridge (1987-1989)

Steve McManaman (1987-1999)

Jamie Carragher (1987-2013)

Glenn Hysen (1989-1992)

Rob Jones (1991-1999)

Stig Inge Bjørnebye (1992-2000)

Neil Ruddock (1993-1998)

Special thanks to Ian Beardsley, Steve Hunter, John Keith, Adrian Killen, John Martin, Peter McDowall, Graeme Riley, Linda Robinson and Nassos Siotropos whose contributions we could not have done without.

Bibliography

Alan A'Court and Ian Hargraves, *My Life in Football*, Bluecoat Press, 2003.

John Barnes, *Autobiography*, Headline Book Publishing, 1999.

Peter Beardsley and Bob Cass, *My Life Story*, HarperCollins Willow, 1996.

Carra, *My Autobiography*, Transworld Publishers, 2009.

Jimmy Case, *Hard Case*, John Blake Publishing Ltd, 2014.

Kenny Dalglish and Henry Winter, *My Home*, 2010.

Derek Dohren, *Ghost on the Wall*, Mainstream, 2004.

Eddie's Golden Years Scrapbook – Liverpool F.C. 1959/60 season, Marksport Publications, 1986.

Tony Evans, *I Don't Know What It Is But I Love It: Liverpool's unforgettable 1983-84 Season*, Penguin UK, 2015.

Gerry Fenlon, *A Tribute to Phil Thompson Liverpool and England - Official Testimonial Brochure*, Phil Thompson Testimonial Committee, 1983.

Robbie Fowler, *My Autobiography*, Pan Macmillan, 2006.

Steven Gerrard, *My Story*, Penguin UK, 2016.

Steven Gerrard, *My Autobiography*, Bantam, 2007.

Steve Heighway, My Team, Souvenir Press Ltd, 1977.

Steven Horton, We Love You Yeah, Yeah, Yeah! The Story of Liverpool's 1963-64 Title Triumph, Vertical Editions, 2014.

Ray Houghton's Liverpool Notebook – Inside Anfield 1988-89, Macdonald Queen Anne Press, 1989.

Simon Hughes, Men in White Suits: Liverpool FC in the 1990s - The Players' Stories, Corgi, 2016.

Simon Hughes, Red Machine: Liverpool FC in the 1980s: The Players' Stories, Mainstream Publishing, 2014.

David Huxley, A Young Family in Wartime at Crosby, Stockport Libraries

Craig Johnston, Walk Alone, Neil Jameson, 2013.

Kevin Keegan, An Autobiography, Magnum, 1978.

Stephen F. Kelly, The Kop: Liverpool's Twelfth Man, Mandarin Paperbacks, 1993.

Ray Kennedy and Andrew J. Lees, Ray of Hope: The Ray Kennedy Story, Pelham Books, 1993.

Phil Neal, Attack From The Back, Littlehampton Book Services Ltd, 1981

Billy Liddell, My Soccer Story, Stanley Paul, 1960.

Ronnie Moran, Testimonial Year 1999-2000 – 50 Years of Loyalty and Glory, 2000.

Bob Paisley, An Autobiography, Littlehampton Book Services Ltd, 1983.

Mark Platt and Andrew Fagan, Joe Fagan: Reluctant Champion: The Authorised Biography, Aurum Press Ltd, 2011.

Ian Rush, Rush: The Autobiography: Liverpool's Greatest Striker, Liverpool's Greatest Era, The True Story, Ebury Press, 2008.

Bill Shankly and John Roberts, Shankly, Arthur Barker, 1976.

BIBLIOGRAPHY

Tommy Smith and Ken Rogers, Over the Top, Breedon Books Publishing Co Ltd, 1998.

Graeme Souness, No Half Measures, Collins, 1985.

Ian St John, My Autobiography, Hodder & Stoughton Ltd, 2005.

Phil Thompson, Stand Up Pinocchio, Trinity Mirror Sport Media, 2005.

Clive Tyldesley, A Tribute to Alan Hansen: Official Testimonial Year, Clive Tyldesley, 1987.

Paul Walsh, Walshy: My Autobiography, Trinity Mirror Sport Media, 2015.

Ronnie Whelan, Walk on: My Life in Red, Simon & Schuster Ltd, 2011.

Mike Yates and Keith Miller, Steven Gerrard, Michael Owen and Me: Mike Yates Tells His Story, Independent Publishing Network, 2014.

Newspapers and publications:

British Soccer Week, Daily Mirror, Guardian, Liverpool Courier, Liverpool Daily Post, Liverpool Echo, Liverpool Evening Express, Liverpool Football Echo, Liverpool Mercury, Morgunbladid, News Chronicle and Daily Dispatch, The Sunday Times, The Times.

Websites:

LFChistory.net, qosfc.com, InDaily.

Documentary:

Bugsy Moran: A Tribute to Liverpool's Sergeant Major, LFC TV, 2015.

FRI. FEB 8ᵗʰ   SNOWING - LIGHT.

   1ˢᵗ TEAM SQUAD:-   TEAM TALK
                      IND. WARM UP
                      4 v 4 (60×40)
                      SPRINTS.

SAT FEB 9ᵗʰ

   1ˢᵗ TEAM   v   ARSENAL (HOME)
                    H.T.
              (CANCELLED)

   A TEAM   v   FORMBY RES (AWAY)
   B TEAM   v
              (BOTH CANCELLED).

MON FEB 11ᵗʰ   10·20AM
   1ˢᵗ TEAM SQUAD:-   ANFIELD
                 WARM UP: 2 FULL LAPS
                            EXERCISES
                            9 - 60YD STRETCHES
                            8 v 8 (60×40)
                            SHUTTLES
                            8 v 8 (60×40 - 2TOUCH)
                            STRETCHES (6 @ 35 YDS)
                      12·10PM